Fish

Fish

Recipes from the sea

Phaidon Press Limited
Regent's Wharf
All Saints Street
London N1 9PA

Phaidon Press Inc.
180 Varick Street
New York, NY 10014

www.phaidon.com

ISBN 978 07148 6387 0

Fish originates from *Il cucchiaio
d'argento*, first published in 1950,
eighth edition (revised, expanded
and redesigned) 1997; from *Primi piatti*,
first published 2004; from *Secondi piatti*,
first published 2005; and from *Antipasti
e contorni*, first published in 2007.
© Editoriale Domus S.p.A.

A CIP catalogue record for this book
is available from the British Library.

Commissioning Editor: Laura Gladwin
Project Editor: Michelle Lo
Production Controller: Vanessa Todd

Designed by Fraser Muggeridge studio
Photography by Andy Sewell
Illustrations by Katie Scott

The Publisher would also like to thank
Joanna de Courcy-Ireland, Carmen Figini,
William Hall, Steve Hatt, Sophie Hodgkin,
CJ Jackson, Phil Jolly, Terri McGeown,
Clelia d'Onofrio (curator of the Italian
edition), Barton Seaver, Adam Whittle
and the team at Billingsgate Fish Market,
for their contributions to the book.

Printed in Italy

FROM SEA TO PLATE

There is something thrilling about taking a whole fish and using it to create a quick and simple meal. The versatility of fish, and the ease with which it can be cooked, are surprising – most fish take no more than a few minutes under the grill (broiler), in a pan or in the oven. The flavours and textures of fish and seafood are very diverse and can be shown off in many different kinds of dish, from a smart but easy dinner-party dish of sea bream with olives and spices, to a hearty casserole of octopus simmered with red wine and herbs, to a quick supper of marinated and chargrilled (charbroiled) squid. In fact, it's perfectly possible to eat fish every day for a whole month without repeating the same species!

Some people worry that fish is difficult to prepare, or are nervous about which fish to buy and how to select them, but often find that it's a lot easier than they imagined. There is plenty of advice in this book about which fish to choose and how to select the best specimens (see the fish descriptions at the beginning of each chapter), and your fish supplier will also be happy to advise you. Of course you can also ask your fish supplier to scale, clean and fillet the fish for you, but if you decide to try doing it yourself, you'll discover that it's a good deal simpler than you thought, and it helps you to get to know the different species (see Basic Techniques on page 286). When it comes to cooking fish, if you follow the recipe carefully, and always err on the side of caution with the cooking times, you'll find that it comes out perfectly.

Fish is also a healthy option and can provide huge nutritional benefits. Many nutritionists and dietitians recommend that we should eat more fish as part of a healthy and balanced diet. White fish, such as sea bass and sole, are very lean and low in fat and are thought to satisfy hunger better than most other types of protein. Oily fish, such as mackerel, salmon and tuna, contain a high amount of omega 3 fatty acids, which are thought to help prevent some diseases and facilitate healthy brain development. Many types of shellfish also provide high levels of omega 3, as well as other nutritional benefits.

COOKING FISH THE ITALIAN WAY

When it comes to cooking with fish, few food cultures do it better than the Italians. In Italy there is a rich tradition of recipes for all kinds of fish, and as with all good home cooking, the basic principles of good-quality ingredients cooked simply are the key to their delicious fish dishes.

Italian cooks are very resourceful and have found many ways to make good use of the types of seafood that are available locally. There is a whole range of recipes for delicious fish soups and stews, from *Zuppa di pesce del pirata* (Pirate's fish soup, page 277), or the classic Livornese fish soup *Cacciucco* (page 280), which vary according to the region, and can be adapted to make use of whatever fish is available – traditionally, the small or under-appreciated fish that the fisherman would otherwise discard. A classic *Fritto misto*, or mixed fried fish (page 175), also makes use of the best fish and seafood that is available at the time. With access to the Mediterranean on the west coast, Adriatic on the east and Tyrrhenian to the north-east, there is plenty of marine fish and seafood available. There are also many rivers and lakes, including Lake Garda and Lake Como in the north, which supply freshwater fish, resulting in delicious dishes such as *Filetti di persico al forno alle noci* (Perch with walnuts, page 187) or *Storione alla paprica* (Sturgeon with paprika, page 201).

Of course, outside Italy, every region in every country has its own iconic fish dishes and favourite species, from Asia to Australia, the Atlantic and Pacific coasts of the USA,

Europe and the Middle East. Although the available species will be different in each country, the general principles discussed here will apply to them all. Even if we don't have access to the same fish and seafood, we can all be inspired by the approach of Italian cooks and adapt the recipes by using the fish and seafood that is available close to home. Every recipe in the book includes suggestions for alternative fish that can be substituted.

WHAT ABOUT SUSTAINABILITY?

The environmental impact of the food we eat has become a consideration that we can't ignore. Some of the particular problems relating to the consumption of fish, such as over-fishing, aggressive fishing methods, global warming and the transportation of fish around the world, have received particular attention, and they are all key areas of concern. However, although the problems are certainly complex and difficult, and vary considerably from country to country, they are not insurmountable, since if they are treated in the right way, fish stocks can recover.

As a consumer, the best approach to take is to seek out and use the varieties of fish and seafood that are available locally. Alternative fish are suggested throughout the book, which will help if there are concerns about a particular species or if the one listed is unavailable for other reasons. There are also some easy points to remember when shopping for fish. As well as choosing locally caught fish, if possible aim for fish that is caught by a day-fishing boat, which usually means a small crew in a small boat. Buy the fish when it is at is best and avoid the when they are developing roe (eggs), which usually occurs during spring. When the fish contains roe, the quality will not be as good, and avoiding it at this time also allows the fish to spawn and create the next generation. A good fish supplier should be able to address any questions about sustainability, and don't be afraid to ask how the fish has been caught. If the answer doesn't satisfy you, try something else. Most of all, try to avoid the most well-known fish, choosing instead something different or untried. There is a huge range of fish available, and eating some of the less well-known species will allow stocks of the more popular fish to recover.

CHOOSING FISH AND SEAFOOD

Many species of fish have their own unique signs of freshness, which are discussed in the individual fish descriptions at the start of each chapter. However, there are some general principles to bear in mind when selecting the freshest fish. At first glance, the fish should look appealing: bright, glossy and standing proud in a box packed with ice. For some fish this is enough to know it is an excellent choice. For whole fish, other key signs of freshness are bright convex eyes, fresh red gills and a firm body with a glossy sheen. Most very fresh fish will be virtually odourless, and some will smell pleasantly fresh and slightly briny. As fish deteriorates it loses its shine and begins to look dry and soft, the eyes sink into the head and begin to cloud over, and the smell becomes stronger.

The flesh side of a fresh fish fillet should not come into direct contact with ice, because this causes freezer burn, which makes it look discoloured or dry. A fillet should look translucent and the flakes should hold together well. Fish fillets vary in colour, but avoid any that have discoloured patches, because they may have been roughly handled. As fillets deteriorate they start to look dull and lose translucency, and the flakes begin to open up so that the skin underneath is visible.

Frozen fish, if it has been rapidly frozen by commercial methods and packaged well, can be an excellent choice, and is often actually fresher than fresh fish, particularly shellfish. For those who don't live close to the coast it is often the best option. The very best frozen fish is usually labelled as being frozen at sea: freezing it early captures the best flavour and it often tastes better than fresh. Good-quality frozen fish will be securely wrapped in very thick plastic. In some cases fish or seafood will have been coated in a protective glaze or thin layer of ice that makes it easier to store and remove from the freezer in small quantities. Avoid any that have an excessively thick layer of ice-glazing. Check for signs of freezer burn, which can happen if the wrapping opens or the fish partially defrosts. In this case the fish will look dry and often white in appearance.

With compact flesh, a mild and distinctive flavour and a pleasant hint of sweetness, seafood often requires little preparation to create delicious meals. There are many things to look for when buying good-quality fresh seafood, and individual signs are listed in the descriptions. As a rule, it's best to buy seafood from a fish supplier that you trust. Crustaceans (crab, lobsters, prawns [shrimp] and langoustines) are usually sold either live or cooked and frozen. Bivalve molluscs (mussels, oysters and clams) should be sold live, and the shells should be mostly closed. If they're alive, the shells will close if tapped sharply, which means they are safe to cook. Any that do not close should be discarded. Scallops can be bought live in their shells, but are also often sold raw and pre-shucked (taken out of the shell), or cooked and frozen.

All fish and seafood will deteriorate quickly if it is not kept cool enough. It is best to store it in the refrigerator in close contact with ice blocks, thereby keeping it as cold as practically possible without freezing it. To store fish at home it is best to remove it from the wrapping in which it was purchased. Place it on a flat tray or large plate and cover it. If it was bought fresh, eat it within a day of purchasing. Keep an eye on the use-by (expiration) date for frozen fish, which tends to be shorter than for other produce. To defrost fish or seafood, put it on a plate and allow it to defrost in the refrigerator.

HOW TO USE THIS BOOK

The book is divided into chapters according to the main types of fish. Each chapter begins with descriptions of the main types of fish, which, along with the illustrations, will help you to identify them. They also describe how to choose and prepare the fish, advise what to ask your fish supplier, and suggest the best cooking methods to try, as well as giving possible alternatives. The descriptions are followed by a collection of delicious, simple and authentic Italian recipes for each kind of fish, including starters (appetizers), first courses and main courses. Each recipe includes suggestions for alternative fish that can be substituted, and an icon directing you to the end of the book, where the step-by-step Basic Techniques section shows you how to prepare the fish you'll need in the recipe. See below for a list of icons.

Fish: Recipes from the Sea offers a unique insight into the delicious traditional fish recipes of Italy. We hope that these, along with the practical guidance included throughout, will inspire and encourage you to discover the wonderful role that fish can play in your everyday cooking.

BASIC TECHNIQUES

These icons will direct you to the relevant preparation techniques for each recipe.

 Trimming, Scaling and Cleaning (page 288)

 Filleting and Skinning Round Fish (page 290)

 Filleting and Skinning Flat Fish (page 292)

 Skinning and Filleting Monkfish (page 294)

Removing Pinbones from a Fillet (page 296)

 Scaling and Gutting Small Oily Fish (page 297)

 Butterfly-Boning Small Oily Fish (page 298)

 Preparing Mussels and Clams (page 300)

 Preparing Octopus (page 301)

 Preparing Squid and Cuttlefish (page 302)

 Preparing Scallops (page 304)

 Shucking Oysters (page 306)

 Preparing Raw Prawns (Shrimp) (page 307)

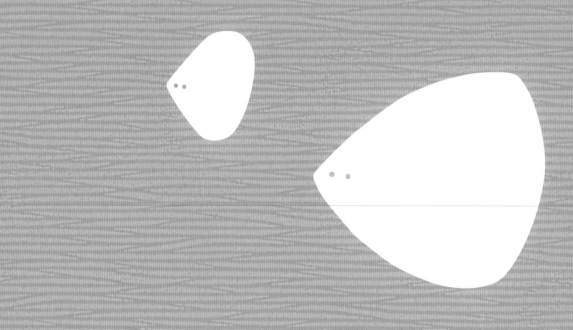

ROUND WHITE FISH

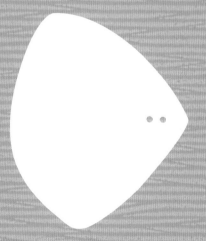

There are two types of white fish: round fish and flat fish. Round white fish include many species such as cod, monkfish, John Dory, the mullets, bass and bream. A round white fish has eyes on both sides of its head, a backbone running along the length of its upper body and a fillet located on both sides. These types of fish can be found in all areas of the ocean, from shallow coasts and seabeds to deep waters.

The texture of white fish varies dramatically. Cod, grouper and snapper have creamy white flaky meat while a monkfish will have a firm and dense texture. To check if the fish is cooked, use the tip of a sharp knife and cut through the thickest part of the fillet. If the fish has been properly cooked, the meat will be opaque, white in colour, not translucent and will look moist.

SEA BASS

Branzino
Dicentrarchus labrax

Average weight range:
450g–2kg (1–4½lb)
Average length: 36–100cm
(14–40 inches)

Recipes on pages 26–31

Often compared to sea bream in texture and flavour, sea bass has a dense covering of small scales, a gleaming silver belly and a well-deserved reputation for its white, lean and delicate flesh. Caught wild in the Atlantic, Pacific and Antarctic oceans, other bass varieties include American striped bass and black bass. It is also known as branzino in the United States.

It is sold both filleted and whole. If it has been filleted, it will already have been scaled, so it is usually unnecessary to remove the skin, although you can if you prefer. With a whole sea bass, the sharp spines on the fins along the back of the fish must be trimmed and the fish should be scaled and cleaned with the gills removed.

With white, lean and delicate flesh, sea bass can be pan-fried, grilled (broiled), roasted or wrapped in a parcel or package before baking or cooking on the barbecue. A simple Italian recipe for bass is *Branzino al forno con carciofi* (Baked sea bass with artichokes, see page 26). It also works nicely with pasta, such as in the delicious *Ravioli di branzino* (Sea bass ravioli, see page 31). Because is widely farmed, sea bass is readily available but should you have problems finding it, good alternatives include the Australian Mulloway, sea bream, red mullet, red snapper, wild striped bass, hybrid striped bass, farmed barramundi and grouper.

GREY / STRIPED MULLET

Cefalo
Mugil cephalus

Average weight range:
600g–2kg (1lb 5oz–4½lb)
Average length: 40–100cm
(16–14 inches)

Recipes on pages 32–34

Despite its name, this fish is not related to red mullet. Beautiful, sleek, silver-grey and densely covered in scales, grey (striped) mullet has an underrated reputation for its earthy flavour. When buying grey mullet, look for very fresh fish that feel firm and have bright eyes, red gills and gleaming scales. It is usually sold whole but you can easily ask to have it trimmed, scaled and cleaned for you. The skin is generally left on fillets to protect the delicate flesh during cooking.

Grey mullet are usually roasted or grilled (broiled) whole, but are also good poached. If the fish is to be cooked whole, it is a good idea to slash both sides part way through to the bone. The fillets can be quite thick, so this allows the heat to penetrate to the centre without overcooking the rest of the fish. To reduce the muddy flavour, marinate the mullet in lemon juice, wine or other acidulated liquid for about 30 minutes.

Cefalo ripieno alle olive (Stuffed grey [striped] mullet with olives, see page 32) is delicious and brings together interesting flavours. Sea bream, sea bass, hybrid striped bass and whiting can be used as alternatives.

Bottarga, a pressed cured grey mullet roe, looks like a firm, light-brown sausage and crumbles when cut.

GROUPER

Cernia
Epinephelus

Average weight range:
1–6kg (2¼–13lb) or more
Average length: 50–90cm
(20–35 inches)

Recipes on pages 35–38

Grouper are among the most highly prized sea fish because their white flesh is tasty and tender. Found in seas around the world, this large family of fish includes rock cod and coral trout in Australia and red grouper, yellowmouth grouper and spotted cabrilla in the United States. The species mainly found in the Mediterranean is the brown or speckled grouper, which has a bullet-shaped body and dappled brown markings on paler skin that is rough to the touch. Their diet comprises of smaller fish and as a result, the flesh is firm, white and meaty with a sweet flavour.

The skin is thick and strong with a layer of fat lying directly underneath it. This layer should be removed along with the skin by cutting into the flesh slightly. If you purchase the fish whole, you can ask for it to be trimmed, deep-skinned and filleted rather than doing it at home.

Grouper are best cooked simply either by poaching (their stock is excellent) or baking. Try it on the barbecue by making *Filetti di cernia con salsa di scalogno* (Grouper with shallot sauce, see page 38). Alternative choices for grouper include members of the cod family, snapper, sea bass, tilapia, catfish, Alaskan pollock, amberjack and cobia.

MONKFISH

Coda di rospo
Lophius piscatorius

Average weight range:
300g–2kg (11oz–4½lb)
Average length: 25–50cm
(10–20 inches)

Recipes on pages 44–46

With a large head and glossy, brown mottled skin, this grotesque fish has a distinctive appearance. In Italy, monkfish are known as *coda di rospo* – toad's tail – because only their long fleshy tails are sold, while in the United States, they were commonly referred to as 'poor man's lobster' due to their dense texture and lobster-like taste. The monkfish is sometimes known as an anglerfish or goosefish.

Monkfish is generally sold with the head removed and the cheeks sold separately. The tail can be purchased on the bone or filleted. If the fillets have not been skinned, simply peel off the skin from the top end to the tail (see page 294). A tough transparent membrane lies underneath and this also needs to be trimmed away with a knife, otherwise it will discolour and shrink during cooking. Occasionally monkfish liver and roe are available, although it is not recommended to eat the liver as they can contain high levels of environmental toxins such as PCBs and dioxins.

The flavoursome flesh has compact fibres and is very tender. With a meaty flesh similar to lobster, monkfish is excellent pan-fried, stir-fried and roasted. In Italy, it is also enjoyed with pasta, such as in *Malloreddus con farro, coda di rospo e carciofi* (Malloreddus with farro, monkfish and artichokes, see page 41). During cooking, the volume of monkfish decreases considerably so this must be taken into account when calculating quantities.

If monkfish is unavailable, prawns (shrimp), huss (dogfish), scallops, lobster and turbot work well in the same recipes.

COD

Merluzzo (fresh)
Stoccafisso (dried)
Baccalà (salted)
Gadidae

Average weight range:
450g–40kg (1–88lb)
Average length: 35–150cm
(14 inches – 5 feet)

Recipes on pages 45–53

Cod is easily identified by its yellow or olive-green speckles and the white line that runs the length of each side. It has superb white, flaky flesh that is almost creamy in consistency. Several species are caught in oceans globally, and in some areas of the North Atlantic, Atlantic cod has been fished to unsustainable levels in some areas. Cod is generally sold filleted but can be purchased whole or in steaks. Cod is the best-known member of a large family of fish that includes haddock, whiting and coley.

Highly versatile, cod can be poached, baked, grilled broiled), pan-fried and deep fried. *Merluzzo agli aromi* (Aromatic cod, see page 48) is simple, healthy and delicious. When buying a fresh cod fillet, make sure that the flakes of flesh are tightly packed; if they are opening enough to reveal the skin, the fish will be past its best.

Salted and dried cod, prepared in the countries bordering the North Sea, is more common than fresh in southern Europe and the Caribbean. Fillets are usually sold with their skin still on because it protects the fish from drying out in the oven; however, the pinbones will need to be removed.

Many Italian specialities are based on salt cod, such as *Frittelle di baccalà* (Salt cod fritters, see page 50), and stockfish, combining them with classic Mediterranean ingredients such as olives, tomatoes, pine nuts and garlic.

Other members of the cod family such as hake, whiting or coley, pollock, Australian flathead and haddock are all good substitutes.

HAKE

Nasello
Merluccius merluccius

Average weight range:
500g–3kg (1lb 2oz–6½lb)
Average length: 40–120cm
(16–48 inches)

Recipes on pages 54–58

Extremely popular in many parts of the Mediterranean, hake is closely associated with cod and has similar white, flaky flesh. With a distinctive silvery, elongated body and pointed snake-like head, large eyes and sharp set of teeth, various species are caught around the globe, notably the Atlantic and Pacific oceans. As such, it has been fished to unsustainable levels in some waters.

Hake is usually cleaned on landing and has soft skin and fins so, apart from removing the gills, a whole fish requires little preparation. Although it may be sold whole, it is more commonly available in fillets or steaks.

Hake has a deceptively soft and delicate flesh, even when very fresh, but the fillets become firm, white and sweet-flavoured when cooked. Hake works well with the same flavours as cod, and it naturally partners with olive oil, citrus, garlic and tomato. It is also excellent poached and seasoned with oil and lemon juice or served with mayonnaise. Good alternatives are other members of the cod or hake families.

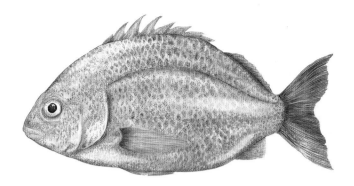

SEA BREAM

Dentice/Orata/Sarago
Sparidae

Average weight range:
300g–2kg (11oz–4½lb)
Average length: 40–70cm
(16–28 inches)

Recipes on pages 58–64

Found in warm waters throughout the world, this large family of fish includes dentex, gilthead sea bream and white sea bream as well as the red porgy, sheepshead bream and scup in the United States, and they can be used interchangeably in the recipes. The species may vary in colour, but their appearance is similar with a deep, rounded body, a slightly domed head and plate-like scales that should be removed before cooking. They are conveniently available year round and are most often sold whole or in fillets. Whole sea bream can be trimmed, scaled, cleaned and the gills removed before filleting – just ask your fish supplier.

Their lean, firm flesh is highly prized and their delicately flavoured cheeks (pearls) may be extracted if the fish is cooked whole. It is suitable for pan-frying, grilling broiling), baking in fillets or whole in a parcel or package, steaming and roasting. A whole fish takes about 20 minutes to cook through, whereas fillets require less than 5 minutes each. A classic Italian recipe is *Sarago al sale* (Sea bream baked in a salt crust, see page 62).

If sea bream is unavailable to you locally, suitable alternatives are sea bass, red mullet, grey (striped) mullet, black sea bass and barramundi. If a larger fish is required, it can be substituted with red snapper.

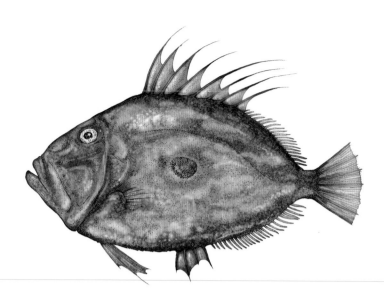

JOHN DORY

San Pietro
Zeus faber

Average weight range:
500g–3kg (1lb 2oz–6½lb)
Average length: 40–120cm
(16–48 inches)

Recipes on pages 65–68

John Dory is also known as Saint Peter's fish because the large spot behind the gills on each side of the body is said to be the thumbprint of the disciple. John Dory are found in the Atlantic and Pacific oceans and the Mediterranean and Adriatic seas. This solitary fish lives on a diet of small shellfish and, in turn, has a sweet, delicately flavoured and firm flesh. Fishermen in Italy would add it to regional fish stews, such as *Brodetto abruzzese*.

It is sold both whole and as fillets and a whole fish will require careful preparation because the fillets are surrounded by sharp spines that must be snipped off (ask your fish supplier to do this). The two fillets obtained from a larger fish are enough to serve two people as a main course. They may be skinned before cooking, but the skin also peels away easily afterwards. The small fish may be cooked whole. Avoid purchasing John Dory in the spring when it spawns: the fish will be full of roe and the fillets will lack flavour.

It is best suited to pan-frying, grilling (broiling) or baking. Because the fillets are firm and dense, they need no more than 4–5 minutes grilling or frying on each side. John Dory goes well with robust Mediterranean flavours such as olives, rosemary and capers. Pomfret, turbot, brill and sablefish are good substitutes for this fish, which can be hard to find in the United States.

SCORPION FISH

Scorfano
Scorpaenidae

Average weight range:
150–500g (5oz–1lb 2oz)
Average length: 20–45cm
(8–18 inches)

Recipes on pages 68–70

There are several types of scorpion fish, which are also known by their French name *rascasse*. Small, rotund, spiny and with large eyes, this easily recognizable fish requires careful handling because the sharp spines can inflict a painful wound. The scorpion fish is closely related to the redfish group that includes rockfish and ocean perch found in the Atlantic and Pacific oceans and the Mediterranean Sea. In the United States, it is not often found in markets but can be substituted with monkfish, lobster, striped bass and members of the cod family.

Smaller specimens are usually sold whole, while larger fish are sold as skinned fillets because the spines are sharp. The many pinbones located near the thicker end of the fillet also need to be extracted and your local fish supplier can do this for you. When buying, choose one that is vibrant in appearance and bear in mind that the bones and head comprise more than half the fish's weight.

Their delicate, white, flaky flesh can be prepared in a number of ways such as pan-frying, poaching and baking, although traditionally in Italy, it is mainly used in soups and stews such as *Brodetto marchigiano* (Marche-style soup, see page 278). It works well with delicate herbs and citrus flavours as combined in *Scorfano al timo* (Scorpion fish with thyme, see page 68). Alternative choices include members of the cod family and gurnard (sea robin).

HUSS /
DOGFISH

Palombo
Squalidae

Average weight range:
700g–9kg (1½–20lb)
Average length: 50–90cm
(20–35 inches)

Recipes on pages 71–73

With its shark-like body, huss (dogfish) is immediately recognizable as a member of the shark family. The sheer number of species is confusing and in Italy several different types – cat sharks and nurse hounds, for example – are caught, often with different regional names. Nevertheless, some members of the shark family have been fished excessively and there are sustainability issues.

Huss (dogfish) is available whole but is usually skinned before purchase. Once the head and skin have been removed, the fish can be filleted in a similar way to monkfish (see page 294). Once the central cartilage has been removed, there are no other bones to extract.

Nutritious, low in fat and easy to digest, the pink, dense and meaty flesh has a strong, game-like taste that works well with robust flavours and in tomato-based soups and stews such as *Palombo con i piselli alla romana* (Roman-style huss [dogfish] with peas, see page 73). It lends itself to the cooking methods used for tuna and swordfish and can also be baked, stir-fried, pan-fried or grilled (broiled). Alternatives include monkfish, cod and skate.

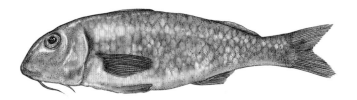

RED MULLET

Triglia
Mullus surmuletus

Average weight range:
200–500g (7oz–1lb 2oz)
Average length: 8–30cm
(3–12 inches)

Recipes on pages 73–77

Red mullet are attractively marked with gradating red flanks. They have copious scales and a fin, called a *barbule*, underneath the chin suggesting the name goatfish (more commonly used in Australia). Various species are found worldwide in warmer waters.

Because the fish is often sold whole and uncleaned, a cook should remove and discard the intestines and save the liver. To prepare the fish, have your fish supplier trim the fins, and scale and clean it, taking care to remove the blood line close to the spine.

Red mullet is best cooked on the bone as this helps retain flavour and a moist texture. Small, very fragile red mullet are best simply fried, but golden mullet can be cooked in a variety of ways – they are very good roasted or baked in a parcel or parcel with herbs such as tarragon, rosemary and basil. If it is filleted, be careful to remove all the pinbones. It is best cooked simply and works well with citrus fruit such as in *Triglia all'arancia* (Red mullet with orange salad, see page 74). During cooking, they should be touched as little as possible and only very gently because their tender flesh breaks up easily. Mullets are also an important ingredient in fish soups.

The flavour is difficult to beat, but good substitutes in red mullet recipes include sea bream, sea bass, red snapper, herring, barramundi and Spanish or Boston mackerel.

Serves 4
Preparation time: 15 mins
Cooking time: 35 mins

· olive oil, for brushing
· 2 garlic cloves, halved
· 1 × 800-g (1¾-lb) sea bass,
  scaled and cleaned
· 100 ml (scant ½ cup) dry
  white wine
· juice of ½ lemon, strained
· 5 baby globe artichokes,
  trimmed and sliced
· salt and pepper
· chopped flat-leaf parsley,
  to garnish

Alternative fish: sea bream,
trout or grey (striped) mullet

 288

Branzino al forno con carciofi

BAKED SEA BASS WITH ARTICHOKES

Preheat the oven to 180°C / 350°F / Gas Mark 4 and brush an ovenproof dish with oil. Put the halved garlic cloves into the cavity of the fish and season inside and out with salt and pepper. Put the fish into the prepared dish and bake for about 5 minutes, then remove from the oven and sprinkle with the wine. Return the fish to the oven and bake for 10 minutes more. Meanwhile, bring a saucepan of water to a boil, add the lemon juice and a pinch of salt, add the artichokes and cook for 5–10 minutes, then drain. Remove the fish from the oven, add the artichokes, return to the oven and cook for an additional 15–20 minutes. Remove from the oven, sprinkle with chopped parsley and serve immediately, straight from the dish.

Photograph opposite

Serves 4
Preparation time: 25 mins
Cooking time: 15 mins

· olive oil, for brushing and
  serving
· 1 rosemary sprig
· 2 garlic cloves, sliced
· 1 × 1-kg (2¼-lb) sea bass,
  scaled and cleaned
· 1 tablespoon chopped
  flat-leaf parsley
· 1 lemon, sliced
· 1 onion, sliced into rings
· 2 spring onions (scallions),
  sliced
· 100 ml (scant ½ cup)
  dry white wine
· salt and pepper
· lemon wedges, to serve

Alternative fish: sea bream,
trout or salmon

 288

Branzino al cartoccio

SEA BASS BAKED IN PAPER

Preheat the oven to 200°C / 400°F / Gas Mark 6. Brush a large sheet of parchment or greaseproof (wax) paper with oil. Put the rosemary and half the garlic in the cavity of the fish and season with salt and pepper. Put the fish on the paper, sprinkle with the parsley, lemon slices, onion rings, spring onions (scallions) and remaining garlic and pour the wine over it. Fold up the paper to enclose the fish and put the parcel on a baking sheet. Bake for 15 minutes, then remove from the oven and serve with extra olive oil, lemon wedges and salt, unwrapping the parcel at the table.

Serves 6
Preparation time: 20 mins
Cooking time: 30 mins

· 1 × 1-kg (2¼-lb) sea bass,
  cleaned and filleted

For the potatoes:
· 1kg (2¼lb) potatoes, peeled
  and cut into chunks
· 150 ml (scant ⅔ cup) olive oil
· 3 tablespoons chopped rocket
  (arugula)
· salt and pepper

For the salmoriglio:
· 100 ml (scant ½ cup) olive oil
· juice of 1 lemon, strained
· 2 tablespoons hot water
· 1 tablespoon chopped
  flat-leaf parsley
· 1 teaspoon chopped oregano
· 1 garlic clove, crushed
· salt and pepper

Alternative fish: salmon or
sea bream

 288   290   296

SEA BASS CARPACCIO WITH SALMORIGLIO

Put the potatoes into a saucepan, add water to cover and a pinch of salt, cover and bring to a boil. Reduce the heat and cook for 25–30 minutes, until tender but not falling apart.

Preheat the oven 180°C/350°F/Gas Mark 4 and line a baking sheet with parchment paper. Cut the fish into thin slices and spread them out on the prepared baking sheet.

To make the salmoriglio, whisk together the oil, lemon juice and hot water in a bowl and season with salt and pepper. Stir in the parsley, oregano and garlic. Brush the slices of fish with the salmoriglio, season with salt and pepper and cook in the oven for 4 minutes. Drain the potatoes, return to the pan and mash, adding just enough oil to produce quite a thick purée. Season with salt and pepper and stir in the rocket (arugula). Serve the fish with the mashed potato.

Serves 4
Preparation time: 30 mins
Cooking time: 20–25 mins

· 2 pomegranates
· 2 teaspoons green peppercorns
· 1 × 1-kg (2¼-lb) sea bass,
  scaled and cleaned
· 100 ml (scant ½ cup) dry
  white wine
· olive oil, for drizzling
· salt

Alternative fish: grouper or
grey (striped) mullet

 288

SEA BASS WITH POMEGRANATES

To remove the pomegranate seeds, cut a thin slice from
one end and stand the pomegranate upright. Using a small,
sharp knife, cut downwards through the skin at intervals
all around the fruit. Bend back the segments and push
out the seeds into a bowl with your fingers. Remove all
traces of the pith and membranes. Preheat the oven to
180°C/350°F/Gas Mark 4. Place a double layer of parchment
or greaseproof (wax) paper onto a baking sheet. Sprinkle
half the pomegranate seeds and half the green peppercorns
in the middle. Place the fish on top and sprinkle with the
remaining seeds and peppercorns. Fold up the sides of
the paper, pour in the wine, drizzle with olive oil and season
with salt. Carefully fold over the edges of the paper to
enclose the fish completely. Bake for 20–25 minutes,
then remove from the oven, transfer to a serving dish
and unwrap it at the table.

Serves 4
Preparation time: 15 mins
Cooking time: 40 mins

· 1 × 1-kg (2¼-lb) sea bass,
  scaled and cleaned
· 2 shallots, chopped
· 2 tablespoons chopped
  flat-leaf parsley
· 100 g (scant 1½ cups) chopped
  button (white) mushrooms
· 1 carrot, sliced into rounds
· 4–5 black peppercorns
· 40 g (3 tablespoons) butter
· 500 ml (2 cups) red wine
· salt

Alternative fish: huss (dogfish)
or grey (striped) mullet

 288

Branzino al vino rosso

SEA BASS IN RED WINE

Put the sea bass into a flameproof casserole (Dutch oven),
add the shallots, parsley, mushrooms, carrot, peppercorns
and a pinch of salt and dot with half the butter. Cover and
cook over low heat for 10 minutes. Pour in just enough
wine to come about halfway up the fish, add the remaining
butter, re-cover the casserole and simmer for about
30 minutes, until the liquid has reduced slightly. Remove
the casserole from the heat and serve immediately.

Serves 6
Preparation time: 1hr 25mins
+ 1hr resting
Cooking time: 20mins

· 350g (3 cups) plain (all-purpose) flour, preferably Italian type 00, plus extra for dusting
· 150g (1¼ cups) durum wheat flour
· 3 eggs
· 4 egg yolks
· salt

For the filling:
· 3 tablespoons olive oil
· 700g (1½lb) sea bass fillets, skinned and chopped
· 3 tablespoons mascarpone
· grated zest of 1 lemon
· 1 teaspoon finely chopped chives
· salt and pepper

For the sauce:
· 90g (6 tablespoons) butter
· 1 tablespoon finely chopped chives

Alternative fish: crab, salmon or hake

288   290   296

SEA BASS RAVIOLI

Sift both kinds of flour into a mound on a work counter and make a well in the middle. Break the eggs into the well and add the egg yolks and a pinch of salt. Knead well, shape into a ball, cover with a clean dish towel and let rest for 1 hour.

Meanwhile, make the filling. Heat the oil in a large frying pan or skillet. Add the fish, season with salt and pepper and cook over low heat, stirring occasionally, for 10 minutes. Remove from the pan and let cool, then combine with the mascarpone, lemon zest and chives in a bowl.

Roll out the dough on a lightly floured work counter into a thin sheet. Put small mounds of the filling in even rows over one half of the pasta sheet. Fold over the other half of the sheet and press around the filling with your fingers to seal. Cut out the ravioli and press the edges together firmly. Cook the ravioli in plenty of salted boiling water until it rises to the surface and is al dente. Drain and toss in a saucepan over a low heat with the butter and chives, then serve.

Serves 4
Preparation time: 15 mins
Cooking time: 20 mins

· 1 orange
· olive oil, for brushing and drizzling
· melted butter, for brushing
· 4 grey (striped) mullet fillets
· 200 ml (scant 1 cup) white wine
· 2 tablespoons coarsely chopped fresh herbs, such as thyme, marjoram and flat-leaf parsley
· salt and pepper

Alternative fish: red mullet or sea bream

GREY (STRIPED) MULLET WITH ORANGE AND HERBS

Preheat the oven to 180°C/350°F/Gas Mark 4. Cut the peel and white pith off the oranges, then cut into thin slices. Brush a large ovenproof dish with a little oil and butter. Put the fish in the prepared dish, season with salt and pepper, drizzle with olive oil and sprinkle with the white wine. Cover with the orange slices, sprinkle with the herbs and bake for 20 minutes. Serve immediately in the dish.

Photograph opposite

Serves 4
Preparation time: 15 mins
+ 10 mins cooling
Cooking time: 22 mins

· 4 bacon rashers (slices)
· 8 sage leaves
· 4 grey (striped) mullet, scaled and cleaned
· 100 ml (scant ½ cup) olive oil
· 2 tablespoons chopped flat-leaf parsley
· 100 ml (scant ½ cup) dry white wine
· 20 mixed green and black olives, pitted and chopped
· salt and pepper

Alternative fish: red mullet or grouper

Cefalo ripieno alle olive

STUFFED GREY (STRIPED) MULLET WITH OLIVES

Put a rasher (slice) of bacon and a sage leaf in the cavity of each fish and season lightly with salt and pepper. Chop the remaining sage leaves. Heat the oil in a large frying pan or skillet, add the chopped parsley and cook over low heat for a few minutes. Remove the pan from the heat and let cool.

Add the fish to the pan, set over medium heat, cover and cook for 5–6 minutes on each side. Sprinkle with the wine and cook, uncovered, for 10 minutes, then add the olives and cook for another 2 minutes. Serve immediately.

Serves 4
Preparation time: 10 mins
Cooking time: 15 mins

· 4 grey (striped) mullet,
  scaled and cleaned
· 12 dill sprigs
· 1 onion, chopped
· 1 garlic clove, chopped
· 1 lemon, sliced
· 100 ml (scant ½ cup) dry
  white wine
· 4 teaspoons brandy
· olive oil, for drizzling
· salt and pepper

Alternative fish: sea bass,
sea bream or grouper

 288

Cefalo in cartoccio all'aneto

GREY (STRIPED) MULLET AND DILL PARCELS

Preheat the oven to 200°C/400°F/Gas Mark 6. Cut out four squares of foil, each large enough to enclose a fish. Season the cavities of the fish with salt and pepper and add a dill sprig to each. Put each fish on a prepared sheet of foil and divide the onion and garlic among them. Lay a few slices of lemon on top of each fish and sprinkle with the white wine and a teaspoonful of brandy each, then drizzle with olive oil.

Wrap up to enclose the fish completely, put the parcels on a baking sheet and bake for about 15 minutes, or until the fish feels firm when pressed. Remove the parcels from the oven and open the foil just before serving at the table.

Serves 4
Preparation time: 20 mins
Cooking time: 20 mins

· olive oil, for brushing and
  drizzling
· 1 × 800-g (1¾-lb) grey (striped)
  mullet, scaled and cleaned
· 1 tablespoon chopped oregano
· 2 tablespoons chopped
  flat-leaf parsley
· 1 garlic clove, chopped
· 100 g (scant 1½ cups) fine
  dry breadcrumbs
· 500 g (1 lb 2 oz) tomatoes,
  peeled, seeded and diced
· juice of 1 lemon, strained
· salt and pepper

Alternative fish: grouper,
grey (striped) mullet or trout

 288

Cefalo al tegame

GREY (STRIPED) MULLET BAKED WITH TOMATOES

Preheat the oven to 180°C/350°F/Gas Mark 4 and brush a large ovenproof dish with oil. Put the fish in the prepared dish, season with salt and pepper and sprinkle evenly with the oregano, parsley, garlic and breadcrumbs.

Top with the diced tomatoes, drizzle with olive oil and bake for about 20 minutes. Remove the dish from the oven, sprinkle the lemon juice over the fish and serve immediately.

Serves 4–6
Preparation time: 20 mins
Cooking time: 30 mins

· 300 g (11 oz) conchiglie
  (pasta shells)
· 3 tablespoons olive oil, plus
  extra for drizzling and brushing
· 1 aubergine (eggplant),
  thickly sliced
· 250 g (9 oz) grouper fillets
· 2 ripe tomatoes, peeled,
  seeded and diced
· juice of 1 lime, strained
· 2 tablespoons vodka
· 1 bunch chives, chopped
· 50 g (⅔ cup) salmon caviar
· salt and pepper

Alternative fish: red mullet
or sea bass

 288   290   296

PASTA SHELLS WITH GROUPER AND SALMON CAVIAR

Preheat the grill (broiler). Meanwhile, bring a large saucepan of salted water to a boil, add the pasta, bring back to a boil and cook for 8–10 minutes, until al dente. Drain, refresh under cold running water and drain again. Tip it into a salad bowl, drizzle with olive oil and stir. Cover with clingfilm (plastic wrap) and chill in the refrigerator.

Brush the aubergine (eggplant) slices with oil and grill (broil) them for 5–10 minutes on each side, until golden. Transfer to a chopping (cutting) board and cut the slices into small cubes. Steam or poach the grouper fillets for 10 minutes, then remove from the steamer or saucepan and let cool. Break up the fish into small pieces. Remove the pasta from the refrigerator and uncover, then add the aubergine cubes, fish and tomatoes and toss lightly.

Whisk together the lime juice, vodka, olive oil and a pinch of salt and pepper in a bowl, add to the salad and toss lightly again. Sprinkle with the chives and salmon caviar and serve immediately.

Serves 6
Preparation time: 30 mins
+ 6 hrs standing
Cooking time: 25 mins

· 400g (14 oz) tomatoes,
  peeled and diced
· 250g (2½ cups) black olives,
  pitted and halved
· 100g (¾ cup) capers
  preserved in salt, rinsed
· 1 teaspoon dried oregano
· 1 garlic clove, unpeeled
· 100ml (scant ½ cup) olive oil
· 1 × 1.3-kg (2¾-lb) grouper,
  cleaned, filleted and skinned
· 2 teaspoons lemon juice
· 900g (2lb) potatoes, cut into
  thin rounds
· salt and pepper

Alternative fish: turbot, brill
or cod

288   290   296

GROUPER WITH MEDITERRANEAN SAUCE

To make the sauce, combine the tomatoes, olives, capers, oregano, garlic clove and olive oil in a bowl, cover and leave to stand in a cool place for 6 hours.

Preheat the oven to 180°C/350°F/Gas Mark 4. Line a large ovenproof dish with a sheet of greaseproof (wax) paper. Cut the fish into six portions and sprinkle the lemon juice over them. Arrange the potato rounds on the paper-lined dish in concentric circles to form a large rosette and season with salt and pepper. Bake for about 15 minutes, until browned.

Remove from the oven and put the pieces of fish in the middle of the rosette, return to the oven and bake for an additional 10 minutes. Remove from the oven and transfer the potatoes and fish, still on the paper, to a serving platter. Remove and discard the garlic from the sauce, then spoon it over the fish and potatoes and serve immediately.

Serves 4
Preparation time: 25 mins
Cooking time: 10 mins

- 20 g (1½ tablespoons) butter
- 5 shallots, finely chopped
- 2 tablespoons finely
  chopped flat-leaf parsley
- 200 ml (scant 1 cup) dry
  white wine
- 150 ml (⅔ cup) double
  (heavy) cream
- 1 egg yolk
- 4 tablespoons olive oil
- juice of 1 lemon, strained
- 4 × 200-g (7-oz) grouper fillets
- salt and pepper

Alternative fish: cod and hake

288   290   296

Filetti di cernia con salsa di scalogno

GROUPER WITH SHALLOT SAUCE

Melt the butter in a frying pan or skillet, add the shallots
and parsley, and cook over low heat, stirring occasionally,
for 5 minutes, until the shallots are softened and translucent.
Add the wine and cook until reduced by half, then turn off
the heat and stir in the cream and egg yolk. Set aside and
keep warm. Whisk together the oil and lemon juice in a bowl
until thoroughly combined, then brush the mixture over the
fish fillets. Season with salt and pepper, place on the grill
of a medium-hot barbecue or under a preheated grill (broiler)
and cook for 5 minutes on each side, brushing frequently
with the oil and lemon mixture. Transfer to a warm platter
and serve immediately, passing around the shallot sauce
separately in a sauceboat.

· ·

Serves 4
Preparation time: 30 mins
Cooking time: 15 mins

- 4 × 200-g (7-oz) grouper fillets
- 50 g (½ cup) plain
  (all-purpose) flour
- 50 g (4 tablespoons) butter
- 2 tablespoons olive oil
- 1 garlic clove, peeled
- 10 sage leaves
- 2 tablespoons hot water
- juice of 1 lemon, strained
- salt
- 4 thin lemon slices, to garnish
- 700 g (1½ lb) cooked new
  potatoes, to serve

Alternative fish: salmon or cod

288   290   296

Cernia alla salvia

GROUPER WITH SAGE

Lightly season the fish fillets with salt and dust with the
flour. Melt the butter with the oil, garlic clove and sage
leaves in a frying pan or skillet and cook over low heat until
the garlic is lightly browned, then remove and discard it.
Slide the fish fillets into the pan and cook, turning once,
for about 15 minutes. Transfer the fish to a serving platter.
Remove the sage leaves from the pan and discard, then
stir in the hot water. Pour this liquid over the fish and
sprinkle over the lemon juice. Garnish each fish fillet with
a lemon slice and surround them with the new potatoes.
Serve immediately.

Photograph opposite

Serves 4
Preparation time: 20 mins
Cooking time: 30 mins

· 4 tablespoons olive oil
· 1 garlic clove, chopped
· ½ onion, chopped
· 4–5 basil leaves, chopped,
  plus extra to garnish
· 250 g (9 oz) monkfish fillet,
  cut into 2-cm (¾-inch) cubes
· 100 ml (scant ½ cup) white wine
· 400 g (14 oz) cherry tomatoes,
  halved
· 1 bay leaf
· 2 baby globe artichokes,
  thinly sliced
· 150 g (5 oz) canned farro, drained
· 40 g (⅓ cup) olives, pitted
  and chopped
· 320 g (11½ oz) malloreddus,
  cavatelli or conchiglie
· salt and pepper

Alternative fish: huss (dogfish)
or hake

288 294

MALLOREDDUS WITH FARRO, MONKFISH AND ARTICHOKES

Heat 3 tablespoons of the oil in a saucepan, add the garlic, onion and basil and cook over low heat, stirring occasionally, for 5 minutes. Add the monkfish, sprinkle over the wine and cook until the alcohol has evaporated, then add the tomatoes, cover and simmer for about 20 minutes.

Meanwhile, heat the remaining oil with the bay leaf in a frying pan or skillet. Add the artichokes and cook for 4–5 minutes, until just tender, then remove from the heat. About 5 minutes before the sauce has finished cooking, add the artichokes, farro and olives to the pan, taste and season with salt and pepper, if necessary.

Bring a large saucepan of salted water to a boil, add the pasta, bring back to a boil and cook for 8–10 minutes, until al dente. Drain and transfer to a serving platter. Add the hot sauce, toss lightly, sprinkle with the remaining basil and serve immediately.

Serves 6
Preparation time: 35 mins
Cooking time: 40 mins

· 1 × 1.2-kg (2½-lb) monkfish tail,
  skinned and filleted
· 80 g (6 tablespoons) butter,
  softened
· 25 g (½ cup) chopped tarragon
· 3 tablespoons olive oil
· 250 g (9 oz) filo (phyllo)
  pastry dough
· 6 lemon balm leaves
· salt and pepper

For the sauce:
· 20 g (1½ tablespoons) butter
· 2 shallots, finely chopped
· 250 ml (1 cup) Fish Stock
  (see page 78)
· 5 tablespoons dry vermouth
· 4 tablespoons cornflour
  (cornstarch)
· 1 tablespoon lemon juice
· 2 tablespoons olive oil
· salt

Alternative fish: salmon or cod

288   294

MONKFISH PARCELS

Cut the fish into 1.5-cm (¾-inch) slices. Beat half the
butter with the tarragon in a bowl until thoroughly mixed,
then set aside. Heat the olive oil into a nonstick saucepan,
add the fish and cook over medium heat, gently stirring
occasionally, for about 10 minutes, until browned. Season
with salt and pepper, remove from the heat and let cool.

Preheat the oven 180°C / 350°F / Gas Mark 4 and line
a baking sheet with foil. Melt the remaining butter. Unroll
three sheets of the filo (phyllo) dough, put them on a work
counter and brush with melted butter. Keep the remaining
sheets of dough covered with a damp dish towel to prevent
them from drying out. Stack the buttered sheets on top
of each other, put two lemon balm leaves in the middle,
add one-third of the monkfish and dot with 1 tablespoon
of the tarragon butter. Fold over the dough to enclose
the contents, brush with melted butter and put the parcel
on the prepared baking sheet. Make two more parcels in
the same way. Bake for 15 minutes, until golden and crisp.

Meanwhile, make the sauce. Melt the butter in a small
frying pan or skillet, add the shallots and cook over low
heat, stirring occasionally, for 5 minutes, until softened.
Season with salt, stir in the stock and vermouth and cook
until the liquid has reduced by half. Stir in the cornflour
(cornstarch), then add the lemon juice and olive oil and
mix well. Remove the pan from the heat and process with
a hand-held blender until smooth. Remove the fish parcels
from the oven, transfer to a serving platter and serve
immediately, passing the sauce separately in a sauceboat.

Serves 4
Preparation time: 20 mins
Cooking time: 20 mins

· 2–3 tablespoons olive oil,
  plus extra for brushing
· 4 slices white bread, crusts
  removed and chopped
· 2 tablespoons chopped
  flat-leaf parsley
· 2 garlic cloves, chopped
· 3 anchovies, preserved in
  salt, rinsed and chopped
· 1.5 kg (3¼ lb) monkfish tail,
  membrane removed
· 6 shallots, sliced into rings
· salt and pepper

Alternative fish: hake or
huss (dogfish)

 288 294

Coda di rospo farcita

STUFFED MONKFISH

Preheat the oven to 200°C/400°F/Gas Mark 6. Brush an ovenproof dish with oil. Mix together the bread, parsley, garlic and anchovies in a bowl and stir in just enough olive oil to make a soft, light stuffing. Put the fish on a chopping (cutting) board with the side where the central bone is most obvious facing upwards. Using a sharp knife cut along either side of the bone, keeping the 2 fillets attached on the underside as far as possible. Lift out and discard the bone. Fill the resulting cavity with the stuffing. Close the fish, season with salt and pepper and tie it with kitchen string at 2.5-cm (1-inch) intervals. Put the fish into the prepared dish, add the shallots and roast for about 40 minutes. Remove the dish from the oven, discard the string from the fish and serve immediately with the cooking juices.

Serves 4–6
Preparation time: 15 mins
Cooking time: 40 mins

· 50 g (4 tablespoons) butter
· 1 shallot, chopped
· ½ carrot, chopped
· 2 tablespoons brandy
· 400 ml (1⅔ cups) red wine
· 3–4 sage leaves
· 1 thyme sprig
· dash of red wine vinegar
· 1 kg (2¼ lb) monkfish fillets,
  cut into even-size chunks
· 1 tablespoon plain
  (all-purpose) flour
· 1 tablespoon olive oil
· 100 g (3½ oz) pickling (pearl)
  onions, chopped
· 100 g (scant 1½ cups) sliced
  button (white) mushrooms
· salt and pepper

Alternative fish: John Dory
or grouper

 288 294

Coda di rospo al vino rosso

MONKFISH IN RED WINE

Melt half the butter in a saucepan, add the shallot and carrot and cook over low heat, stirring occasionally, for 5 minutes, until softened. Sprinkle with the brandy and cook until the alcohol has evaporated, then add the red wine, herbs and vinegar and season with salt and pepper. Cover and simmer gently for about 20 minutes, then strain, pour back into the pan and reheat. Add the fish and cook for 10 minutes, then remove with a slotted spoon and keep warm. Increase the heat to high. Mix the the flour and remaining butter into a paste and beat a little at a time into the boiling sauce. Continue to cook, stirring constantly, for 10 minutes, until thickened, then turn off the heat. Heat the oil in another saucepan, add the onions and cook over low heat, stirring frequently, for 5 minutes, until softened. Add the mushrooms and stir in the red wine sauce, then add the fish and simmer over low heat for 5 minutes. Transfer to a serving dish and serve immediately.

Serves 4
Preparation time: 30 mins
Cooking time: 45 mins

· 4 courgettes (zucchini),
  thinly sliced
· plain (all-purpose) flour,
  for dusting
· 6 tablespoons olive oil
· 1 onion, chopped
· 1 celery stalk, chopped
· 200 ml (scant 1 cup) passata
  (puréed canned tomatoes)
· 1 tablespoon capers, drained,
  rinsed and chopped
· 100 g (1 cup) pitted green
  olives, chopped
· 600 g (1 lb 5 oz) cod fillets,
  cut into chunks
· salt and pepper

Alternative fish: hake, turbot
or brill

COD STEW WITH OLIVES AND CAPERS

Lightly dust the courgettes (zucchini) with flour, shaking off the excess. Heat half the olive oil in a large frying pan or skillet, add the courgette slices, in batches if necessary, and cook over medium heat, stirring occasionally, for about 5 minutes, until they are golden brown on both sides. Remove with a slotted spoon and drain on paper towels, then sprinkle with salt and keep warm. Heat the remaining olive oil in a large saucepan, add the onion and celery and cook over low heat, stirring occasionally, for 5 minutes. Add the passata (puréed canned tomatoes), capers and olives and simmer for about 10 minutes. Increase the heat to high, add the cod and cook for an additional few minutes. Season with salt and pepper, add the courgettes, lower the heat, cover and simmer for 30 minutes. Serve immediately.

Serves 6
Preparation time: 30 mins
+ 2 hrs marinating
Cooking time: 35 mins

· 1.2 kg (2½ lb) cod fillets,
  skinned and cut into chunks
· 1 tablespoon yellow mustard
  seeds, crushed
· 50 g (4 tablespoons) butter
· 2 shallots, finely chopped
· 500 g (3½ cups) shelled fresh
  or frozen peas
· 150 ml (⅔ cup) single
  (light) cream
· 2 tablespoons olive oil
· salt
· chopped dill, to garnish

Alternative fish: salmon
or hake

 288   290   296

SAUTÉED COD WITH PEA CREAM

Put the chunks of cod into a dish, sprinkle with the ground mustard seeds and let marinate for 2 hours. Melt the butter in a frying pan or skillet, add the shallots and cook over low heat, stirring occasionally, for 5 minutes, until softened. Add 400 g (2¾ cups) of the peas and 200 ml (scant 1 cup) water and season with salt. Cover and cook for 20 minutes.

Meanwhile, cook the remaining peas in plenty of salted boiling water in another pan for 5–10 minutes, until tender, then drain and transfer to a food processor. Process at high speed, then add the cream and process again. Check the seasoning and add more salt if necessary. Pour the mixture into a saucepan and keep warm over low heat, but do not let the mixture boil. Heat the oil in a frying pan or skillet, add the chunks of cod and cook over high heat, turning occasionally, for 5–6 minutes. Season lightly with salt.

Spoon a layer of the pea sauce on a serving platter and put the fish chunks on top. Spoon the shallot and pea mixture around the fish, sprinkle with dill and serve.

Serves 4
Preparation time: 15 mins
+ 1 hr resting
Cooking time: 20 mins

· 25 g (2 tablespoons) butter
· 175 ml (¾ cup) olive oil
· 8 cod fillets

For the batter:
· 100 g (scant 1 cup) plain
  (all-purpose) flour
· 1 egg, separated
· 120 ml (½ cup) beer, at
  room temperature
· salt
· home-made or ready-made
  tomato sauce, to serve

Alternative fish: hake or
John Dory

Filetti croccanti di merluzzo in pastella alla birra

CRISPY COD FILLETS IN BEER BATTER

First, make the batter. Sift the flour with a pinch of salt
into a bowl and stir in the egg yolk. Gradually stir in the
beer until the batter is smooth and creamy, then cover
and let rest for 1 hour. Whisk the egg white in a grease-free
bowl until stiff, then fold into the batter.

Melt the butter with the oil in a wide frying pan or skillet
and heat until hot. Dip the cod fillets carefully into the
batter, drain off the excess and add to the hot oil mixture.
Cook for about 10 minutes, until golden brown. Remove
from the pan with a fish slice (spatula) and drain on paper
towels. Serve immediately with tomato sauce on the side.

Serves 4
Preparation time: 20 mins
+ 10 mins standing
Cooking time: 20 mins

· 1 garlic clove, chopped
· 1 onion, chopped
· 1 chilli, seeded and chopped
· 1 tablespoon chopped thyme
· 2 teaspoons chopped rosemary
· 800 g (1¾ lb) cod fillets
· olive oil, for brushing
· salt

Alternative fish: hake or trout

Merluzzo agli aromi

AROMATIC COD

Mix together the garlic, onion, chilli, thyme and rosemary
in a small bowl and sprinkle the mixture all over the fish,
rubbing it well into the flesh. Let stand for 10 minutes.

Brush a large non-stick frying pan or skillet with oil,
add the fish fillets and cook for about 10 minutes, until a
golden crust has formed on the undersides. Turn with
a fish slice (spatula) and cook for another 10 minutes, until
golden brown. Season with salt and serve immediately.

Serves 6
Preparation time: 20 mins
+ 2 hrs marinating
Cooking time: 10 mins

· 6 × 175-g (6-oz) pieces of cod,
  sliced 4 cm (1½ inches) thick
· 50 g (2 oz) salted anchovies,
  rinsed, filleted and chopped
  (see page 110)
· ½ tablespoon mild mustard
· 1 large flat-leaf parsley
  sprig, chopped
· pinch of dried oregano
· 2 egg yolks
· juice of ½ lemon juice, strained
· 200 ml (scant 1 cup) olive oil
· oil for frying
· plain (all-purpose) flour,
  for dusting
· salt and pepper

Alternative fish: hake or
monkfish

 288   290   296

COD WITH HERBS AND MUSTARD

Spread out the cod fillets in a single layer on a large plate. Mix together the anchovies, mustard, parsley, oregano, egg yolks and a pinch each of salt and pepper in a bowl. Add the lemon juice, then gradually beat in enough olive oil to make a thick, mayonnaise-like sauce. Spread this sauce evenly over the cod fillets, cover and let marinate in the refrigerator for 2 hours.

Meanwhile, heat the oil for frying in a deep frying pan or skillet. Coat the pieces of cod with flour. Add to the pan in batches and cook in batches for about 3 minutes each, turning occasionally. Drain on paper towels and sprinkle with a little salt.

Serves 4
Preparation time: 20 mins
Cooking time: 30 mins

· 3 tablespoons olive oil, plus
  extra for brushing
· 2 rosemary sprigs
· 6 basil leaves
· 100 ml (3½ oz) salted anchovies,
  heads removed, cleaned and
  filleted (see page 110), soaked
  in cold water for 10 mins
  and drained
· 1 × 1-kg (2¼-lb) cod, scaled
  and cleaned
· 50 g (1 cup) fresh breadcrumbs
· 4 black olives, pitted and sliced
  for garnish (optional)
· salt and pepper

Alternative fish: hake or
monkfish

 288

Merluzzo alla siciliana

SICILIAN COD

Preheat the oven to 200°C/400°F/Gas Mark 6. Brush
an ovenproof dish with olive oil. Chop the needles
from 1 rosemary sprig and chop 4 basil leaves. Chop the
anchovies. Heat 2 tablespoons of the olive oil in a saucepan,
add the anchovies and cook, mashing with a wooden spoon
until they have almost completely disintegrated. Spoon
a little of the anchovy mixture inside the cavity of the cod
and add the rosemary sprig, the remaining whole basil
leaves and remaining olive oil, then close the cavity. Spoon
the remaining anchovy mixture into the prepared dish, add
the fish, sprinkle with the chopped rosemary, chopped basil
and breadcrumbs, season with salt and pepper and bake for
30 minutes. Garnish with the olives and serve immediately.

Photograph opposite

Serves 6
Preparation time: 30 mins
+ 1 hr cooling
Cooking time: 15 mins

· 250 g (9 oz) presoaked salt cod,
  skinned and cut into small pieces
· ½ onion, chopped
· 1 tablespoon lemon juice
· 175–250 ml (¾–1 cup) milk
· oil, for deep-frying

For the batter:
· 3 tablespoons plain
  (all-purpose) flour
· 1 egg
· 1 tablespoon olive oil
· 1 tablespoon finely chopped
  flat-leaf parsley
· 1 garlic clove, finely chopped
· salt and pepper

Alternative fish: salt pollock

 288   290

Frittelle di baccalà

SALT COD FRITTERS

Put the fish into a bowl, add the onion and lemon juice,
pour in enough milk to cover and let marinate for at
least 1 hour. Meanwhile, make the batter. Sift the flour
into a bowl and beat in the egg, then stir in the olive oil,
parsley, garlic and a pinch each of salt and pepper until
thoroughly combined. Heat the oil in a deep-fryer to
180–190°C/350–375°F or until a cube of day-old bread
browns in 30 seconds. Drain the salt cod pieces thoroughly
and stir them into the batter. Add tablespoonfuls of
the mixture to the hot oil, a few at a time, and cook for
3–5 minutes, until golden brown. Remove with a slotted
spoon and drain on paper towels. Keep warm while you
cook the remaining batches, then serve immediately.

Serves 4
Preparation time: 35 mins
Cooking time: 30 mins

· 500 g (1 lb 2 oz) tomatoes,
  peeled, seeded and coarsely
  chopped
· 4 tablespoons olive oil, plus
  extra for drying
· 2 garlic cloves
· 100 g (1 cup) black olives,
  pitted and sliced
· 2 tablespoons capers preserved
  in salt, rinsed and chopped
· 50 g (½ cup) pine nuts
· 50 g (⅓ cup) raisins
· 600 g (1 lb 5 oz) presoaked
  salt cod, skinned, boned
  and cut into pieces
· plain (all-purpose) flour,
  for dusting
· salt and pepper

Alternative fish: salt pollock

 288   290

Baccalà alla partenopea

NEAPOLITAN SALT COD

Put the tomatoes into a blender or food processor and
process to a purée. Put the olive oil, puréed tomatoes,
garlic, olives, capers, pine nuts and raisins into a frying pan
or skillet, add a pinch each of salt and pepper and 150 ml
(⅔ cup) water. Cook over low heat, stirring occasionally, for
20 minutes. Preheat the oven to 180°C/350°F/Gas Mark 4.
Heat the oil in a deep-fryer to 180–190°C/350–375°F or until
a cube of day-old bread browns in 30 seconds. Dust the
pieces of fish with flour, shaking off the excess, add to
the hot oil and cook for 5–8 minutes, until golden brown.
Remove with a fish slice (spatula) and drain on paper
towels. Put the fish in an ovenproof dish, spoon the tomato
sauce over them and bake for 30 minutes.

- -

Serves 4
Preparation time: 20 mins
Cooking time: 40 mins

· 2 tablespoons olive oil, plus
  extra for frying
· 4 garlic cloves, finely chopped
· 2 leeks, finely chopped
· 300 g (11 oz) tomatoes, peeled
  and sieved (strained)
· 800 g (1¾ lb) presoaked salt cod,
  skinned and cut into pieces
· plain (all-purpose) flour,
  for dusting
· 2 tablespoons chopped
  flat-leaf parsley
· salt and pepper

Alternative fish: salt pollock

 288   290

Baccalà con pomodori

SALT COD WITH TOMATOES

Heat the olive oil in a frying pan or skillet, add the garlic
and leeks and cook over low heat, stirring occasionally,
for 5–7 minutes, until softened. Add the tomatoes, season
with salt and pepper and simmer, stirring occasionally, for
15 minutes. Dust the pieces of fish with flour, shaking off
any excess. Pour oil to a depth of 4–5 cm (1½–2 inches) into
a large frying pan or skillet and heat. Add the fish and cook
for 8–10 minutes on each side until golden. Remove the
salt cod with a fish slice (spatula), drain on paper towels and
transfer to the pan with the vegetables. Sprinkle with the
parsley and cook over low heat for a few minutes. Transfer
the fish and sauce to a serving platter and serve immediately.

Photograph opposite

Serves 4
Preparation time: 1hr
Cooking time: 15 mins

· 400 g (14 oz) live mussels,
  scrubbed and beards removed
· 2 tablespoons olive oil
· 1 garlic clove, finely chopped
· ½ onion, chopped
· 150 g (2 cups) sliced chestnut
  (cremini) mushrooms
· 12 black olives, pitted and sliced
· 4 tomatoes, diced
· 1 tablespoon chopped
  flat-leaf parsley
· 2 hake, cleaned and filleted
· dry white wine
· salt and pepper

Alternative fish: cod or monkfish

Cartoccio di nasello e cozze

HAKE AND MUSSEL PARCEL

Put the mussels into a saucepan and cook over high heat, shaking the pan occasionally, for 4–5 minutes, until the shells have opened. Remove from the heat and discard any closed mussels. Remove the mussels from the shells and set aside. Preheat the oven to 180°C/350°F/Gas Mark 4. Heat the oil in a saucepan, add the garlic and onion and cook over low heat, stirring occasionally, for 5 minutes, until softened. Add the mushrooms and cook, for 7–8 minutes, then add the mussels, olives and tomatoes and season. Simmer for 5 minutes and sprinkle with parsley. Put the fish in a roasting pan, pour in the wine, season and bake for 10 minutes. Remove the hake from the oven and increase the temperature to 190°C/375°F/Gas Mark 5. Cut a sheet of parchment paper and spoon one-third of the sauce into the middle. Top with the fish and spoon the remaining sauce over it. Wrap up and bake for 15 minutes. Serve unwrapped.

Photograph opposite

···

Serves 6
Preparation time: 35 mins
Cooking time: 45 mins

· 500 g (1lb 2 oz) fennel bulbs,
  chopped
· 300 g (11 oz) potatoes, diced
· 1 × 1.5-kg (3¼-lb) hake,
  cleaned and filleted
· 100 ml (scant ½ cup) olive oil
· 3 tablespoons Pernod
· 25 g (½ cup) chopped dill
· salt and pepper

Alternative fish: cod or
huss (dogfish)

Nasello con pure di finocchi

HAKE WITH FENNEL PURÉE

Cook the fennel in salted boiling water for about 15 minutes, then add the potatoes and continue cooking for about another 15 minutes or until tender. Meanwhile, cut the hake fillets into medium-size pieces. Drain the vegetables, transfer to a food processor and process until smooth and creamy. Scrape the fennel purée into a bowl, stir in half the oil, then stir in the Pernod. Season with a pinch each of salt and pepper, set aside and keep warm. Cook the pieces of hake in a steamer for 3–4 minutes, until the flesh flakes easily, then transfer to a serving platter and pour the sauce over them. Garnish with the dill, drizzle with the remaining oil, season with a pinch of pepper and serve immediately.

Serves 4
Preparation time: 15 mins
Cooking time: 10 mins

· 2 tablespoons olive oil,
  plus extra for brushing
· 4 × 225-g (8-oz) hake steaks
· 1 onion, chopped
· 1 flat-leaf parsley sprig,
  chopped
· 1 celery stalk, chopped,
  plus a few leaves
· juice of 1 lemon, strained
· salt and pepper

Alternative fish: cod, conger
eel or salmon

 288

Nasello in salsa verde

HAKE IN GREEN SAUCE

Preheat the oven to 200°C/400°F/Gas Mark 6. Brush
an ovenproof dish with oil, put the fish in it and bake
for about 10 minutes.

Meanwhile, heat the olive oil in a saucepan, add the
onion and cook over low heat, stirring occasionally, for
5 minutes, until softened. Season with salt and pepper,
remove from the heat and keep warm. Stir in the parsley,
the celery and its leaves and the lemon juice. Serve the
hake with the green sauce.

Photograph opposite

Serves 4
Preparation time: 30 mins
Cooking time: 30 mins

· olive oil, for brushing
  and drizzling
· 4 potatoes, thinly sliced
· 800 g (1¾ lb) hake fillets
· 1 thyme sprig
· 1 rosemary sprig
· salt and freshly ground
  white pepper

Alternative fish: sea bream
or conger eel

 288   290   296

Nasello con patate

HAKE WITH POTATOES

Preheat the oven to 200°C/400°F/Gas Mark 6. Brush an
ovenproof dish with olive oil and put half the potato slices
in an even layer on the bottom. Put the fish on top, add
the thyme and rosemary and season with salt and pepper.
Cover with the remaining potato slices and drizzle with
olive oil. Bake for 30 minutes and serve immediately.

Serves 4
Preparation time: 15 mins
Cooking time: 30 mins

· 600 g (1 lb 5 oz) hake, cleaned, filleted and skinned
· 3 tablespoons olive oil
· 2 onions, finely chopped
· 1 garlic clove, chopped
· 1 bunch flat-leaf parsley, chopped
· 2 anchovies preserved in salt, rinsed and chopped
· 1 tablespoon Fish Stock (see page 78)
· 250–300 ml (1–1¼ cups) milk
· 8 slices cooked and set polenta (see page 125)
· salt and pepper

Alternative fish: cod or sea bass

 288   290   296

HAKE WITH MILK, ONIONS AND POLENTA

Cut the hake into pieces. Heat the oil in a frying pan or skillet, add the onions, garlic and parsley and cook over low heat, stirring occasionally, for a few minutes. Add the anchovies and stir, then add the hake. Add the stock and pour in just enough milk to cover the fish. Season to taste with salt and pepper. Cook over low heat, uncovered, for 20–30 minutes, until the cooking liquid has reduced to a smooth cream. Meanwhile, toast the polenta slices under a preheated grill (broiler) for about 3 minutes on each side. Transfer the hake to a serving platter, surround with the toasted polenta and serve immediately.

. . . .

Serves 6
Preparation time: 30 mins
Cooking time: 20 mins

· 2 × 900-g (2-lb) sea bream fillets
· 1 teaspoon ground coriander
· 6 green cardamom pods, split
· 6 tablespoons vegetable stock
· 3 tomatoes, peeled, seeded and chopped
· 20 black olives, pitted and chopped
· 2 tablespoons dry vermouth
· salt and pepper

For the sauce:
· 250 ml (1 cup) olive oil
· 100 ml (scant ½ cup) hot water
· juice of 1 lemon, strained
· ½ teaspoon chopped flat-leaf parsley
· pinch of chopped oregano
· salt and pepper

Alternative fish: sea bass

288   290   296

SEA BREAM WITH OLIVES AND SPICES

Preheat the oven to 180°C / 350°F / Gas Mark 4. Sprinkle the fish fillets with the ground coriander and cardamom seeds and season with salt and pepper. Pour the stock into an ovenproof dish and add the fish, tomatoes and olives. Sprinkle with the vermouth and bake for 20 minutes.

Meanwhile, make the sauce. Put all the ingredients into a blender or food processor and process until thoroughly combined, then pour into a sauceboat. Remove the dish from the oven and serve immediately, straight from the dish, and pass the cold sauce separately.

Photograph opposite

Serves 4
Preparation time: 20 mins
+ 3 hrs marinating
Cooking time: 6–8 mins

· juice of 3 lemons, strained
· 1 garlic clove, finely chopped
· 1 mint sprig, finely chopped
· 1 thyme sprig, finely chopped
· 1 oregano sprig, finely chopped
· 1 flat-leaf parsley sprig,
  finely chopped
· 5 tablespoons olive oil
· 4 sea bream fillets
· salt and pepper

Alternative fish: cod or sea bass

 288   290   296

Sarago marinato

MARINATED SEA BREAM SLICES

Combine the lemon juice, garlic, mint, thyme, oregano, parsley and 1 tablespoon of the olive oil in a dish. Add the fish, turning to coat, and let marinate in a cool place for 3 hours.

Heat the remaining oil in a frying pan or skillet. Drain the fish, reserving the marinade, and add them to the pan. Cook over high heat for 3–4 minutes, then sprinkle with 2 tablespoons of the reserved marinade. Gently turn over and cook for another 3–4 minutes. Season lightly with salt and pepper and carefully transfer the fish to a serving dish using a fish slice (spatula). Serve immediately.

Photograph opposite

· ·

Serves 4
Preparation time: 20 mins
Cooking time: 30 mins

· olive oil, for brushing
  and drizzling
· 4 leeks, thinly sliced
· 1 carrot, thinly sliced
· 1 × 1-kg (2¼-lb) sea bream,
  scaled and cleaned
· 2 tablespoons chopped
  flat-leaf parsley
· 200 ml (scant 1 cup) dry
  white wine
· salt and pepper

Alternative fish: hake or cod

 288

Sarago con i porri

SEA BREAM WITH LEEKS

Preheat the oven to 200°C/400°F/Gas Mark 6. Brush an ovenproof dish with oil and add half the leek and carrot slices. Lay the fish on top, cover with the remaining leek and carrot slices, sprinkle with chopped parsley and season with salt and pepper. Pour over the wine and drizzle with olive oil, then bake for 30 minutes. Remove from the oven, carefully lift out the fillets and serve with the vegetables.

Serves 6
Preparation time: 15 mins
Cooking time: 45 mins

· 1 × 1.5-kg (3¼-lb) sea bream,
  scaled and cleaned
· 1.8kg (8 cups) coarse
  sea salt
· olive oil, for drizzling
· juice of 1 lemon, strained
· salt and pepper

Alternative fish: sea bass
or grey (striped) mullet

 288

SEA BREAM BAKED IN A SALT CRUST

Preheat the oven to 200°C/400°F/Gas Mark 6. Season
the cavity of the fish with salt and pepper. Line a roasting
pan with a sheet of foil, sprinkle 400g (1¾ cups) of the
sea salt on the bottom and put the fish on top. Cover it
completely with the remaining salt and bake for about
45 minutes (allow 15 minutes per 500g/1lb 2oz). Remove
the pan from the oven, break the salt crust and lift out
the fish. Remove and discard the skin, brushing away all
traces of salt, and put the fish on a warm serving dish.
Drizzle with olive oil and the lemon juice and serve
immediately.

Photograph opposite

Serves 4
Preparation time: 15 mins
+ 3 hrs marinating
Cooking time: 30 mins

· 1 × 1-kg (2¼-lb) sea bream,
  scaled, cleaned and cut
  into pieces
· juice of 5 lemons, strained
· 500g (1lb 2oz) onions, sliced
· 3 garlic cloves, crushed
· 1 fresh chilli, chopped
· plain (all-purpose) flour,
  for dusting
· 3 tablespoons olive oil
· salt and pepper

Alternative fish: sea bass
or red mullet

 288

SEA BREAM WITH LEMON

Put the fish into a bowl, add the lemon juice, onions, garlic
and chilli and let marinate for 3 hours. Remove the pieces
of fish from of the bowl, pat dry with paper towels and dust
with flour. Strain the marinade into a bowl and reserve the
onions, garlic and chilli. Heat the olive oil in a frying pan
or skillet, add the pieces of fish and cook over medium heat
for 4 minutes on each side, then remove from the pan and
keep warm. Add the onions, garlic and chilli to the pan
and cook over low heat, stirring occasionally, for 5 minutes.
Return the fish to the pan, pour in the reserved marinade
and season with salt and pepper. Cover and simmer for
15 minutes, then serve.

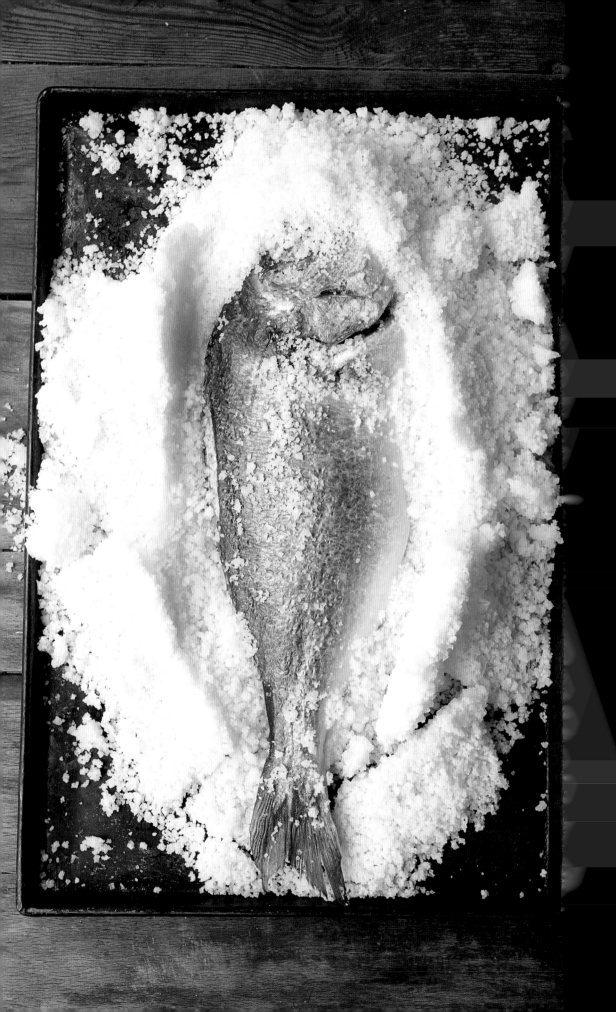

Serves 4
Preparation time: 10 mins
+ 3 hrs marinating
Cooking time: 50 mins

· 1 × 1-kg (2¼ lb) gilthead or
  other sea bream, scaled
  and cleaned
· 1 litre (4¼ cups) dry white wine
· 1 carrot, coarsely chopped
· 1 onion, coarsely chopped
· 1 tablespoon coarsely chopped
  flat-leaf parsley
· 1 bay leaf
· 1 garlic clove, coarsely chopped
· 50 g (⅓ cup) sultanas or
  golden raisins
· 25 g (2 tablespoons) butter
· salt

Alternative fish: sea bass or
grey (striped) mullet

 288   290

Sarago con uva sultanina

SEA BREAM WITH GOLDEN RAISINS

Put the fish into a flameproof casserole (Dutch oven) just large enough to hold it, pour in sufficient wine to cover it, add the carrot, onion, parsley, bay leaf and garlic and season with salt. Simmer over low heat for about 45 minutes, until the flesh flakes easily. Carefully remove the fish from the casserole, draining it well, then halve and remove the backbone and any attached bones. Put the fish on a serving plate and keep warm.

Strain the cooking liquid into a bowl and divide it into 2 batches, reserving the vegetables in the sieve (strainer) but discarding the bay leaf. Pour 1 batch into a blender or food processor, add the reserved vegetables and process. Pour the other batch into a saucepan, add the sultanas and cook over medium-high heat until the liquid has reduced. Stir in the processed cooking liquid and the butter and heat until very hot. Pour the sauce over the fish and serve immediately.

Serves 4
Preparation time: 10 mins
Cooking time: 25 mins

· 3 tablespoons olive oil, plus
  extra for brushing
· 50g (½ cup) fine
  dry breadcrumbs
· 4 × 200-g (7-oz) John Dory
  fillets
· 2 tablespoons chopped
  flat-leaf parsley
· large pinch of dried oregano
· 1 garlic clove, chopped
· 400 ml (1⅔ cups) dry white wine
· salt and pepper

Alternative fish: hake or turbot

 288   290   296

JOHN DORY GRATIN

Preheat the oven to 180°C/350°F/Gas Mark 4. Brush
a flameproof baking dish with oil. Sprinkle 3 tablespoons
of the breadcrumbs over the bottom of the prepared
dish and put two fish fillets on top. Sprinkle with half the
parsley, half the oregano, 3 tablespoons of the remaining
breadcrumbs and half the chopped garlic and season
with salt and pepper. Add the remaining fish fillets and
sprinkle with the remaining parsley, remaining oregano,
3 tablespoons of the remaining breadcrumbs and the
remaining garlic. Drizzle with the wine, set the dish over
medium heat and cook until the wine has completely
evaporated. Transfer the dish to the oven and bake, basting
occasionally, for 8 minutes. Remove the dish from the
oven, sprinkle with the remaining breadcrumbs, drizzle
with the olive oil and return to the oven. Bake for another
7–12 minutes, until the fish flakes easily and the topping
is golden brown. Serve immediately.

Serves 4
Preparation time: 45 mins
Cooking time: 10–15 mins

· 100g (scant ½ cup) butter
· 500g (1lb 2oz) mangetouts
  (snow peas), trimmed
· 1.5-kg (3¼-lb) John Dory,
  cleaned and filleted
· plain (all-purpose) flour,
  for dusting
· salt and pepper
· fennel fronds, to garnish

Alternative fish: cod or brill

 288   290   296

JOHN DORY WITH
MANGETOUTS (SNOW PEAS)

Melt half the butter in a frying pan or skillet, add the
mangetouts (snow peas) and cook over low heat, stirring
occasionally, for about 5 minutes, then season with salt
and pepper. Add 150 ml (⅔ cup) water, cover and simmer
for 30 minutes. Lightly dust the fish with flour, shaking
off the excess. Melt the remaining butter in a frying pan or
skillet, add the fish and cook over medium heat until golden
brown all over and cooked through. Drain the mangetouts
and transfer them and the fish fillets to a warm serving
dish. Garnish with fennel fronds and serve immediately.

Serves 4
Preparation time: 15 mins
+ 3 hrs marinating
Cooking time: 50 mins

· 3 tablespoons olive oil
· 1 onion, thinly sliced
· 1 celery stalk, thinly sliced
· 1 carrot, thinly sliced
· ½ garlic clove
· 200 g (7 oz) tomatoes,
  coarsely chopped
· 2 tablespoons finely chopped
  flat-leaf parsley
· 1 tablespoon finely chopped basil
· 1 chilli, seeded and finely chopped
· 100 ml (scant ½ cup) dry
  white wine
· dash of balsamic vinegar
· 4 John Dory fillets
· salt and pepper

Alternative fish: turbot or hake

288   290   296

Filetti di San Pietro all'acqua pazza

JOHN DORY POACHED IN PIQUANT SAUCE

Heat the oil in a large flameproof casserole (Dutch oven), add the onion, celery, carrot, garlic, tomatoes, parsley, basil and chilli and cook over low heat, stirring occasionally, for 10 minutes. Season with salt and pepper, pour in 400 ml (1⅔ cups) water and the wine, sprinkle with a dash of balsamic vinegar and simmer for 15 minutes. Meanwhile, preheat the oven to 180°C/350°F/Gas Mark 4. Add the John Dory fillets to the casserole, transfer it to the oven and cook for about 20 minutes, until the fish flakes easily. Remove the casserole from the oven and transfer the fish fillets to a serving platter. Set the casserole over medium-high heat and cook until the liquid has reduced and thickened, then ladle this over the fish fillets. Serve immediately.

Photograph opposite

Serves 4
Preparation time: 20 mins
+ 2 hrs standing
Cooking time: 8–10 mins

· 5 tablespoons olive oil
· 1.5 kg (3¼ lb) John Dory fillets
· salt

For the sauce:
· 750 g (1 lb 10 oz) tomatoes,
  peeled, seeded and diced
· zest of 1 lemon, chopped
· 6 basil leaves, chopped
· ½ garlic clove, chopped
· pinch dried thyme
· 1 teaspoon chopped
  flat-leaf parsley
· 5 tablespoons olive oil
· salt and pepper

Alternative fish: cod or brill

288   290   296

Filetti di San Pietro al pomodoro ed erbe di stagione

JOHN DORY WITH TOMATOES AND HERBS

First make the sauce. Put the tomatoes in a colander and set aside to drain for 15 minutes. Combine the lemon zest, basil, garlic and thyme in a bowl, add the tomatoes, parsley and olive oil and season with salt and pepper. Stir well, cover and set aside in the refrigerator for 2 hours for the flavours to mingle. Preheat the oven to 200°C/400°F/Gas Mark 6. Pour the oil into an ovenproof dish, add the fish fillets and season lightly with salt and pepper. Bake for 8–10 minutes, until the flesh flakes easily. Meanwhile, transfer the sauce to a saucepan and heat gently without boiling. Remove the dish from the oven and transfer the fish to a serving platter. Serve immediately, handing the sauce separately in a sauceboat.

Serves 4
Preparation time: 10 mins
Cooking time: 20 mins

· 2 tablespoons olive oil
· 4 John Dory fillets
· juice of 1 lemon, strained
· 120 ml (½ cup) Marsala
· 2 tablespoons chopped basil
· salt and pepper

Alternative fish: monkfish
or huss (dogfish)

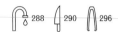

288   290   296

San Pietro al marsala

JOHN DORY WITH MARSALA

Heat the oil in a frying pan or skillet, add the fish and cook
over high heat for 5 minutes on each side, until browned.
Season with salt and pepper, sprinkle with the lemon juice
and Marsala and cook for 10 minutes more. Sprinkle with
the basil, remove from the heat and serve immediately.

Serves 4
Preparation time: 25 mins
Cooking time: 20–30 mins

· 4 scorpion fish, spines trimmed,
  scaled and cleaned
· ½ bunch thyme, chopped
· 4 tablespoons olive oil
· juice of 1 lemon, strained
· 100 g (3½ oz) salted anchovies,
  heads removed, cleaned and
  filleted (see page 110), soaked
  in cold water for 10 minutes
  and drained
· 100 g (½ cup) butter, softened
· salt and pepper

Alternative fish: red mullet
or trout

288

Scorfano al timo

SCORPION FISH WITH THYME

Preheat the oven to 180°C/350°F/Gas Mark 4. Season the
cavities of the fish with salt and pepper and fill with some
of the thyme. Sprinkle the remainder of the thyme in an
ovenproof dish, add the fish and season with salt and
pepper. Whisk together the olive oil and lemon juice and
pour the mixture over the fish. Bake, basting frequently,
for 20–30 minutes.

Meanwhile, chop the anchovy fillets. Pass the anchovies
through a sieve (strainer) into a bowl and mash with the
butter in a bowl until thoroughly combined. Serve the fish
with the anchovy butter.

Photograph opposite

Serves 4
Preparation time: 25 mins
Cooking time: 20–30 mins

· 50 g (4 tablespoons) butter,
  plus extra for greasing
· 200 g (3 cups) mushrooms,
  thinly sliced
· 1 × 800-g (1¾-lb) scorpion fish,
  heads removed, spines trimmed,
  scaled and cleaned
· 3 lemon slices
· 175 ml (¾ cup) dry white wine
· salt and pepper

Alternative fish: grey (striped)
mullet or trout

 288

SCORPION FISH WITH MUSHROOMS

Preheat the oven to 180°C/350°F/Gas Mark 4. Grease an ovenproof dish with butter. Spread out the mushrooms in the dish, season the fish with salt and pepper and put it on top of them. Dot with butter, top with the lemon slices and pour in the wine. Bake, basting frequently, for 20–30 minutes. Serve immediately, straight from the dish.

Serves 4
Preparation time: 25 mins
+ cooling
Cooking time: 15–20 mins

· 2 × 300-g (11-oz) scorpion
  fish, heads removed, spines
  trimmed, scaled and cleaned
· 3 tablespoons olive oil
· 4 tomatoes, peeled, seeded
  and diced
· 1 garlic clove, finely chopped
· pinch of saffron threads
· 500 ml (2 cups) dry white wine
· salt and pepper

Alternative fish: red mullet
or trout

 288

SCORPION FISH WITH WHITE WINE AND SAFFRON

Put the fish in a flameproof casserole (Dutch oven) and add the olive oil and tomatoes. Season with salt and pepper, add the garlic and saffron and pour in the wine. Bring to a boil, cover and simmer over medium heat for 15–20 minutes. Remove from the heat and let the fish cool in the cooking liquid. Serve cold with the white wine sauce.

Serves 4
Preparation time: 15 mins
+ 2 hrs marinating
Cooking time: 10 mins

· 4 large huss (dogfish) steaks

For the marinade:
· 1 onion, thinly sliced
· 2 garlic cloves, thinly sliced
· 1 basil sprig, coarsely chopped
· 2 flat-leaf parsley sprigs,
  coarsely chopped
· 1 chilli, seeded and chopped
· 1 clove
· juice of 1 lemon, strained
· 100 ml (scant ½ cup) olive oil
· salt and pepper

Alternative fish: monkfish
or turbot

288   290

Palombo marinato

MARINATED HUSS (DOGFISH)

First, make the marinade. Mix together the onion, garlic, basil, parsley, chilli, clove, lemon juice, oil and a pinch each of salt and pepper in a dish. Add the fish and let marinate in the refrigerator, turning frequently, for 2 hours. Preheat the grill (broiler) or light the barbecue. Drain the fish and reserve the marinade. Cook the fish under the grill or on the barbecue, brushing occasionally with reserved marinade, for 5 minutes on each side. Transfer to a serving platter and serve immediately.

Serves 4
Preparation time: 10 mins
Cooking time: 20 mins

· 800 g (1¾ lb) huss (dogfish)
  fillets, sliced
· plain (all-purpose) flour,
  for dusting
· 4 tablespoons olive oil
· 4 shallots, finely chopped
· 1 canned anchovy fillet,
  drained and chopped
· 2 tablespoons chopped
  flat-leaf parsley
· 200 ml (scant 1 cup) dry
  white wine
· salt and pepper

Alternative fish: turbot or cod

288   290   296

Palombo al vino bianco

HUSS (DOGFISH) WITH WHITE WINE

Dust the slices of fish with flour, shaking off the excess. Heat half the oil in a frying pan or skillet, add the fish and cook over high heat for about 5 minutes on each side, until browned, then season with salt and pepper and turn off the heat. Meanwhile, heat the remaining oil in another frying pan or skillet, add the shallots and cook over low heat, stirring occasionally, for 5 minutes, until softened. Add the anchovy and parsley, sprinkle with the wine, increase the heat and cook until the liquid has almost completely reduced. Stir in 1 tablespoon water and season with a pinch each of salt and pepper. Pour the sauce over the slices of fish and simmer for a few minutes until heated through, then serve.

Serves 6
Preparation time: 10 mins
Cooking time: 45 mins

· 2 tablespoons olive oil
· ½ onion, chopped
· 1 kg (2¼ lb) peas, shelled
  (yields about 500 g/3½ cups)
· 250 ml (1 cup) passata (puréed
  canned tomatoes)
· 800 g (1¾ lb) huss (dogfish)
  fillets
· salt and pepper
· chopped flat-leaf parsley,
  to garnish

Alternative fish: monkfish
or hake

288   290   296

ROMAN-STYLE HUSS (DOGFISH) WITH PEAS

Heat the oil in a large frying pan or skillet, add the onion and cook over low heat, stirring occasionally, for 5 minutes. Add the peas, the passata (puréed canned tomatoes) and just enough water to cover the peas, and cook for 35 minutes. Add the fish, season with salt and pepper and simmer gently for 5 minutes, until the fish flakes easily and the liquid has thickened slightly. Transfer to a serving dish, garnish with the parsley and serve immediately.

Photograph opposite

Serves 6
Preparation time: 20 mins
Cooking time: 40 mins

· 1.2 kg (2⅔ lb) red mullet
  or red snapper, cleaned
  and filleted, heads and
  bones reserved
· 150 ml (⅔ cup) olive oil
· 50 g (1¼ cups) chopped leek
· 300 ml (1¼ cups) Friuli Tocai
  wine
· 30 fresh basil leaves
· salt and pepper

Alternative fish: grey (striped)
mullet or scorpion fish

288   290   296

Filetti di triglia al vino bianco

RED MULLET WITH WINE

Cut out and discard the gills from the fish heads. Heat 5 tablespoons of the oil in a large saucepan, add the leek and cook over low heat, stirring occasionally, for 5 minutes, until softened. Add the fish heads and bones, pour in 250 ml (1 cup) of the wine and cook until the liquid has reduced. Pour in 350 ml (1½ cups) water and simmer for 15 minutes. Remove from the heat and strain into a clean saucepan. Bring to a boil and continue to boil until the sauce becomes syrupy. Season to taste with salt and pepper and remove the pan from the heat. Tear half the basil leaves into small pieces. Heat the remaining oil with the torn basil leaves in a frying pan or skillet, add the fish fillets and cook for 3–4 minutes, then sprinkle with the remaining wine and cook until evaporated. Transfer the fish and any pan juices to a serving platter, pour the wine sauce over it, garnish with the remaining basil and serve immediately.

Serves 4
Preparation time: 20 mins
+ 15 mins marinating
Cooking time: 20–30 mins

· 3 oranges
· 150 ml (⅔ cup) olive oil, plus
  extra for brushing
· 12 × 100-g (3½-oz) red mullet or
  red snapper, scaled and cleaned
· 3 spring onions (scallions),
  finely chopped
· 2 pinches of fennel seeds
· 1 tablespoon chopped
  flat-leaf parsley
· salt and pepper

Alternative fish: grey (striped)
mullet or cod

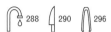

Triglia all'arancia

RED MULLET WITH ORANGE SALAD

Squeeze the juice from 1 orange and whisk it with the olive oil in a jug (pitcher). Pour half of this mixture into a dish, add the fish and let marinate for 15 minutes. Meanwhile, peel the remaining oranges with a sharp knife, cutting away all the pith, then slice thinly. Put the slices into a salad bowl, add the spring onions (scallions), season with salt and pepper and sprinkle with the remaining oil and orange juice mixture. Toss gently and set aside. Line a griddle (grill) pan with aluminum foil. Drain the fish, add to the pan, skin side down, season with salt and pepper and sprinkle with the fennel seeds. Cook for 3 minutes, then turn over and cook for another minute. Transfer the fish to a serving dish and sprinkle with the parsley. Serve immediately, passing the salad separately.

Photograph opposite

Serves 4
Preparation time: 30 mins
Cooking time: 30 mins

· 1 bundle asparagus, washed
  and trimmed
· 100 ml (scant ½ cup) olive oil,
  plus extra for drizzling
· 1 garlic clove, peeled
· 1 large tomato, peeled, seeded
  and diced
· 1 courgette (zucchini), diced
· 10 fresh basil leaves, finely
  chopped
· 12 red mullet or red snapper
  fillets
· semolina, for coating
· salt and freshly ground
  white pepper

Alternative fish: scorpion fish
or grouper

Triglia di scoglio al basilico

RED MULLET WITH BASIL

Cut the asparagus into thin julienne strips and blanch for 30 seconds in a saucepan of boiling water, then drain and refresh under cold running water. Heat 3 tablespoons of the oil with the garlic in a frying pan or skillet. When the garlic starts to colour, remove and discard it. Add the asparagus to the pan, together with the tomato and courgette (zucchini). Stir, season with salt and pepper and cook for 10 minutes. Meanwhile, press the basil leaves onto the skin of the fillets with the palm of your hand, then season with salt and pepper and roll them in the semolina to coat. Heat the remaining oil in a large frying pan or skillet. Working in batches, add the fish, skin side down, and cook for 3 minutes, then turn over and cook for another minute. Lift out the fillets with a fish slice (spatula) and drain on paper towels. Spoon the vegetable mixture evenly over a serving platter and place the fillets on top. Drizzle with olive oil and serve.

Serves 4
Preparation time: 15 mins
+ 5 mins standing
Cooking time: 30 mins

· 4 tablespoons olive oil, for
  brushing
· 6 thick slices of crusted bread
· 2 × 500-g (1lb 2-oz) red mullet,
  scaled and cleaned
· 150 g (5 oz) tomatoes, peeled
  and diced
· 1 garlic clove, chopped
· 1 onion, chopped
· 6–8 small, tender celery leaves
· 100 ml (scant ½ cup) dry
  white wine
· salt and pepper

Alternative fish: sea bass or
sea bream

 288

Crostino di triglia

RED MULLET WITH TOMATOES ON TOAST

Preheat the oven to 200°C / 400°F / Gas Mark 6. Brush
a large ovenproof dish with oil, put the slices of bread
in it in a single layer and put the fish on top. Sprinkle the
tomatoes, garlic, onion and celery leaves over the fish,
season with salt and pepper and drizzle with the olive oil
and white wine.

Transfer to the oven and roast for about 30 minutes.
Remove from the oven and let stand for 5 minutes, then
serve straight from the dish.

Photograph opposite

- -

Serves 6
Preparation time: 30 mins
+ cooling
Cooking time: 1½ hrs

· butter, for greasing
· 400 g (14 oz) assorted fish fillets,
  such as cod, hake and tuna
· 400 g (2 cups) mashed potatoes
· 200 ml (scant 1 cup) double
  (heavy) cream
· 2 egg yolks
· 3 tablespoons capers, rinsed
· 3 hard-boiled eggs, sliced
· salt and pepper

Alternative fish: salmon

 288   290   296

Gâteau di pesce alla casalinga

FISH TIMBALE

Preheat the oven to 180°C / 350°F / Gas Mark 4. Grease an
ovenproof dish or loaf pan with butter. Put the fish fillets,
potatoes and cream in a food processor and process until
smooth and combined. With the motor running, add the egg
yolks one at a time, then the capers. Season with salt and
pepper. Transfer half the fish mixture to the prepared dish
and smooth the surface. Cover with the sliced hard-boiled
eggs, then spoon the remaining fish mixture on top and
smooth the surface. Cover tightly with foil. Stand the dish
in a roasting pan and pour in boiling water to come about
halfway up the side. Cook in the oven for 1½ hours. Remove
the dish the oven and let cool completely before then
turning out. This makes a tasty starter (appetizer) served
with slices of toast.

Serves 8
Preparation time: 30 mins
Cooking time: 1 hr

· 2.5 kg (5½ lb) mixed fish
  (see method), cleaned and
  cut into chunks if necessary
· 175 ml (¾ cup) olive oil
· 1 onion, chopped
· 1 sprig fresh flat-leaf
  parsley, chopped
· 2 cloves garlic, chopped
· 1 small fresh chilli, de-seeded
  and chopped
· 500 ml (2 cups) red or white wine
· 300 g (11 oz) tomatoes, peeled,
  de-seeded and chopped
· Fish Stock (see below), optional
· 500 g (1 lb 2 oz) mussels,
  scrubbed and beards removed
· salt and pepper
· toast rubbed with garlic, to serve

CACCIUCCO

For this fish soup that's typical of Livorno in northwest Italy, you need a few slices of monkfish, a conger or freshwater eel, a few squid or cuttlefish and some mussels. Heat the olive oil in a flameproof casserole (Dutch oven), preferably earthenware, add the onion, parsley, garlic and chilli, season with salt and pepper and cook over low heat, stirring occasionally, for about 10 minutes, until the onion is golden brown. Add the wine and cook for 10 minutes, then add the tomatoes and simmer for another 10 minutes. Add the firmer fish (such as eel and monkfish), pour in a little warm water or fish stock and cook over high heat for 10 minutes. Gradually add the more delicate fish, finishing with the mussels. (Discard any with broken shells or that do not shut immediately when sharply tapped, and any that remain closed after cooking.) Simmer for 30 minutes. Serve with slices of toast rubbed with garlic.

Photograph opposite

Serves 4–6
Preparation time: 10 mins
Cooking time: 1 hr

· 1 fresh flat-leaf parsley sprig
· 1 sprig fresh thyme
· 1 onion, chopped
· 1 carrot, sliced
· 1 celery stick, sliced
· 1 tablespoon black peppercorns,
  lightly crushed
· 1 kg (2¼ lb) white fish or white
  fish bones and heads, gills
  removed
· salt

 288

FISH STOCK

Pour 2 litres (8½ cups) water into a large saucepan, add the herbs, onion, carrot, celery and peppercorns and season with salt. Gradually bring to a boil, then reduce the heat and simmer for 30 minutes. Remove from the heat, leave to cool, then add the fish (the water should just cover). Return to the heat, bring just to the boil, then reduce the heat and simmer for 20 minutes. Remove from the heat and leave the fish to cool in the stock for a stronger flavour. Strain the stock. If using only bones and heads, add to the pan with the herbs and vegetables and simmer for 30 minutes. Leave to cool slightly, then strain.

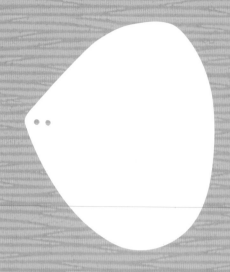

FLAT WHITE FISH

Flat fish start life as round fish but as they develop, they turn onto their sides and the eyes move to the top exposed fillet. The colour of the fish changes too and the top fillet will take on camouflage colouring to match the seabed. The underside of the fillet often remains white and pearlescent, so is masked by the sun or daylight shining through the water, which protects the fish from underside attack.

Similar to round white fish, flat fish have white, textured flesh with natural oils in the liver and delicate flaky fillets – although some members of the sole group, and turbot, are meaty. Skates and rays also come under the heading of flat fish, and they too have lean, white flesh, although the flesh is fibrous. These fish are classified as cartilaginous, which means they have a soft frame, made from cartilage rather than bones.

Smaller flat fish – such as common sole, plaice and flounder – provide a top and bottom fillet that is often cut in half to present quarter fillets. Large fish, including turbot and halibut, are most often cut into steaks with the bone running through the main part of the body. They can be filleted and skinned ready for rolling to poach or pan-frying flat.

Flat white fish are often at their best after they have been out of the water for a day or so and kept very well chilled on ice. The flavour develops a little and the fish tends to become firmer in texture.

TURBOT

Rombo
Psetta axima

Average weight range:
500g – 8kg (1lb 2oz – 17½lb)
Average length: 20 – 35 cm
(8–14 inches)

Recipes on pages 86–95

The Italian name for this fish – *rombo*, meaning rhombus – derives from its shape. Both brill and turbot (which belong to the same family) are called *rombo*, and the former is preferred in Italy. The mottled skin on its upper surface is a contrast to the pure white belly.

Turbot is farmed extensively in Europe to feed a demanding market and brill is only wild caught. Smaller farmed turbot are usually sold whole, but a large turbot is often either filleted and skinned or cut into *tronçons* (a slice of flat fish cut on the bone).

The white, sweet flesh of turbot and brill has such a fine flavour that they are best simply pan-fried or poached with a flavoured butter or olive oil and a squeeze of lemon. In Italy, they are often simply dusted with flour and pan-fried and served with classic sauces such as white wine and anchovy and tomato. Because turbot is firmer and meatier than brill, it suits a range of cooking methods including roasting, char-grilling (charbroiling) and stir-frying. Alternative fish are sole, John Dory, flounder, halibut or the lesser-known relative, megrim.

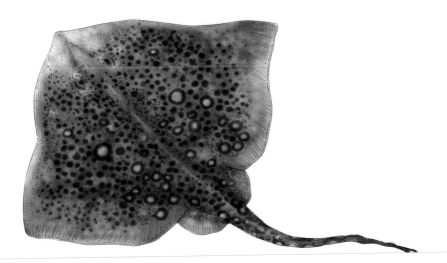

SKATE

Razza
Rajidae

Average weight range:
300g–2kg (11oz–4½lb)
Average length: 50–90cm
(20–35 inches)

Recipes on pages 96–99

Found in all the oceans of the world, skates (also known as rays) are kite-shaped, cartilaginous, flat fish with long thin tails. The skin colour varies from species to species, but the flavour and texture are virtually the same. The flesh of these fish is unique and instantly recognizable because it peels away from the cartilage in long strands. It has a distinctive, strong and slightly earthy flavour.

A whole skate is an uncommon sight because only the fins (usually known as the wings) and cheeks (also known as the knobs) can be eaten. The skin is difficult to remove so it is often better to ask for your fish supplier to skin the wings. Look for a fresh smell and avoid any that smell of ammonia, which is a sign that they are not fresh.

Wings and knobs can be poached, fried, baked or cooked in a parcel or package of greaseproof (wax) paper or aluminum foil. Generally cooked with the cartilage intact, a large wing will be dense in texture and can be poached to perfection in 12 minutes. Classic partners for skate are capers, lemon and *beurre noir*, a melted butter that is cooked over low heat until the milk solids turn a very dark brown. In Italy, they are traditionally served in tomato sauce or fried in butter and served with anchovy sauce. Their distinctive texture make them difficult to substitute, but huss (dogfish) or monkfish are possible alternatives.

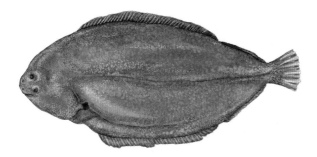

SOLE

Sogliola
Solea solea

Average weight range:
150g–1kg (5oz–2¼lb)
Average length: 24–40cm
(10–16 inches)

Recipes on pages 100–105

The common sole has a chocolate-brown, slightly mottled and rough skin, and is highly prized in Europe. True sole, which is sold in the United Kingdom as Dover sole (named after the port where it was traditionally landed), is highly prized across Europe for its densely textured white fillets and sweet flavour. Many members of the true sole are found worldwide.

Sole is at its best a couple of days after it has been caught, when the flavour has developed and it is much easier to skin. The fish supplier will trim, skin and fillet the fish if required, but it is usually sold and cooked on the bone because the fillets are long and thin. It is best to ask for the heads, fins and the blood line to be removed and for the fish to be skinned ready for cooking whole.

Sole can be pan-fried, baked, roasted or grilled (broiled). Brushing the skinned fish with melted butter or oil will keep it from drying out during cooking. Flavoured butters, such as maître d'hotel or anchovy butter, will add flavour and richness to cooked fish. It is perfectly acceptable to cook sole with the skin on because it will peel away easily afterwards. In Italy, sole has several regional names, such as *sfogi* in Veneto and *sfoglie* near the Adriatic coast. It works well in risotto such as *Risotto allo zafferano e filetti di sogliola* (Sole and saffron risotto, see page 103) and as a light and colourful *Filetti di sogliole insalata* (Sole salad, see page 104). Alternative fish that can be substituted for sole recipes are lemon sole, flounder, dab and plaice.

Serves 6
Preparation time: 20 mins
Cooking time: 20 mins

· 250 g (4 cups) button (white)
  mushrooms, sliced
· 6 baby globe artichoke
  hearts, sliced
· juice of 2 lemons, strained
· 70 ml (⅓ cup) olive oil
· 1.2 kg (2½ lb) turbot fillet
· 1½ teaspoons mild curry powder
· 120 ml (½ cup) Fish Stock
  (see page 78)
· 50 g (4 tablespoons) butter
· salt and pepper

Alternative fish: brill or halibut

 288   292

TURBOT WITH MUSHROOMS AND ARTICHOKES

Preheat the oven to 200°C / 400°F / Gas Mark 6. Put the mushroom and artichoke strips into a bowl, stir in the lemon juice and cover with clingfilm (plastic wrap). Sprinkle the curry powder over the fish and rub it in. Season with salt and pepper. Heat the oil in a flameproof casserole over medium heat. Brown the fish fillets on both sides, 1-2 minutes. Place the casserole in the oven, uncovered for 5 minutes. Lift out the fish and remove and discard the skin. Put the fish in a serving dish and keep warm.

Pour the fish stock into the casserole and heat, stirring well, then remove from the heat and stir in the butter. Heat the remaining oil in a frying pan or skillet. Drain the strips of mushroom and artichoke, add to the pan and cook, stirring occasionally, for about 10 minutes, until lightly browned. Remove from the heat. Sprinkle the vegetables over the fish, pour the sauce all over the dish and serve immediately.

Serves 6
Preparation time: 40 mins
Cooking time: 20 mins

· 2½ tablespoons sultanas
  or golden raisins
· 1 × 2-kg (4½-lb) turbot,
  cut into slices, trimmings
  and bones reserved
· 4 tablespoons olive oil
· 400 g (14 oz) onions, very
  thinly sliced
· 175 ml (¾ cup) dry white wine
· 100 ml (scant ½ cup) white
  wine vinegar
· large pinch of saffron threads,
  crushed
· 100 g (scant ½ cup) blanched
  almonds, finely chopped
· salt and pepper

Alternative fish: brill or halibut

 288   292

Rombo in bottaggio

TURBOT WITH SAFFRON, ALMONDS AND WINE

Put the sultanas or golden raisins in a bowl, pour in water to cover and let soak for 20 minutes, then drain. Meanwhile, put the fish trimmings and bones into a saucepan, pour in water to cover and bring to a boil, then reduce the heat and simmer for 30 minutes.

Remove the pan from the heat and strain the stock into a bowl. Heat the oil in a large frying pan or skillet, add the onions and cook over low heat, stirring occasionally, for about 5 minutes, until translucent. Pour in the wine, vinegar and enough fish stock to cover the onions completely and cook for about 20 minutes, until tender. Meanwhile, mix the saffron with 2 tablespoons of the remaining fish stock in a small bowl. When the onions are tender, stir in the saffron, almonds and drained sultanas and cook, stirring constantly, until the liquid has reduced. Add the slices of fish to the pan and cook for about five minutes, then season with salt and pepper and serve.

Serves 6
Preparation time: 1¼ hrs
Cooking time: 25–30 mins

· 250 g (1⅓ cups) lentils
· 3 bay leaves
· 175 ml (¾ cup) olive oil
· 2 shallots, chopped
· 50 g (1¾ oz) bacon, diced
· 175 ml (¾ cup) dry white wine
· 250 ml (1 cup) Fish Stock
  (see page 78)
· 1 × 2-kg (4½-lb) turbot,
  cleaned and filleted
· pinch of curry powder
· 40 g (3 tablespoons) butter,
  cut into small pieces
· 1 marjoram sprig, chopped
· salt

Alternative fish: John Dory,
brill, halibut or grouper

 288 292

BAKED TURBOT WITH LENTILS

Put the lentils and 1 of the bay leaves in a saucepan,
pour in water to cover and bring to a boil, then reduce
the heat and simmer for 30–45 minutes until tender.
Drain well and discard the bay leaf. Preheat the oven to
180°C / 350°F / Gas Mark 4. Heat 2 tablespoons of the olive
oil in a saucepan, add one-quarter of the shallots, the
bacon and a bay leaf and cook over low heat, stirring
frequently, for 5 minutes. Add the lentils, 4 tablespoons
of the wine and 5 tablespoons of the stock and simmer
for about 5 minutes.

Remove from the heat, transfer half the mixture to a food
processor and process to a purée, then scrape into a clean
saucepan. Heat the remaining olive oil, stock, wine, bay leaf
and chopped shallot in a roasting pan. Lightly season the
fish fillets with salt, add to the pan and cook for 5 minutes,
then transfer to the oven and bake for another 15 minutes.
Remove the pan from the oven, transfer the fish to a serving
dish and keep warm. Strain the cooking juices into a bowl
and stir in the curry powder. Add the mixture to the lentil
purée, heat gently and gradually whisk in the butter.
Sprinkle the marjoram over the fish and serve with the
lentil mixture and sauce.

Serves 6
Preparation time: 15 mins
Cooking time: 45 mins

· 150 g (5 oz) smoked pancetta
  or streaky (lean) bacon
· 1.2 kg (2½ lb) turbot fillets
· 6 tablespoons olive oil, plus
  extra for drizzling
· 750 g (1¾ lb) onions, very
  thinly sliced
· 2 tablespoons granulated sugar
· 3 tablespoons white wine vinegar
· 3 tablespoons red wine vinegar
· 2 tablespoons sherry vinegar
· 1 tablespoon freshly squeezed
  orange juice
· salt and pepper

Alternative fish: John Dory
or grouper

 288   292

TURBOT WITH ONION JAM

Stretch the pancetta or bacon with the back of a table knife, then wrap around the fish fillets. Secure with a cocktail stick. Heat half the oil in a saucepan, add the onion and cook over high heat, stirring frequently, for 15 minutes. Sprinkle with the sugar, reduce the heat and cook, stirring frequently, for another 15 minutes, or until they begin to caramelize. Season with salt and pepper, then add alternate tablespoons of the white wine vinegar and red wine vinegar, scraping up the deposit from the pan.

When the onions are good golden brown, cook for 5 minutes more, then remove from the heat and keep warm. Heat the remaining 2 tablespoons of oil in a non-stick frying pan, add the fish fillets and brown for 1–2 minutes on each side, then sprinkle with the sherry vinegar and continue cooking for 10 minutes. Spread out the onion jam on a serving platter, put the fish fillets on top and drizzle with olive oil and the orange juice. Serve immediately.

Serves 6
Preparation time: 40 mins
Cooking time: 20 mins

- 4 tablespoons olive oil,
  plus extra for drizzling
- 1 shallot, chopped
- 300 g (11 oz) potatoes, peeled
  and cut into wedges
- 300 ml (1¼ cups) Fish Stock
  (see page 78)
- 1 garlic clove, peeled
- 1.2 kg (2½ lb) turbot fillets
- plain (all-purpose) flour,
  for dusting
- 200 ml (scant 1 cup) dry
  white wine
- salt and pepper
- 500 g (4 cups) cooked green
  beans, to serve

  For the pesto:
- 100 ml (scant ½ cup) olive oil
- 4 shallots, chopped
- 80 g (¾ cup) pine nuts
- 50 g (½ cup) walnuts
- 1 ice cube
- 50 g (1 cup) coarsely chopped
  fresh basil
- 50 g (1 cup) coarsely chopped
  flat-leaf parsley
- coarse sea salt

  Alternative fish: John Dory,
  halibut or brill

288   292

TURBOT WITH PESTO

First make the pesto. Heat 1 tablespoon of oil in a
small saucepan, add the shallots and cook over low heat,
stirring occasionally, for 5 minutes, until softened. Add
2 tablespoons water and simmer for 10 minutes. Put the
pine nuts, walnuts, remaining olive oil and the shallots into
a food processor and process, then add the ice cube, basil,
parsley and salt to taste and process again. Set aside.

Heat half the oil in a saucepan, add the shallot and cook
over low heat, stirring occasionally, for 5 minutes. Add the
potato wedges, stir and pour in the stock. Bring to a boil
and cook for 15–20 minutes, until the potatoes are tender
but not falling apart. Remove from the heat, drain and
pass through a potato ricer or mash with a potato masher.
Put the mashed potato mixture into a saucepan, set over
low heat and stir in the pesto.

Heat the remaining oil with the garlic clove in a frying pan
or skillet. When the garlic starts to brown, remove and
discard it. Dust the fish fillets with flour, season with salt
and pepper, add to the pan and cook for 1–2 minutes on
each side. Pour in the wine and cook for about 10 minutes.
Serve the fish with the pesto-flavoured mashed potato
and the cooked green beans, drizzled with a little oil.

Serves 6
Preparation time: 1¼ hrs
Cooking time: 40 mins

· 1 × 1.2-kg (2½-lb) turbot,
  skinned
· olive oil
· 2 tablespoons chopped
  flat-leaf parsley
· salt and pepper

For the sauce:
· 450 g (1lb) carpet shell or
  cherrystone clams
· 4 tablespoons olive oil
· 150 ml (⅔ cup) dry white wine
· 1 garlic clove, peeled
· 1 shallot, chopped
· 150 g (½ cup) diced potatoes
· 1 ripe tomato, peeled and
  diced
· 150 ml (⅔ cup) Fish Stock
  (see page 78)
· pinch of saffron threads,
  lightly crushed
· 80 g (6 tablespoons) butter
· pinch of dried chilli flakes
· salt and pepper

Alternative fish: John Dory
or cod

 288 292 300

TURBOT WITH SAFFRON AND CLAM SAUCE

First make the sauce. Wash the clams thoroughly and discard any that are damaged or do not shut when sharply tapped. Put them in a frying pan or skillet with the olive oil, 100 ml (scant ½ cup) of the wine and the garlic. Cook over high heat for a few minutes, until the shells have opened. Remove the pan from the heat, let cool and remove the clams from their shells. Discard any clams that have remained shut. Strain the cooking juices into a bowl and reserve.

Heat the remaining oil in a saucepan, add the shallot and cook over low heat, stirring occasionally, for 7–8 minutes, until it starts to brown. Stir in the potatoes and tomato, sprinkle with the remaining wine and cook until the alcohol has evaporated. Pour in the fish stock and reserved cooking juices, bring to a boil and cook for 10 minutes, until the potatoes are tender. Meanwhile put the saffron into a small bowl, add 2 tablespoons water and let soak. Preheat the oven to 180°C/350°F/Gas Mark 4. Transfer half the potato mixture to a blender or food processor and process to a purée. Scrape the purée back into the pan and mix well. Add the clams, season with salt and pepper and stir in the butter, then whisk with a hand-held mixer until the mixture is light and fluffy. Stir in the saffron and dried chilli flakes.

Season the fish fillets with salt and pepper. Brush an ovenproof dish with oil, add the fish fillets and cook in the oven for 7 minutes. Remove the dish from the oven, transfer the fish to a serving platter and pour the sauce over it. Sprinkle with parsley and serve immediately.

Serves 6
Preparation time: 20 mins
Cooking time: 16 mins

· 6 tablespoons olive oil
· 6 baby courgettes (zucchini),
  diced
· pinch of saffron threads,
  lightly crushed
· 2 large red onions, diced
· 1 tablespoon tomato
  purée (paste)
· 1 garlic clove, peeled
· 1.5 kg (3¼ lb) turbot fillets
· salt and pepper

Alternative fish: brill or halibut

 288   292

TURBOT WITH COURGETTES (ZUCCHINI) AND RED ONION SAUCE

Heat 2 tablespoons of the oil in a saucepan, add the courgettes (zucchini), sprinkle with a little salt and cook for a few minutes, then remove the pan from the heat. Put the saffron into a small bowl, add 2 tablespoons water and let soak. Heat 2 tablespoons of the remaining oil in another saucepan, add the onions and cook over low heat, stirring occasionally, for 5 minutes, until translucent. Add the saffron and its soaking water, the tomato purée (paste) and 175 ml (¾ cup) water, season with salt and pepper and cook over low heat for 10 minutes, but do not let the onions brown.

Heat the remaining oil with the garlic in a non-stick frying pan or skillet. When the garlic starts to colour, remove and discard it. Add the fish fillets and cook for 3 minutes on each side, then remove from the pan. Remove and discard the skin, season very lightly with salt and serve with the courgettes and onions.

Serves 4
Preparation time: 20 mins
Cooking time: 15 mins

· 2 tablespoons finely
 chopped basil
· 2 tablespoons finely
 chopped chives
· 2 tablespoons capers,
 finely chopped
· 2 tablespoons finely
 chopped flat-leaf parsley
· 1 garlic clove, finely
 chopped
· grated zest of ½ lemon
· juice of 1 lemon, strained
· 6 tablespoons olive oil
· 4 × 150-g (5-oz) skate wings
· plain (all-purpose) flour,
 for dusting
· salt and pepper

Alternative fish: cod or hake

 288

Razza in salsina verde alle erbe

SKATE WITH GREEN HERB SAUCE

Put the basil, chives, capers, parsley, garlic, lemon zest
and lemon juice in a bowl. Stir in half the olive oil and
season with salt and pepper to taste. Heat the remaining
oil in a frying pan or skillet. Dust the skate wings with flour,
season with salt and pepper and add to the pan. Cook for
4–5 minutes on each side, until the flesh has turned snowy
white and is beginning to come away from the cartilage.

Pour the prepared herb sauce over the fish and cook over
low heat for another few minutes, then transfer to a serving
platter and serve immediately.

Photograph opposite

Serves 6
Preparation time: 40 mins
+ cooling
Cooking time: 15 mins

· 4 × 150-g (5-oz) skate wings
· 80 g (6 tablespoons) butter,
 plus extra to garnish
· 2 tablespoons hot mustard

For the court-bouillon:
· 1 onion, coarsely chopped
· 2 carrots, coarsely chopped
· 1 bunch mixed herbs
· 12 black peppercorns
· 1 teaspoon salt
· 300 ml (1¼ cups) dry
 white wine
· 5 tablespoons white
 wine vinegar

Alternative fish: turbot
or cod

 288

Razza alla senape

SKATE WITH MUSTARD

First, make a court-bouillon. Put the onion, carrots, herbs,
peppercorns, salt, wine and vinegar into a large saucepan,
pour in 1.2 litres (5 cups) water and bring to a boil. Reduce
the heat and simmer for 20 minutes, then remove the pan
from the heat and let cool. Put the skate wings into a large
saucepan, strain the cooled court-bouillon over them and
bring to a boil. Reduce the heat to low and poach very
gently for about 15 minutes. Meanwhile, melt the butter in
a heatproof dish set over a saucepan of barely simmering
water or in the microwave. Lift out the fish with a fish slice
(spatula) and pat dry with paper towels. If the wings have
not already been skinned, carefully remove the black skin.
Put about 1½ teaspoons mustard on each of 6 warmed
plates and top with a skate wing, skinned side down. Drizzle
with the melted butter and dot with a few curls of butter to
garnish. This dish is good with a salad of raw tomatoes and
cold boiled potatoes sprinkled with fresh parsley.

Serves 4
Preparation time: 15 mins
Cooking time: 20 mins

· 4 × 150-g (5-oz) skate wings
· 1.5 litres (6¼ cups) Fish Stock
  (see page 78)
· 80 g (6 tablespoons) butter
· 150 ml (⅔ cup) red wine vinegar
· 2 tablespoons capers, rinsed
· 2 tablespoons chopped
  flat-leaf parsley

Alternative fish: John Dory
or halibut

 288

FRIED SKATE WITH BUTTER AND CAPERS

Cut the skate wings into fairly large pieces, put them into a large saucepan and pour in the fish stock. Bring just to a boil, then reduce the heat so that the surface of the stock is barely shivering and poach for 15 minutes. Remove the fish from the pan with a fish slice (spatula) and remove and discard the skin.

Melt the butter in a frying pan or skillet. When it has turned a pale golden brown, add the skate pieces and cook for a few seconds, then turn them over, sprinkle with the vinegar and cook very briefly. As soon as the vinegar comes to a boil, remove the pan from the heat. Transfer the fish to a warm serving platter, sprinkle with the capers and parsley and serve immediately.

Serves 4
Preparation time: 15 mins
Cooking time: 10 mins

· 16 sole fillets, skinned
· plain (all-purpose) flour,
  for dusting
· 25 g (2 tablespoons) butter
· 4 tablespoons olive oil
· 16 sole fillets
· generous 1 teaspoon
  Dijon mustard
· grated zest and juice of 1 lemon
· 2 teaspoons coriander seeds,
  coarsely crushed
· 1 tablespoon chopped fresh
  coriander (cilantro)
· 40 g (⅓ cup) blanched almonds,
  toasted and chopped
· salt and pepper

Alternative fish: plaice or turbot

 288   292

DELICIOUS SOLE

Lightly dust the fish fillets with flour, shaking off the excess. Melt the butter with 2 tablespoons of the oil in a frying pan or skillet, add the sole fillets, in batches, and cook wfor 2 minutes on each side. Season with salt and pepper, then remove from the heat, transfer to a serving platter and keep warm. Whisk together the remaining oil, the mustard, lemon zest and juice, coriander seeds, chopped coriander (cilantro) and almonds in a bowl until thoroughly combined, then pour into the pan and heat for a few minutes. Pour the sauce over the fish and serve immediately.

Photograph opposite

. . . .

Serves 4
Preparation time: 20 mins
Cooking time: 25 mins

· 3 tablespoons cornflour
  (cornstarch)
· 650 g (1 lb 7 oz) sole fillets,
  very finely chopped
· 4 tablespoons iced water
· 1 teaspoon sugar
· plain (all-purpose) flour,
  for dusting
· olive oil
· salt

Alternative fish: brill or plaice

 288   292

Polpette di sogliola

SOLE FRITTERS

Mix the cornflour (cornstarch) to a paste with a little water in a small bowl. Combine the fish, iced water, sugar, cornflour paste and a pinch of salt in a bowl. Shape this mixture into 8 flattened balls and dust them lightly with flour. Heat plenty of oil in a frying pan or skillet, add the fish fritters and cook for 15 minutes, or until pale golden brown.

Meanwhile, preheat the oven to 200°C / 400°F / Gas Mark 6 and line a baking sheet with greaseproof (wax) paper. Remove the fritters with a slotted spoon and drain on paper towels, then transfer to the prepared baking sheet and place in the oven for 10 minutes to crisp up. Serve immediately.

Serves 4
Preparation time: 15 mins
Cooking time: 35 mins

- 4 tablespoons olive oil
- 1 garlic clove, peeled
- 4 soles, skinned and filleted
- 200 ml (scant 1 cup) dry white wine
- 2 tomatoes, peeled, seeded and diced
- 1.2 litres (5 cups) Fish Stock (see page 78)
- pinch of saffron threads, lightly crushed
- 1 onion, thinly sliced
- 320 g (1⅔ cups) risotto rice
- 2 tablespoons chopped flat-leaf parsley
- salt and pepper

Alternative fish: brill or cod

288   292

SOLE AND SAFFRON RISOTTO

Heat half the oil with the garlic clove in a frying pan or skillet. When the garlic starts to colour, remove and discard it. Add the sole fillets, sprinkle with half the wine and cook until the alcohol has evaporated, then add the tomatoes to the pan and cook for 10 minutes. Meanwhile, pour the fish stock into a saucepan and bring to a boil, then reduce the heat to a simmer. When the fish is cooked, season with salt and pepper, remove from the heat and keep warm. Transfer a ladleful of the hot stock to a heatproof bowl, stir in the saffron and let stand.

Heat the remaining oil in a flameproof casserole (Dutch oven), add the onion and cook over low heat, stirring occasionally, for 5 minutes, until softened. Add the rice and cook, stirring constantly, for 1–2 minutes, until all the grains are coated in oil. Pour in the remaining wine and cook, stirring, until it has been absorbed, then add a ladleful of the hot stock. Cook, stirring constantly, until it has been absorbed. Continue adding the hot stock, a ladleful at a time, and cook until it has been absorbed. This will take 18–20 minutes. About halfway through the cooking, stir in the saffron mixture. When the rice is tender and creamy, remove the casserole from the heat and spoon it onto a serving platter. Put the sole fillets on top and spoon the fish cooking juices over them. Sprinkle with the parsley and serve immediately.

Serves 4
Preparation time: 40 mins
+ 2 hrs chilling

· 8 large sole fillets, skinned
· juice of 2 lemons, strained
· 2 green bell peppers, halved,
  seeded and diced
· 1 yellow bell pepper, halved,
  seeded and diced
· 1 carrot, thinly sliced
· 1 cucumber, thinly sliced
· 2 tomatoes, peeled, seeded
  and diced
· 4–5 tablespoons olive oil
· 1 tablespoon rosemary needles,
  chopped
· 1 tablespoon white wine vinegar
· salt and pepper

Alternative fish: scallops or
sea bass

 288   292

Filetti di sogliole insalata

SOLE SALAD

Put the fish fillets into a non-metallic dish, pour the lemon juice over them and cover with clingfilm (plastic wrap). Chill in the refrigerator for 2 hours.

Put the bell peppers, carrot, cucumber and tomatoes into a salad bowl. Whisk together the olive oil, rosemary and vinegar in a small bowl, season with salt and pepper and pour the dressing over the salad. Drain the fish and dice, then add to the salad and toss. Season with salt and serve.

Photograph opposite

. . . .

Serves 4
Preparation time: 20 mins
Cooking time: 15 mins

· 50 g (4 tablespoons) butter,
  plus extra for greasing
· 4 × 200-g (7-oz) sole, trimmed
  and skinned
· 1 shallot, chopped
· 2 tablespoons chopped
  flat-leaf parsley
· 1 tablespoon chopped thyme
· 1 bay leaf
· 300 ml (1¼ cups) dry white wine
· 4 tablespoons plain
  (all-purpose) flour
· 2 tablespoons double
  (heavy) cream
· salt and pepper

Alternative fish: plaice or hake

 288   292

Sogliole al vino bianco

SOLE WITH WHITE WINE

Preheat the oven to 180°C/350°F/Gas Mark 4. Grease a flameproof ovenproof dish with butter and put the fish into it in a single layer. Season with salt and pepper and fill the spaces between the fish with the shallot. Melt half the butter and sprinkle it over the fish. Sprinkle them with parsley and thyme, add the bay leaf, then pour in just enough wine to cover the fish. Bring to a boil over medium heat, then transfer the dish to the oven and cook for 10 minutes, until the flesh flakes easily. Put the remaining butter into a bowl, add the flour and work with a fork until combined into a smooth paste. Remove the dish from the oven and transfer the sole to a platter with a fish slice (spatula). Strain the cooking liquid into a small saucepan and bring to simmer over low heat. Whisk in the paste, in small pieces at a time, making sure each addition has been incorporated before adding the next. Stir in the cream and cook for 1 minute. Pour the sauce over the fish and serve.

OILY FISH

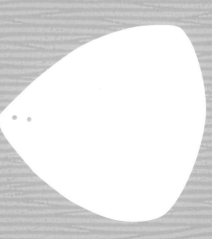

The flesh of oily fish contains essential fatty acids and fat-soluble vitamins that are vital for good health. Most of these fish live in open water, as opposed to near the coast or the sea bed, and swim in large shoals. They are traditionally caught in large numbers, so the need to make the most of the catch led to the many methods of preserving of these fish.

Oily fish include tuna, salmon, sardines, herring, mackerel and anchovies. Unlike white fish, which keep well for a short time period when well iced and stored at a very low temperature, oil-rich species spoil very easily. They are best eaten very fresh and ideally within a few hours of landing. Oily fish such as salmon and herring contain less fat than meat and poultry. When choosing between white and oily fish, bear in mind that the nutritional value of white fish is usually lower than that of oily fish.

All these fish have a delicate texture that breaks easily during cooking, so minimal turning of the fish is recommended when cooking.

HERRING

Aringhe
Clupeidae

Average weight range:
200–400g (7–14oz)
Average length: 20–40cm
(8–16 inches)

Recipes on pages 118–122

This silver shoaling fish is caught in large quantities
in northern European waters and herring fishing is an
important industry off the Pacific Coast of the United States
and Canada. When very fresh, it has shiny silver skin with
blue-green iridescent colours along the back and large
loose scales. It is highly seasonal: in England, the herring
season runs from October to December, while in the United
States they are mostly fished in summer months. Many of
these fish end up as bait used in other fisheries. Shad, or
river herring, come from the herring family and can be used
interchangeably but they have a deeper body and spawn in
rivers. There are some sustainability issues in the US due
to the large amounts of river herring by-catch, which occurs
when they are caught unintentionally.

Herring and shad have an oily and creamy flesh with a
delicate flavour. Their prized roe is often sold separately.
To prepare fresh herrings, remove the skins and heads, slit
open the backs and remove the bones using the technique
on page 298, without disturbing the roe. The blood line along
the backbone and the bitter gills should always be removed.
Fresh herring is simple to cook and can be pan-fried, roasted
and grilled (broiled).

Herring is also preserved by salting, smoking and pickling
to produce such specialities as kippers and rollmops.
To prepare preserved herring, soak the fillets in a mixture
of water and vinegar for 4 hours to remove the salt, then
drain and sprinkle with garlic, oregano and chilli.

In the United States, herring are often sold canned and
labelled as sardines. For fresh fish, sardines and mackerels
make good substitutes.

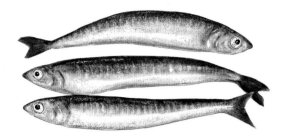

ANCHOVIES

Acciughe
Engraulis encrasicolus

Average weight range:
10–50g (⅓–1¾ oz)
Average length: 10–15cm
(4–6 inches)

Recipes on pages 122–129

Fresh anchovies are startlingly attractive with vivid, deep blue backs and shiny, silver flanks. A close relative to sardines and herring, they are a finger-length, slim fish that swim in huge shoals in warmer waters such as the Indian and Pacific oceans. Outside their native regions, they are only very occasionally available from specialist fish suppliers from June to December.

Oily yet delicate, they do not transport well and lose condition extremely rapidly, so anchovies are often salted, canned or cured in vinegar. Whole salted anchovies, which are popular in Italy, can be substituted with tinned or bottled fillets in oil. Their popularity as a preserved fish has led to relentless fishing, which has threatened some stocks.

Anchovies can be prepared in a variety of ways. Whole ones can be salted and fillets are salted and canned in oil. To fillet a whole salted anchovy, cut off its head and tail, and press along the backbones with your thumb. Turn it over and remove the bones, which should come away easily. For a fish its size, anchovies have unusually large scales. To scale, scrape them from the tail to the head with a butter knife. To reduce the messiness, it can be done under cold, running water or over a bowl of ice water. To clean anchovies, snap their backbones just behind the heads with your fingers, then pull off the heads. Most of the innards will come with them. Slit open the bellies and remove any remaining innards, cut off the tails, then rinse and dry the fish.

Fresh anchovies can either be simply pan-fried with sage or cured in white wine vinegar and salt for a few hours, then be drained and marinated in olive oil, herbs and lemon overnight.

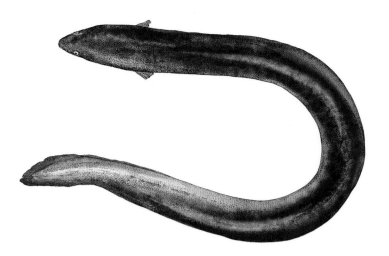

EEL

Anguilla
Anguilla anguilla

Average weight range:
225g–1.6kg (8oz–3½lb)
Average length: 30–90cm
(1–3 feet)

Recipes on pages 130–134

Snake-like in appearance, eel has a distinctive texture and flavour. Conger eel is a sea dweller with a dense texture and a flavour resembling pork. It is notorious for the mass of small bones, especially in the tail end, which is best used for making stock. There are serious sustainability issues surrounding both freshwater and conger eels, so for the time being alternatives should be considered.

With a distinctive flavour and texture, eel is meaty, oil-rich and gelatinous. They should be freshly killed (having been kept alive until required) or smoked. Eels must be skinned for some recipes and it's best to ask the fish supplier to prepare them for you. Otherwise, use a small, sharp, pointed knife and make a T-shaped cut under the head. Take hold of the two flaps and pull the skin inside out. Because eels are slippery, it is advisable to hold them firmly with a dish towel. Eel can be gutted and cut into small steaks or filleted in the same way as for monkfish (see page 294).

Eel has a pronounced flavour and goes particularly well with robust herbs and spices, such as rosemary, sage, smoked paprika and cumin, as seen in *Terrina d'anguilla e carciofi* (Eel and artichoke terrine, see page 132). Classic Italian recipes include *Anguilla al vino rosso* (Eel in red wine, see page 133). Prawns (shrimp), monkfish and huss (dogfish) can be substituted for texture, and freshwater fish with a similar flavour include carp and pike.

WHITEBAIT

Bianchetti
Clupeidae

Average weight range:
10–25g (½–1oz each)
Average length: 5cm (2 inches)

Recipes on pages 134–136

Whitebait are tiny members of the herring family and can include both herring and sprats – in fact, there are about 150–180 fish in every 600g (1lb 5oz) of whitebait. They are fished in quantities in the tidal waters of many estuaries and the season in Europe is usually between February and August, although most are now sold frozen. In the United States, the term whitebait is used for silversides or sand-eels, which are cooked in a similar way to whitebait. They are immature fish that do not have the chance to spawn and because they have been relentlessly harvested, their survival is threatened.

Although occasionally available fresh, they are most often sold frozen. Whitebait are traditionally pan- or deep-fried and served with lemon, although they can be cooked very rapidly in simmering water. They can also be rolled in seasoned flour or dipped into a batter and fried, such as in *Bianchetti fritti* (Fried whitebait, see page 136) and *Bianchetti in pastella* (Whitebait in batter, see page 136).

Alternatives are other small but more mature members of the same fish family, such as sprats, sardines or smelt.

SWORDFISH

Pesce Spada
Xiphias gladius

Average weight range as a loin:
1.5–4kg (3¼–9lb)
Average size steak: 150–250g
(5–9oz)

Recipes on pages 137–141

This dynamic, aggressive and handsome fish group
is easily recognizable with its distinctive long 'sword',
dark back and silvery flanks. Caught in warmer waters
around the globe, swordfish is highly valued and often
expensive. Because of its size, it is usually filleted into
long loins for sale and then cut into steaks. The advantage
of this is that there are no bones and usually no skin,
so it requires virtually no preparation. Smoked swordfish
is also available.

With a dense and meaty flesh, the flavour is delicate,
sweet and ideal for a wide range of recipes, many of
which are also suitable for fresh tuna. Fresh swordfish is
perfect for the barbecue and for pan-frying – a swordfish
steak requires only 3–4 minutes on each side. It is best
accompanied by strongly aromatic herbs, such as oregano
and basil, and works well with *salsa verde*, especially when
gherkins, garlic and anchovy are added. Contemporary
Italian recipes use it for carpaccio but more creative recipes
includes the delicious *Millefoglie di pesce spada e verdure
al timo* (Swordfish layered with vegetables and thyme,
see page 139).

Alternatives include tuna, huss (dogfish) and amberjack.

SALMON

Salmone
Salmo salar

Average weight range:
750g–7kg (1lb 10oz–15lb)
Average length: 40–80cm
(16–31 inches)

Recipes on pages 142–153

Among the most highly prized of all fish, salmon live in the ocean but swim upstream against the current to reproduce in the rivers in which they were born. Caught in both the West and East Atlantic, wild salmon is now a rare and very expensive sight. It is, however, extensively farmed in Norway, Scotland and Chile, which provides an excellent source for a demanding market worldwide. Although not native to the southern hemisphere, salmon farming in Tasmania has made it a popular fish in Australia and New Zealand. Wild caught Alaskan salmon is sustainable and is available fresh from spring through the end of autumn (fall).

Salmon's striking silver-scaled skin is speckled with black spots and its firm, oily, flamingo-pink flesh has a delicious flavour. It is available whole and cleaned, filleted or cut into steaks, with or without skin. Salmon should be scaled before cooking because the scales will otherwise loosen and stick to the flesh – you can ask for this to be done for you. If filleted, the pinbones should also be removed.

Fresh salmon has a moist, flaky texture and suits a variety of cooking methods from poaching and pan-frying to grilling (broiling) and roasting. A salmon steak requires only 8–10 minutes to cook through and the tail end of the salmon – popular because it is boneless – requires only 4–5 minutes cooking. Salmon can be enjoyed cold in *Tartara di salmone* (Salmon tartare, see page 150) or hot smoked.

Alternatives can include sea trout (also known as salmon trout) and rainbow trout, which have a similarly coloured flesh. Arctic char, rainbow trout and whitefish, another relative, can also be substituted.

SARDINES

Sarde/Sardine
Sardina pilchardus

Average weight range:
50–150 g (2–5 oz)
Average length: 11–20 cm
(4–8 inches)

Recipes on pages 153–159

Startlingly attractive with deep blue-green backs and shiny silver flanks, sardines are very small pilchards and are related to others in the herring family. An important fish for southern European countries, shoals of sardines are caught off the coasts of the East Atlantic and in the Mediterranean. They are seasonal fish found in spring and autumn (fall).

They are usually sold whole, but you can ask for them to be scaled and cleaned for you. The scales are already quite loose and only need to be scraped gently with the back of a knife or your hand because the skin underneath is delicate and can tear easily. When cooking them, in some cases you will need to cut off their heads and remove the bones. To do this, open them out, place skin side up and press along the backbones with your thumb. Turn them over, cut through the ends of their bones and remove. Rinse well and pat dry with paper towels.

Sardines are popular pan-fried and require only 2–3 minutes on the barbecue. Olive oil, basil, lemon and other traditional Mediterranean flavours are the perfect partners. *Sardine marinate al basilico* (Marinated sardines with basil, see page 157) and the very simple *Sardine al rosmarino* (Sardines with rosemary, see page 153) are tasty, classic Italian dishes.

Herring, mackerel and sprats can all be used as substitutes in sardine recipes.

MACKEREL

Sgombro
Scomber scombrus

Average weight range:
300g–2kg (11oz–4½lb)
Average length: 50–90cm
(20–35 inches)

Recipes on pages 160–163

With a streamlined, bullet-shaped body, an iridescent shine and rainbow hues along its flanks, the mackerel belongs to what is known in Italy as the 'blue scale' (*pesce azzuro*) fish family. Like tuna, mackerel are caught in huge shoals in northern and southern European waters. In the United States mackerel are commercially fished in southern New England and mid-Atlantic coastal waters as well as in the Gulf of Maine. There are sustainability concerns about fish caught by large trawlers, so the best choice is those that have been caught by hook and line. Mackerel are available year-round, but are at their best during the summer. They are best avoided during the spring when the fish will produce roe and the flesh can be disappointing.

Mackerel boasts an unbeatable delicate flavour and creamy texture when straight out of the water. As the fish loses its initial freshness, the flavour becomes stronger and more pronounced. They are sold whole and as fillets. If buying whole fish, make sure that the gills and blood line (found running close to the backbone) are removed as these have a bitter taste that can taint the flavour of the fish. The fine skin is usually left on.

Best grilled (broiled) or roasted, a single fillet of mackerel requires less than 4 minutes cooking time under the grill (broiler) and as it is quite thin, it doesn't require turning during cooking. Rich and oily, it is a natural partner to gooseberries but teams up well with mint, such as in *Filetti di sgombri marinati alla menta* (Marinated mackerel with mint, see page 163). Alternative options include herring and pilchards (large or Cornish sardines).

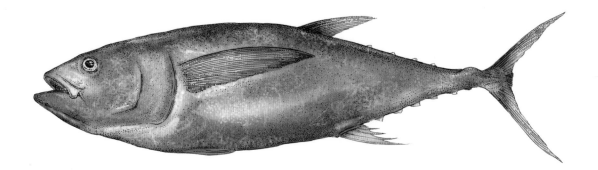

TUNA

Tonno
Thunnus thynnus

Average weight range of
whole loin: 1.5–4kg (3¼–9lb)
Average size of steak:
150–250g (5–9oz)

Recipes on pages 164–171

Tuna fishing in the Mediterranean is highly profitable because the fish are greatly appreciated and demand is high. Blue-fin tuna is thought to be on the brink of extinction and should be avoided. Catching tuna with a pole and line is considered to be the most sustainable method of fishing since the fish are caught one-by-one and the process is harmless to other sea life. Yellow fin tuna is often considered the most sustainable, but both bonito and mackerel make good alternatives as smaller members of the same family.

Tuna tend to reach a considerable size, so while they are sold commercially as whole fish, they are mostly filleted into loins and then cut into steaks for sale to the public. Usually sold skinned and boneless, tuna requires no preparation.

A fresh tuna steak is best simply char-grilled (charbroiled) or pan-fried since direct contact with heat tends to brown the flesh and gives it a more appetizing appearance. Canned tuna often appears on Italian tables, but fresh tuna is seen rather less frequently because it is quite expensive. *Tonno alle mandorle, pinoli e olive* (Tuna with almonds, pine nuts and olives, see page 169) marries bold Italian flavours with different textures.

Serves 6
Preparation time: 10 mins
Cooking time: 20 mins

- 150 ml (⅔ cup) olive oil
- 2 garlic cloves, chopped
- 1 red chilli, chopped
- 1 kg (2¼ lb) herring, cleaned and filleted
- about 12 slices bread, crusts removed and slightly toasted
- salt
- flat-leaf parsley, chopped, to serve
- lemon wedges, to serve

Alternative fish: sardines or mackerel

 288   290

Aringhe alla calabrese

CALABRESE-STYLE HERRING

Heat 2 tablespoons of the oil in a frying pan or skillet, add the garlic and chilli and cook over low heat, stirring occasionally, for a few minutes. Lay the herring fillets on top, season lightly with salt, increase the heat to medium and cook for about 15 minutes, occasionally mashing it with the back of a spoon, until the fish have broken up completely in the sauce. Spread the hot herring mixture on the slices of bread, put them on a serving platter, drizzle with the remaining oil, sprinkle with parsley and serve immediately with lemon wedges.

Photograph opposite

Serves 4
Preparation time: 25 mins
Cooking time: 5 mins

- 1 cauliflower, cut into florets
- 1 × 120-g (4-oz) jar of herring fillets in oil, drained and halved lengthwise
- 175 ml (¾ cup) double (heavy) cream
- 1 tablespoon Dijon mustard
- 1 tablespoon red wine vinegar
- 3 tablespoons olive oil
- 1 baby (pearl) onion, chopped
- 1 loose-leaf lettuce heart, such as lollo rosso, chopped
- 1 red onion, thinly sliced
- salt and pepper

Alternative fish: sardines or mackerel

Insalata d'aringhe con cavolfiori

HERRING AND CAULIFLOWER SALAD

Cook the cauliflower in a saucepan of salted boiling water for 5 minutes. Drain and refresh under cold running water. Roll up the herring fillet halves and secure with a wooden cocktail stick or toothpick. Mix together the cream, mustard, vinegar, olive oil and baby (pearl) onion in a bowl and season with salt and pepper. Put the lettuce and red onion in a large salad bowl and top with the cauliflower and herring rolls. Pour the dressing over the salad and keep in a cool place until ready to serve.

Serves 4
Preparation time: 15 mins
+ 12 hrs soaking and 15 mins
chilling

· 2 tablespoons white wine
  vinegar
· 8 smoked herring fillets
· 4 tablespoons olive oil
· juice of 1 grapefruit, strained
· juice of ½ lemon, strained
· 1 teaspoon Dijon mustard
· 1 fennel bulb, very thinly sliced
· pinch of chopped dill
· salt and pepper

Alternative fish: sardines
or mackerel

 288   290

Aringhe al pompelmo

HERRING WITH GRAPEFRUIT

Partly fill a non-metallic bowl with water, stir in the vinegar
and add the herring fillets. Let soak for 12 hours, then drain.
Whisk together the olive oil, grapefruit juice, lemon juice,
mustard and a pinch each of salt and pepper in a bowl until
combined. Spread out the fennel slices on a serving platter,
put the herring fillets on top and drizzle with the grapefruit
dressing. Sprinkle with a pinch of chopped dill and chill in
the refrigerator for 15 minutes before serving.

Serves 4
Preparation time: 25 mins
Cooking time: 35 mins

· 4 tablespoons olive oil
· 1 carrot, finely chopped
· 1 onion, finely chopped
· 1 garlic, cove, finely chopped
· 1 celery stalk, finely chopped
· 1 flat-leaf parsley sprig,
  finely chopped
· 6 plum tomatoes, peeled,
  seeded and chopped
· 800 g (1¾ lb) shad, scaled
  and cleaned
· 1 tablespoon capers, rinsed
· salt

Alternative fish: herring
or mackerel

 288

Agoni al pomodoro

SHAD WITH TOMATO

Heat the oil in a large saucepan, add the carrot, onion,
garlic, celery and parsley and cook over low heat, stirring
occasionally, for 5 minutes. Add the tomatoes, cover and
simmer for 10 minutes, until slightly thickened. Meanwhile,
cut each fish into 3 pieces. Add the fish and capers to
the pan, season with salt, cover and simmer for 20 minutes.
Serve immediately.

Photograph opposite

Serves 4
Preparation time: 20 mins
+ 24 hrs marinating
Cooking time: 45 mins

· 800 g (1¾ lb) shad, scaled
  and cleaned
· plain (all-purpose) flour,
  for dusting
· 100 ml (scant ½ cup) olive oil
· 1 onion, thinly sliced
· 1 celery stalk, chopped
· 1 garlic clove, thinly sliced
· 4 sage leaves
· 1 bay leaf
· 1 rosemary sprig
· 6 black peppercorns
· 300 ml (1¼ cups) red wine vinegar
· 1 tablespoon olive oil
· salt

Alternative fish: herring
or mackerel

 288

Agoni in carpione

SOUSED SHAD

Dust the fish with flour, shaking off excess any excess. Heat the oil in a frying pan or skillet, add the fish, in batches, and cook for 3–4 minutes on each side. Remove with a fish slice (spatula) and drain on paper towels. Season with salt and transfer to a serving dish.

To make the marinade, put the onion, celery, garlic, sage, bay leaf, rosemary, peppercorns, vinegar and oil in a saucepan and bring to a boil over high heat. Reduce the heat and cook until the mixture comes back to a boil. Remove the pan from the heat and pour the mixture over the fish. Let marinate in a cool place for 24 hours before serving.

Serves 4
Preparation time: 20 mins
+ 3–4 hrs marinating

· 500 g (1 lb 2 oz) very fresh
  small anchovies
· juice of 3 lemons, strained
· 50 g (1 cup) chopped
  fresh parsley
· 2 garlic cloves, chopped
· 50 g (½ cup) black olives,
  pitted and chopped
· 100 ml (scant ½ cup) olive oil
· 1 dried chilli, crumbled

Alternative fish: sprats
or smelts

Acciughe alle olive

ANCHOVIES WITH OLIVES

Pinch off the heads of the anchovies and pull them away (the innards will come with them). Pinch along the top edge of each fish and pull out the spines. Open them out like a book. Rinse and pat dry, then put them in a bowl, pour the lemon juice over them and let marinate for 3–4 hours. Mix together the parsley, garlic and olives in another bowl. Drain the anchovies and arrange them on a serving platter, drizzle with the olive oil and sprinkle with the parsley mixture. Serve immediately.

Photograph opposite

Serves 4
Preparation time: 20 mins
+ 24 hrs marinating

- 16 fresh anchovies, scaled
  and cleaned (see page 110)
- juice of 2 lemons, strained
  or 120 ml (½ cup) white
  wine vinegar
- 2 tablespoons chopped
  fresh parsley
- 2 spring onions (scallions),
  chopped
- olive oil, for drizzling
- salt

Alternative fish: herring
or sardines

Acciughe al limone

ANCHOVIES MARINATED WITH LEMON

Open out the fish and put them skin side uppermost
on a chopping (cutting) board. Press firmly along the
backbone of each fish until it is flat, then turn over and
pull the backbone away, snipping it off at the tail. Fold the
fish back into shape and put them in a non-metallic dish,
packed together in a single layer. Sprinkle lightly with salt
and add enough lemon juice or vinegar to cover. Cover
and let marinate in the refrigerator for 24 hours. Drain
off and discard the marinade and transfer the anchovies
to a serving dish. Sprinkle with chopped parsley and the
spring onions (scallions), drizzle with olive oil and chill
until just before serving.

Serves 4
Preparation time: 20 mins
Cooking time: 15 mins

- 4–5 tablespoons olive oil,
  plus extra for brushing
- 800 g (1¾ lb) fresh anchovies,
  scaled and cleaned
  (see page 110)
- 4 tablespoons
  white wine vinegar
- ½ teaspoon dried oregano
- 1 garlic clove, chopped
- salt and pepper

Alternative fish: sprats
or sardines

Acciughe gratinate

ANCHOVY GRATIN

Preheat the oven to 200°C/400°F/Gas Mark 6. Brush an
ovenproof dish with olive oil. Place the anchovies skin side
up and press along the backbones with your thumb, then
turn over and remove the bones, leaving the fish joined
along their backs. Put the anchovies in the prepared dish.

Mix together the vinegar, olive oil, oregano and garlic in
a bowl and season with salt and pepper. Pour the mixture
over the anchovies and bake for 15 minutes. Transfer to
a serving dish and serve hot or cold.

Serves 4
Preparation time: 1¼ hrs
+ 4–5 hrs setting
Cooking time: 20 mins

- 350 g (scant 2½ cups) polenta
- 200 g (7 oz) salted anchovies, rinsed
- 25 g (2 tablespoons) butter, melted, plus extra for greasing
- 350 ml (1½ cups) passata (puréed canned tomatoes)
- 3 tablespoons chopped flat-leaf parsley
- salt

Alternative fish: sprats or sardines

POLENTA WITH ANCHOVIES

First make the polenta. Pour 1.2 litres (5 cups) water into a large saucepan and bring to a boil, then add a generous pinch of salt. Sprinkle in the polenta, stirring constantly, and cook, stirring constantly, for 35–45 minutes, until the polenta has thickened and starts to come away from the sides of the pan. Dampen a work counter. Remove the polenta from the heat and pour it onto the prepared surface, smoothing it level to a thickness of 2 cm (¾ inch) with a rubber spatula dipped in water. Let cool and set (this can take up to 5 hours).

Meanwhile, prepare the anchovies. Pinch off the heads and pull them away – the innards will come with them. Pinch along the top edge of each fish and pull out the spines. Rinse and pat dry. Preheat the oven to 180°C/350°F/ Gas Mark 4. Grease a terrine or loaf pan with butter. Cut the set polenta into squares and use some of them to line the prepared terrine or pan. Fill the terrine with alternate layers of anchovies, passata (puréed canned tomatoes) and parsley and top with a layer of polenta squares. Brush the top with the melted butter and bake for 20 minutes. Remove from the oven and serve immediately.

Serves 4
Preparation time: 10 mins
Cooking time: 30 mins

· 2 tablespoons olive oil
· 1 garlic clove
· 2 preserved anchovies, cleaned
  and filleted (see page 110)
· 400 g (14 oz) tomatoes, peeled
  and diced or canned chopped
  tomatoes
· 1 chilli, seeded and chopped
· 300 g (11 oz) penne
· 2 tablespoons capers,
  drained and rinsed
· 1 tablespoon chopped
  flat-leaf parsley
· salt

Alternative fish: sprats
or smelts

PENNE WITH TOMATO AND ANCHOVIES

Heat the oil with the garlic clove in a saucepan over low heat. When the garlic begins to colour, remove and discard it. Add the anchovies to the pan and cook, stirring and mashing with the spoon, until they have almost completely disintegrated. Stir in the tomatoes and chilli and cook for 20 minutes.

Meanwhile, bring a large saucepan of salted water to a boil, add the pasta, bring back to a boil and cook for 8–10 minutes, until tender but still firm to the bite. Stir the capers and parsley into the sauce. Drain the pasta, tip it into the sauce, toss lightly and transfer to a serving dish. Serve immediately.

Serves 4
Preparation time: 35 mins
Cooking time: 1hr

· olive oil, for brushing
  and drizzling
· 1 flat-leaf parsley sprig
· 1 garlic clove
· 8 mint leaves
· 600g (1lb 5oz) fresh anchovies,
  scaled and cleaned
  (see page 110)
· juice of 2 lemons, strained
· 600g (1lb 5oz) potatoes,
  thinly sliced
· 200ml (scant 1 cup)
  dry white wine
· 80g (1½ cups) fresh
  breadcrumbs
· salt and pepper

Alternative fish: sprats
or sardines

Patate al forno con acciughe

POTATOES BAKED WITH ANCHOVIES

Preheat the oven to 180°C / 350°F / Gas Mark 4. Brush an ovenproof dish with oil. Chop the parsley, garlic and half the mint leaves together. Place the anchovies skin side up and press along the backbones with your thumb, then turn over and pull out the backbones, snipping them off at the tail and leaving the fish joined along their backs. Put a layer of anchovies, skin side down and still opened out, in the prepared dish, sprinkle with a little of the herb mixture, season with salt and pepper and drizzle with lemon juice and olive oil. Cover with a layer of potatoes, sprinkle with more of the herb mixture and season with salt and pepper.

Continue making alternate layers until all the ingredients have been used, then pour in the wine. Chop the remaining mint leaves and mix with the breadcrumbs, then sprinkle them over surface. Bake for 1 hour, then remove from the oven and serve immediately.

Serves 4
Preparation time: 30 mins
Cooking time: 20 mins

· 2 slices white bread,
  crusts removed
· 4 tablespoons milk
· 1 garlic clove, chopped
· 1 large flat-leaf parsley sprig,
  chopped
· 1 small oregano sprig, chopped
· 4 basil leaves, chopped
· 600 g (1 lb 5 oz) fresh anchovies,
  scaled and cleaned
  (see page 110)
· plain (all-purpose) flour,
  for dusting
· 1 egg, lightly beaten
· 120–150 g (1⅓–2 cups)
  dry breadcrumbs
· 5 tablespoons olive oil
· salt and pepper
· lemon wedges, to garnish

Alternative fish: sprats
or sardines

Acciughe ripiene

STUFFED ANCHOVIES

Tear the bread in to pieces, put them into a bowl, add the
milk and let soak until required. Meanwhile, mix together
the garlic, parsley, oregano and basil in a bowl.

Rub off the scales from the fish with your fingers. Cut off
and discard the heads, then slit the fish open along the
belly and pull out the innards. Rinse the cavities. Place the
anchovies skin side up and press along the backbones with
your thumb, then turn over and remove the bones, leaving
the fish joined along their backs. Rinse and pat dry, then
put them on a large plate, opened out and skin side down.

Squeeze out any excess milk from the bread, stir it into
the herb mixture and season with salt and pepper. Season
the anchovies lightly with salt and divide the stuffing among
half of them, spreading it evenly. Put the other anchovies on
top, skin side uppermost, pressing together gently to form
little sandwiches. Dust them with flour, dip in the beaten
egg and press both sides into the breadcrumbs. Heat the oil
in a large frying pan or skillet, add the anchovy sandwiches,
in batches, and cook, turning them once, until golden brown
on both sides. Remove with a fish slice (spatula), drain on
paper towels and keep warm while you cook the remaining
batches. Serve garnished with lemon wedges.

Serves 4
Preparation time: 15 mins
Cooking time: 1hr

· 2 tablespoons olive oil
· 100 g (¾ cup) baby (pearl)
  onions, chopped
· 200 g (1½ cups) baby carrots,
  chopped
· 1 celery stalk, chopped
· 1 bunch of fresh parsley,
  chopped
· 1 garlic clove, chopped
· 800 g (1¾ lb) eel, skinned and
  cut into 5-cm (2-inch) pieces
  (see page 111)
· 100 ml (scant ½ cup)
  dry white wine
· 350 g (12 oz) tomatoes, peeled
  and coarsely chopped
· 350 g (2¼ cups) cooked peas
· 20 g (¾ oz) preserved anchovies,
  rinsed, dried, filleted and
  crushed
· salt and pepper

Alternative fish: monkfish
or huss (dogfish)

EEL WITH PEAS AND CARROTS

Heat the oil in a frying pan or skillet, add the chopped onions, carrots, celery, parsley and garlic and cook over low heat, stirring occasionally, for 10 minutes. Add the pieces of eel, increase the heat to medium and cook for about 5 minutes on each side, until lightly browned. Add the wine and cook until the alcohol has evaporated. Season to taste with salt and pepper, reduce the heat, cover and simmer for 15 minutes.

Add the tomatoes, peas and anchovies, stir well, reduce the heat to very low and cook for about 40 minutes. Remove the pan from the heat, transfer the mixture to a serving platter and serve immediately.

Serves 12
Preparation time: 1¼ hrs
+ 5 days marinating and chilling
Cooking time: 1hr

· 2 tablespoons olive oil, plus
  extra for drizzling
· 1.2 kg (2½ lb) eel, skinned and
  cut into 3–4-cm (1¼–1½-inch)
  slices (see page 111)
· 1 onion, chopped
· 2 celery stalks, chopped
· 1 carrot, chopped
· 1 litre (4¼ cups) Fish
  (see page 78), chicken
  or vegetable stock
· juice of 1 lemon, strained
· 8 globe artichokes
· 200 g (7oz) smoked pancetta,
  sliced
· 2 bay leaves
· 1 head curly lettuce, separated
  into leaves
· balsamic vinegar, for drizzling
· salt and pepper

For the marinade:
· 100 ml (scant ½ cup)
  dry white wine
· 100 ml (scant ½ cup)
  dry vermouth
· 1 tablespoon chopped thyme
· 1 tablespoon chopped tarragon
· 2 tablespoons chopped
  flat-leaf parsley
· 2 tablespoons olive oil

Alternative fish: monkfish
or huss (dogfish)

EEL AND ARTICHOKE TERRINE

Pour the white wine and vermouth into a large bowl, add
the thyme, tarragon, parsley and olive oil. Season with
salt and pepper, and add the pieces of eel, turning to coat.
Cover with clingfilm (plastic wrap) and let marinate in the
refrigerator overnight.

The following day, heat the olive oil in a large flameproof
casserole (Dutch oven), add the onion, celery and carrot
and cook over low heat, stirring occasionally, for 5 minutes.
Pour in the stock and bring to a boil. Drain the eel, reserving
the marinade, add to the casserole and cook for 2 minutes.
Remove from the heat and set aside.

Fill a bowl halfway with water and add half the lemon juice.
Working on them one at a time, break off the artichoke
stems, discard all the tough outer leaves and the chokes
and cut into chunks, then immediately add to the acidulated
water to prevent discolouration. Bring a saucepan of water
to a boil and add the remaining lemon juice. Drain the
artichokes, add to the pan and cook for 7–8 minutes. Drain
with a slotted spoon and let cool.

Preheat the oven to 180°C/350°F/Gas Mark 4. Line a terrine
with the slices of pancetta, letting them hang over the
sides, and fill it with alternate layers of eel and artichokes,
ending with a layer of eel. Drizzle with some of the reserved
marinade and season with salt and pepper. Cover the top
by folding over the overhanging slices of pancetta, lay the
bay leaves on top and cover with foil. Put the terrine into
a roasting pan, pour in hot water to come about halfway
up the sides and bake for 1 hour. Remove the terrine from
the oven, lift it out of the roasting pan, remove the foil and
weigh it down with a 1-kg (2½-lb) weight. Let cool, then put
in the refrigerator for 4 days.

When ready to serve, wrap a warm cloth around the terrine,
turn it out and cut it into thin slices. Put the lettuce into
a bowl, drizzle with oil and balsamic vinegar and season salt
and pepper. Divide among 12 individual serving plates, top
with a slice of terrine and serve.

Serves 6
Preparation time: 10 mins
Cooking time: 15 mins

· 1 × 900-g (2-lb) eel, skinned
  and filleted (see page 111)
· plain (all-purpose) flour,
  for dusting
· 4 tablespoons olive oil
· 2 bay leaves
· 1 carrot, chopped
· 50 g (½ cup) chopped celery
· 1 medium onion, chopped
· 1 garlic clove, chopped
· 500 ml (2 cups) red wine
· ½ tablespoon black peppercorns
· salt

Alternative fish: monkfish
or grouper

Anguilla al vino rosso

EEL IN RED WINE

Cut the eel fillets into pieces and dust them with flour.
Heat half the oil with the bay leaves in a frying pan or skillet,
add the pieces of eel and cook over high heat for 2 minutes
each side, until lightly browned, then remove from the heat.

Heat the remaining oil in another frying pan or skillet,
add the carrot, celery and onions and cook over low heat,
stirring occasionally, for 5 minutes. Add the garlic and cook
for another 2 minutes. Add the pieces of eel to the pan of
vegetables, season with salt, add the peppercorns, pour
in the red wine and simmer over medium heat for about
10 minutes. Remove from the heat and serve immediately.

Serves 4
Preparation time: 10 mins
+ 2 hrs marinating
Cooking time: 30 mins

· 1 kg (2¼ lb) eel, skinned and
  cut into 5-cm (2-inch) pieces
  (see page 111)
· 5 tablespoons olive oil
· 120 g (1¼ cups) dry breadcrumbs
· 2 garlic cloves, crushed
· 4–5 sage leaves
· 2 tablespoons hot water
· salt and pepper

Alternative fish: monkfish
or huss (dogfish)

Anguilla alla fiorentina

FLORENTINE-STYLE EEL

Put the pieces of eel into a shallow dish, add 3 tablespoons
of the oil, season with salt and pepper and let marinate
for 2 hours. Preheat the oven to 180°C/350°F/Gas Mark 4.
Drain the pieces of eel and coat in the breadcrumbs.
Heat the remaining oil in a large flameproof casserole
(Dutch oven), add the garlic and sage leaves and cook for
a few minutes. Add the pieces of eel, transfer the casserole
to the oven and cook, turning the fish occasionally, for
25 minutes, until browned. Remove the casserole from the
oven, sprinkle the eel with the hot water, return to the oven
and cook for another 5 minutes, until it has evaporated.
Serve immediately.

Serves 4
Preparation time: 45 mins
+ 5 hrs soaking
Cooking time: 1½ hrs

· red wine vinegar, for soaking
· 1 eel, cut into 4-cm (1½-inch) slices (see page 111)
· plain (all-purpose) flour, for dusting
· 2 tablespoons olive oil
· 1 garlic clove, chopped
· pinch of dried oregano
· 200 ml (scant 1 cup) dry white wine
· 350 g (12 oz) tomatoes, peeled and chopped
· salt and pepper
· 350 g (scant 2½ cups) polenta, freshly cooked (see page 125), to serve

Alternative fish: cod or swordfish

Polenta e anguilla

EEL WITH POLENTA

Mix together equal quantities of water and vinegar in a bowl, add the pieces of eel and let soak for about 5 hours. Drain the pieces of eel, pat dry with paper towels and dust with flour. Heat the oil in a frying pan or skillet, add the garlic and oregano and cook over low heat, stirring frequently, for 2–3 minutes. Add the pieces of eel and cook for about 5 minutes on each side, until lightly browned. Add the wine and cook until the alcohol has evaporated, then stir in the tomatoes. Simmer gently for 30 minutes, then season with salt and pepper. Serve immediately with the polenta.

Serves 4
Preparation time: 10 mins
+ cooling
Cooking time: 2–3 mins

· 300 g (11 oz) whitebait, rinsed and drained
· 150 ml (⅔ cup) olive oil
· juice of 1 lemon, strained
· 1 teaspoon Dijon mustard
· salt

Alternative fish: sprats or anchovies

Bianchetti all'olio e limone

WHITEBAIT WITH OIL AND LEMON

Cook the whitebait in a saucepan of salted boiling water for 2–3 minutes, then drain and let cool. Whisk together the olive oil, lemon juice and mustard in a bowl, pour the mixture over the fish and serve.

Photograph opposite

Serves 4
Preparation time: 20 mins
Cooking time: 20 mins

· 400 g (14 oz) whitebait,
  rinsed and drained
· 15 g (1 tablespoon) butter
· 100 ml (scant ½ cup) olive oil
· ½ onion, finely chopped
· 120 g (1 cup) plain
  (all-purpose) flour
· 3 eggs
· 100 g (generous 1 cup) grated
  Parmesan cheese
· 100 ml (scant ½ cup) milk
· salt and pepper

Alternative fish: sprats
or anchovies

Bianchetti in pastella

WHITEBAIT IN BATTER

Rinse the fish and let drain in a colander. Melt the butter
with ½ tablespoon of the oil in a small frying pan or skillet,
add the onion and cook over low heat, stirring occasionally,
for 8–10 minutes, until golden brown. Remove from the
heat and let cool. Sift the flour into a bowl, add the eggs
and beat well with a whisk until smooth. Stir in the cooled
onion, grated cheese and milk and season with salt and
pepper. Beat well with a whisk to make a smooth pouring
batter, adding a little more milk if necessary. Gently stir
in the whitebait. Heat the remaining oil in a frying pan or
skillet. Drop tablespoonfuls of the mixture into the oil, in
batches, and cook until golden brown on the undersides,
then turn with a fish slice (spatula) and cook until browned
on the second side. Remove from the pan with a fish slice
and drain on paper towels. Keep warm while you cook the
remaining batches. Serve immediately.

Serves 6
Preparation time: 10 mins
Cooking time: 10 mins

· 700 g (1½ lb) whitebait,
  rinsed and drained
· plain (all-purpose) flour,
  dusting
· olive or vegetable oil,
  for deep-frying
· salt
· parsley sprigs and lemon
  wedges, to garnish

Alternative fish: sprats
or anchovies

Bianchetti fritti

FRIED WHITEBAIT

Put the whitebait in a colander and wash briefly in salted
water then pat dry. Dust with flour, shaking off any excess.
Heat the oil in a deep-fryer to 180–190°C (350–375°F) or
until a cube of day-old bread browns in 30 seconds. Add
the fish to the hot oil and cook for 2 minutes, separating
them with a slotted spoon. Drain on paper towels, season
lightly with salt and serve hot, garnished with parsley
and lemon wedges.

Serves 4
Preparation time: 25 mins
Cooking time: 1hr

· 4 swordfish steaks
· 1 small bay leaf
· 1 garlic clove, peeled
· 1 chervil sprig, chopped
· 1 basil sprig, chopped
· 2 tablespoons olive oil, plus
  extra for drizzling
· 3–4 tablespoons dry white wine
· 1 onion, chopped
· 1 celery stalk, chopped
· 1 carrot, chopped
· 300g (11oz) tomatoes, peeled,
  seeded and chopped
· 2 tablespoons capers, rinsed
· 50g (½ cup) black olives, pitted
· 40g (1½oz) Parmesan cheese,
  flaked
· salt, pepper

Alternative fish: monkfish

SWORDFISH BAKED WITH TOMATOES AND PARMESAN

Put the fish steaks in a roasting pan with the bay leaf and garlic clove. Sprinkle with chervil and basil, drizzle with olive oil and season with salt and pepper. Cook over medium-low heat, turning the fish occasionally, for 30 minutes. Meanwhile, preheat the oven to 180°C/350°F/ Gas Mark 4. Transfer to the oven and cook, drizzling occasionally with the wine, for about 12 minutes. Meanwhile, heat the oil in a saucepan, add the onion, celery and carrot and cook over low heat, stirring occasionally, for 5 minutes. Add the tomatoes, capers and olives and cook for another 10 minutes. If necessary, stir in a tablespoon of water. Remove the roasting pan from the oven, pour the tomato sauce over the fish and sprinkle with the Parmesan. Return to the oven and cook for another 15 minutes. Remove from the oven and let stand for a few minutes before serving.

Serves 6
Preparation time: 20 mins
+ 5 mins standing
Cooking time: 40 mins

· 150 ml (⅔ cup) olive oil,
  plus extra for brushing
· 1kg (2¼lb) potatoes,
  thinly sliced
· 1 onion, cut into rings
· 700g (1½lb) swordfish
  fillets, sliced
· 1 red chilli, chopped
· 1 garlic clove, chopped
· 1 bunch flat-leaf parsley,
  chopped
· salt and pepper

Alternative fish: tuna

BAKED SWORDFISH WITH POTATOES

Preheat the oven to 180°C/350°F/Gas Mark 4. Brush an ovenproof dish with oil and make a layer of half the potato slices and then a layer of half the onion rings. Season the fish pieces on both sides with salt and pepper and lay them on top of the vegetables, then sprinkle with the chilli and drizzle with half the oil. Cover with a second layer of potatoes and a second layer of onion and sprinkle with the garlic and parsley. Season with salt and pepper and drizzle with the remaining oil. Bake for 40 minutes. Remove from the oven and let stand for 5 minutes, then serve.

Serves 4
Preparation time: 20 mins
+ 5 mins standing
Cooking time: 45 mins

· 1 courgette (zucchini),
  cut into long, thin slices
· olive oil, for brushing
  and drizzling
· 2 potatoes, sliced into
  thin rounds
· 1 tablespoon chopped thyme
· 1 × 400-g (14-oz) swordfish
  fillet, cut into thin slices
· grated zest of 1 lemon
· salt and pepper

Alternative fish: monkfish
or tuna

SWORDFISH LAYERED WITH VEGETABLES AND THYME

Preheat the grill (broiler). Spread out the courgette (zucchini) slices on a baking sheet, lightly brush oil with oil and grill (broil) for 4–5 minutes, until lightly coloured. Turn over, lightly brush with oil and grill for another 4–5 minutes, then transfer to a plate. Repeat with the potato rounds. Drizzle with a little oil, season with salt and pepper, sprinkle 1 teaspoon of the thyme and let stand for the flavours to mingle.

Meanwhile, preheat the oven to 150°C/300°F/Gas Mark 2. Line a baking sheet with greaseproof (wax) paper. Brush the swordfish pieces with oil, and sprinkle with the remaining thyme and the grated lemon zest and season with salt and pepper. Make 4 stacks, alternating a layer of fish pieces with a layer of vegetables, ending with a layer of fish. Bake for about 15 minutes. Remove from the oven and let stand for 5 minutes, then transfer to a serving platter and serve.

Serves 6
Preparation time: 1hr
+ 30 mins marinating

· juice of ½ lemon, strained
· 250g (9oz) carrots
· 250g (9oz) cucumber
· 300g (11oz) courgettes (zucchini)
· 150g (5oz) radishes
· 175g (6oz) celeriac
· 150ml (⅔ cups) olive oil
· 2 tablespoons Worcestershire
  sauce
· 2 tablespoons chopped shallot
· 4 tablespoons chopped basil
· 1.2kg (2½lb) swordfish steaks,
  cut into wafer-thin slices
· fine sea salt
· freshly ground white pepper

Alternative fish: tuna

Pesce spada marinato allo scalogno e basilico

SWORDFISH MARINATED WITH SHALLOTS AND BASIL

Fill a large bowl with ice-cold water and stir in the lemon juice. Cut the carrots, cucumber, courgettes (zucchini), radishes and celeriac into very thin julienne strips, adding them immediately to the acidulated water. Pour the oil into a blender, add the Worcestershire sauce, shallot and basil, season with salt and white pepper and process until smooth. Put the swordfish slices on a serving platter, slightly overlapping each other, season with salt and white pepper and drizzle with the blended dressing. Leave to stand for 30 minutes. Drain the vegetables well, spoon them on top of the fish and serve.

Photograph opposite

Serves 4
Preparation time: 10 mins
+ 10 mins soaking
Cooking time: 20 mins

· 4 swordfish steaks
· 100ml (scant ½ cup) milk
· 1 tablespoon butter
· plain (all-purpose) flour,
  for dusting

For the sauce:
· 100g (½ cup) butter
· ½ teaspoon ground cinnamon
· 1 clove
· 100ml (scant ½ cup) cider
  (apple) vinegar
· 2 tablespoons balsamic vinegar
· salt and pepper

Alternative fish: tuna

Pesce spada all'aceto balsamico

SWORDFISH IN BALSAMIC VINEGAR

Put the fish in a shallow dish, pour in the milk and let soak for 10 minutes, then drain and pat dry. Melt the butter in a large frying pan or skillet. Dust the fish with flour, add to the pan and cook over medium heat for 5 minutes on each side, until lightly browned. Season with salt and pepper, remove from the pan with a fish slice (spatula) and drain on paper towels, then transfer a serving dish and keep warm.

To make the sauce, melt the butter over low heat, add the cinnamon and clove and pour in both kinds of vinegar. Stir well and simmer for about 10 minutes, until thickened. Pour the sauce over the fish and serve immediately.

Serves 6
Preparation time: 1¼ hrs
Cooking time: 30 mins

· 1kg (2¼ lb) spinach
· 4 × 175-g (6-oz) salmon fillets
· 40g (3 tablespoons) butter,
  plus extra for greasing
· 50g (½ cup) plain (all-purpose)
  flour, plus extra for dusting
· 500 ml (2 cups) milk
· pinch of freshly grated nutmeg
· pinch of dried thyme
· 100g (scant 1 cup) grated
  Gruyère cheese
· 100 ml (scant ½ cup) double
  (heavy) cream
· 200g (7oz) shortcrust pastry
  (basic pie dough), thawed
  if frozen
· salt and pepper

Alternative fish: trout or a
smoked fish such as haddock

288   290   296

SALMON AND SPINACH PIE

Put the spinach into a saucepan with just the water clinging
to leaves after washing and cook for 5–10 minutes, then
drain well. Squeeze out the excess moisture and chop.
Put the fish into a shallow saucepan, pour in water to cover,
add a pinch of salt and bring just to a boil, then reduce the
heat to low and simmer for 10 minutes. Remove the fish with
a fish slice (spatula), discard the skin and flake the flesh.
Reserve the cooking liquid.

Preheat the oven to 160°C/325°F/Gas Mark 3. Lightly grease
a pie dish (plate) with butter. Melt the butter in a saucepan,
stir in the flour and cook over low heat, stirring constantly,
for 2 minutes. Gradually stir in the milk and 2 ladlefuls of the
reserved cooking liquid. Season with salt and pepper, stir
in the nutmeg and thyme and remove the pan from the heat.
Stir in the cheese, cream, spinach and salmon.

Roll out the pastry dough into a round on a lightly floured
counter and use to line the prepared pie dish. Line with
a sheet of parchment paper, fill with baking beans (pie
weights) and bake blind for 15 minutes. Remove the dish
from the oven and increase the oven temperature to
180°C/350°F/Gas Mark 4. Remove the baking beans and
paper from the pastry case (shell). Spoon the spinach
and salmon mixture into the pastry case and bake for
30 minutes. Remove the pie from the oven and serve warm.

Serves 4
Preparation time: 15 mins
Cooking time: 25 mins

· 25 g (2 tablespoons) butter
· 3 fennel bulbs, sliced
· 120 ml (½ cup) double
  (heavy) cream
· 80 g (3 oz) smoked salmon,
  chopped
· 4 dill sprigs, chopped
· salt and pepper

Alternative fish: salmon roe
or smoked trout

CREAM OF FENNEL SOUP WITH SMOKED SALMON

Melt the butter in a saucepan, add the fennel and 5 tablespoons water and cook over low heat for about 20 minutes. Stir in another 5 tablespoons water, transfer the mixture to a blender or food processor and process to a purée. Pour into a clean saucepan and stir in the cream and 250 ml (1 cup) water. Season with salt and pepper to taste.

Reheat over medium heat but do not allow to boil. Ladle into individual soup bowls, garnish with the chopped salmon and dill, and serve.

Serves 4
Preparation time: 18 mins
+ 5 mins standing
Cooking time: 28 mins

· 1 litre (4½ cups) chicken stock
· 40g (3 tablespoons) butter
· 2 tablespoons olive oil
· 1 leek, chopped
· 100g (¾ cup) diced pumpkin
· 150 ml (⅔ cup) Marsala
· 280g (1½ cups) risotto rice
· 100g (3½ oz) salmon fillet, diced
· 5 hazelnuts, chopped
· 40g (½ cup) grated
  Parmesan cheese
· salt and pepper

Alternative fish: trout or
prawns (shrimp)

 288   290   296

RISOTTO WITH SALMON, LEEKS AND HAZELNUTS

Pour the stock into a saucepan and bring to a boil, then reduce the heat and simmer gently. Meanwhile, melt half the butter with the oil in a separate saucepan, add the leek and cook over low heat, stirring occasionally, for 5–6 minutes, until softened. Stir in the pumpkin and cook for about 5 minutes, until lightly browned. Pour in the Marsala and cook until the alcohol has evaporated, then season lightly with salt.

Add the rice and stir well, then pour in just enough of the simmering stock to cover. Bring back to a boil and cook, stirring constantly and adding more stock when necessary, for about 12 minutes.

Add the salmon and hazelnuts and cook, stirring constantly, for another 8 minutes, until the rice is tender. Remove from the heat and stir in the remaining butter and the Parmesan and season with pepper. Cover and let stand for 5 minutes, then serve.

Serves 4
Preparation time: 30 mins
Cooking time: 45 mins

· 3 tablespoons olive oil, plus
  extra for brushing
· 2 courgettes (zucchini), cut
  into thin strips
· 2 artichoke hearts, sliced
· 1 leek, sliced
· 300 ml (1¼ cups) dry white wine
· 500 g (1lb 2oz) puff pastry dough,
  thawed if frozen
· plain (all-purpose) flour,
  for dusting
· 1½ teaspoons butter, melted
· 1 × 500-g (1lb 2-oz) salmon
  fillet, skinned
· 1 shallot, chopped
· 4–5 black peppercorns
· 1 tablespoon chopped
  flat-leaf parsley
· salt

For the saffron sauce:
· pinch of saffron threads,
  lightly crushed
· 250 ml (1 cup) Fish Stock
  (see page 78)
· 20 g (3 tablespoons) butter
· 3 tablespoons plain
  (all-purpose) flour
· 1½ tablespoons double
  (heavy) cream

Alternative fish: trout or pike

SALMON IN PASTRY WITH SAFFRON SAUCE

Preheat the oven to 200°C/400°F/Gas Mark 6. Brush a baking sheet with oil. Heat 2 tablespoons of the oil in a frying pan or skillet, add the courgettes (zucchini), artichoke hearts and leek and cook over low heat, stirring occasionally, for 5–8 minutes, until lightly browned. Add 200 ml (scant 1 cup) of the wine and cook until the alcohol has evaporated, then season with salt and pepper and cook for another 5 minutes. Remove the pan from the heat. Roll out the dough into a thin sheet on a lightly floured counter. Brush with melted butter and spoon half the vegetable mixture evenly on top. Cover with the salmon fillet and top with the remaining vegetables. Fold over the dough to enclose it completely, pinching the edges to seal, and prick a few holes in it with a cocktail stick or toothpick. Put the pastry parcel on the prepared baking sheet and bake for 30 minutes.

Meanwhile, heat the remaining oil in a small frying pan or skillet, add the shallot and cook over low heat, stirring occasionally, for 5 minutes, until translucent. Add half the remaining white wine and the peppercorns, season with salt and simmer for another 10 minutes, then strain into a clean saucepan.

To make the saffron sauce, put the saffron threads into a small bowl, add 1 tablespoon of the stock and let soak. Melt the butter in a saucepan over low heat, stir in the flour and cook, stirring constantly, until the mixture is a light golden colour. Gradually stir in the stock, a little at a time, then bring to a boil, stirring constantly. Simmer very gently over the lowest possible heat for 20–25 minutes, until thick and creamy. Strain the sauce into the pan with the shallot and wine mixture and heat gently. Stir in the cream, remaining wine and saffron with its soaking liquid and cook, stirring constantly, for 2 minutes, then remove the pan from the heat. Pour a few tablespoons of sauce onto a serving platter and sprinkle with the parsley. Remove the salmon parcel from the oven, cut into small slices and put them on the platter. Serve immediately, handing the remaining sauce separately in a sauceboat.

Serves 4
Preparation time: 25 mins
+ overnight marinating
Cooking time: 20–25 mins

- 1 × 300-g (11-oz) salmon fillet
- grated zest of 1 lemon
- grated zest of 1 orange
- 1 bunch of dill, chopped
- 250 g (1¼ cups) caster
  (superfine) sugar
- 250 g (scant 1 cup) fine salt
- 4 waxy salad (new) potatoes
- 100 g (3½ oz) lamb's lettuce
  (mâche)
- 175 ml (¾ cup) olive oil
- salt and freshly ground
  white pepper

Also works with trout or
sea bass

 288 290 296

MARINATED SALMON
AND POTATO SALAD

Put the salmon fillet, skin side down, on the rack of
a fish kettle (poacher) or other perforated tray set over
a container to let the juices drain off as it marinates.
Sprinkle with the grated lemon and orange zest and
half the dill. Mix together the sugar and salt in a bowl
and sprinkle the mixture over the fish to cover completely.
Chill overnight in the refrigerator.

Cook the potatoes in salted boiling water for about
20 minutes, until tender but not falling apart, then drain
and let cool. Remove the fish from the refrigerator, drain
off the liquid, scrape off the of sugar and salt crust and
cut the fish diagonally into wafer-thin slices, like smoked
salmon. Slice the potatoes. Put the lamb's lettuce (mâche)
and the potatoes on a serving platter and top with the
salmon slices. Mix together the oil and remaining dill
in a bowl and season with salt and white pepper. Serve
the potato and salmon salad, handing the dill dressing
separately in a sauceboat.

Serves 4
Preparation time: 35 mins
+ 3–5 hrs chilling

· 300g (11oz) very fresh
  salmon fillet, skinned
· olive oil, for drizzling
· juice of 2 lemons, strained
· 50g (2oz) rocket (arugula)
· 1 bunch of chervil
· 1 bunch of radishes, trimmed
  and halved
· 1 lemon, thinly sliced
· salt and pepper

Alternative fish: monkfish
or scallops

 288   290   296

SALMON WITH LEMON AND MIXED GREENS

Chill the salmon fillet in the refrigerator for about 3 hours or in the freezer for 1 hour to firm up. Using a very sharp knife, cut it into paper-thin slices. Put the slices on a serving platter, drizzle with olive oil and the lemon juice and season with salt and pepper. Cover with clingfilm (plastic wrap) and chill in the refrigerator for about 2 hours. Finely chop the rocket (arugula), chervil and radishes together and sprinkle over the salmon. Drizzle with a little more olive oil, season with salt and pepper, garnish with the lemon slices and serve.

Photograph opposite

Serves 4
Preparation time: 30 mins
+ 20 mins marinating

· 3 lemons
· 5 tablespoons olive oil
· dash of Tabasco sauce
· 600g (1lb 5oz) salmon fillet,
  skinned and diced
· 2 yellow bell peppers, seeded
  and cut into squares
· 50g (scant ½ cup) capers,
  drained and rinsed
· 8 green olives, pitted
  and chopped
· 4 egg yolks
· 1 tablespoon chopped
  flat-leaf parsley
· salt and pepper

Alternative fish: tuna or
scallops

 288   290   296

SALMON TARTARE

Peel one of the lemons, removing all traces of white pith, and chop the flesh. Squeeze the juice from the remaining lemons. Mix together the olive oil, lemon juice and Tabasco in a bowl and season with salt and pepper. Mix together the salmon, bell peppers, capers, olives and chopped lemon in a dish, add the lemon dressing, mix well and let marinate for 20 minutes. Divide the mixture among 4 individual dishes and put an egg yolk in the middle of each. Garnish with the parsley and serve.

Serves 6
Preparation time: 10 mins
Cooking time: 30 mins

· 130 g (4½ oz) fresh rosemary
  leaves, chopped
· 6 × 200-g (7-oz) salmon steaks
· 3 tablespoons whipping cream
· 200 ml (scant 1 cup) mayonnaise
· 2 tablespoons dry vermouth
· 50 g (1 cup) chopped mixed
  fresh herbs, such as flat-leaf
  parsley, dill and thyme
· 2 pickled gherkins, finely
  chopped
· salt and pepper

Alternative fish: tuna or
sea bass

Salmone croccante al rosmarino

GRILLED SALMON WITH ROSEMARY

Preheat the grill (broiler), line the grill (broiler) pan with foil and sprinkle the chopped rosemary over it. Put the salmon steaks on top, season with salt and pepper and grill (broil) for about 5 minutes on each side.

Meanwhile, whip the cream, then fold it gently into the mayonnaise. Gently stir in the vermouth, herbs and gherkins. To serve, put the salmon steaks on one side of a serving platter, slightly overlapping each other, and spoon the creamy mayonnaise sauce on the other side.

Photograph opposite

Serves 4
Preparation time: 30 mins
+ cooling
Cooking time: 20 mins

· 900 g (2 lb) sardines, scaled,
  cleaned and butterflied
· 2 rosemary sprigs, chopped
· 1 garlic clove, chopped
· olive oil, for drizzling
· 1 tablespoon red wine vinegar
· salt and pepper

Alternative fish: herring or
mackerel

 297 298  296

Sardine al rosmarino

SARDINES WITH ROSEMARY

Press firmly along the backbone with your thumb or the palm of your hand. When the fish is completely flat, turn it over, pull away the backbone and snip it off at the tail end. Remove any remaining small bones with tweezers. Prepare the remaining sardines in the same way. Mix together the rosemary and garlic in a bowl, drizzle with olive oil and season with salt and pepper. Put alternate layers of sardines and the rosemary mixture in a saucepan and cook gently over low heat for about 10 minutes. Add the vinegar and cook for 10 minutes. Remove from the heat and let cool before serving.

Serves 6
Preparation time: 45 mins
+ 10 mins marinating

· olive oil, for drizzling
· 24 sardines, scaled, cleaned
  and butterflied
· 200 ml (scant 1 cup)
  cider vinegar
· 3 pink grapefruit
· 1 head endive, shredded
· 2 fennel bulbs, trimmed and
  thinly sliced
· 50 g (⅓ cup) pine nuts, toasted
· 1 bunch of chives, chopped
· salt

Alternative fish: anchovies
or sprats

 297   298   296

MARINATED SARDINES WITH ENDIVE, FENNEL AND PINE NUT SALAD

Put the sardines, skin side uppermost, in a single layer in a serving dish, season with salt, drizzle with the cider vinegar and let marinate for 10 minutes.

Meanwhile, peel the grapefruit over a plate to catch the juice, making sure that you have removed all traces of the bitter white pith. Cut out the grapefruit segments from between the membranes and squeeze out the membranes over the plate of juice before discarding.

Remove the sardines from the marinade and pat dry with paper towels, then put them in a bowl and drizzle with olive oil and the reserved grapefruit juice. Put the endive and fennel into another bowl, drizzle with oil, season with salt and toss lightly, then transfer to a serving platter. Add the sardines, garnish with the grapefruit segments, pine nuts and chives and serve.

Serves 4
Preparation time: 30 mins
+ 24 hrs marinating

· 24 sardines, scaled, cleaned
  and butterflied
· 150 ml (⅔ cup) olive oil
· juice of 1 lemon, strained
· 2 red bell peppers, seeded
  and sliced
· 10 black olives, pitted and
  chopped
· 1 basil sprig, leaves torn
· salt and pepper

For the sauce:
· 1 egg yolk
· 1 tablespoon white wine vinegar
· 3 canned anchovy fillets in oil,
  drained
· 5 basil leaves

Alternative fish: herring
or sprats

 297 298  296

MARINATED SARDINES WITH BASIL

Place the sardines in a shallow dish. Whisk together the olive oil, lemon juice and a pinch each of salt and pepper in a bowl and pour the mixture over the sardines. Cover with clingfilm (plastic wrap) and let marinate in the refrigerator for 24 hours. Drain the sardines, reserving the marinade and put them on a serving dish.

To make the sauce, put the egg yolk, vinegar, anchovy fillets, basil and reserved marinade in a blender and process on low speed until thoroughly combined. Garnish the sardines with red bell peppers, olives and basil leaves, spoon the sauce over them and serve.

Photograph opposite

Serves 4
Preparation time: 20 mins
+ 2 days chilling
Cooking time: 50 mins

· 4 tablespoons olive oil,
  plus extra for frying
· 1 kg (2¼ lb) sardines, scaled,
  cleaned and butterflied
· plain (all-purpose) flour,
  for dusting
· 600 g (1 lb 5 oz) white onions,
  very thinly sliced
· 600 ml (2½ cups) white
  wine vinegar
· 2 bay leaves
· salt and pepper

Alternative fish: herring
or mackerel

 297 298  296

FRIED SARDINES 'IN SAOR'

Heat the oil for frying in a large frying pan or skillet. Dust the sardines with flour, add to the pan, in batches, and cook for about 6 minutes. Remove from the pan with a fish slice (spatula), drain on paper towels, set aside and keep warm. Heat four tablespoons of oil in another frying pan or skillet, add the onion, cover and cook over low heat for 20–25 minutes. Sprinkle with the vinegar, bring to a boil and cook for a few minutes, then remove the heat. Put the bay leaves into a terrine, add a layer of sardines, season lightly with salt and top with some of the onion and vinegar mixture. Continue making layers, ending with a layer of onions and vinegar mixture. Cover and chill in the refrigerator for two days before serving. Turn out and cut into slices to serve.

Note: Some Italian cooks like to add pine nuts and raisins that have been soaked in dry white wine to each onion layer.

Serves 4
Preparation time: 30 mins
Cooking time: 10 mins

· 175 g (1⅓ cups) fine couscous, cooked
· 1 teaspoon ground cumin
· 1 teaspoon paprika
· 2 garlic cloves, chopped
· ½ small bunch fresh coriander (cilantro), chopped
· 16 sardines, scaled, cleaned and butterflied
· 1 tablespoon olive oil, plus extra for brushing
· salt
· slices of crusty wholemeal (whole wheat) bread, to serve

Alternative fish: sprats or anchovies

 297 298 296

SARDINES STUFFED WITH HERBS AND COUSCOUS

Preheat the grill (broiler). Mix together the couscous, cumin, paprika, garlic and coriander (cilantro) in a bowl and stir in the oil. Divide this mixture among the fish cavities, brush the fish with oil and grill (broil) for 3–5 minutes on each side.

Remove the sardines from the grill and drain on paper towels. Season lightly with salt and serve very hot with slices of crusty bread.

Photograph opposite

Serves 4
Preparation time: 20 mins
Cooking time: 20 mins

· olive oil, for brushing and drizzling
· 8 sardines, scaled, cleaned and butterflied
· 4 tablespoons chopped flat-leaf parsley
· 1 garlic clove, chopped
· 50 g (½ cup) plain (all-purpose) flour
· 1 egg
· 80 g (1½ cups) fresh breadcrumbs
· salt and pepper
· lemon wedges, to serve

Alternative fish: sprats or herring

 297 298 296

Sardine al forno

BAKED SARDINES

Preheat the oven to 200°C/400°F/Gas Mark 6. Generously brush a roasting pan with oil. While the sardines are still opened out, drizzle with olive oil and season with pepper, then divide the parsley and garlic among them. Close up the sardines and press gently together.

Spread out the flour in a shallow dish, lightly beat the egg with a pinch of salt in another shallow dish and spread out the breadcrumbs in third. Dip the fish first in the flour, then in the egg and, finally, in the breadcrumbs and put them in a ingle layer on the prepared roasting pan. Drizzle with a little more olive oil. Bake for 15 minutes, until browned, and serve immediately with lemon wedges.

Serves 4
Preparation time: 30 mins
Cooking time: 20 mins

- 350 g (2½ cups) redcurrants
- 4 mackerel, cleaned
- 25 g (2 tablespoons) butter
- 1 onion, chopped
- 1 garlic clove, finely chopped
- 175 ml (¾ cup) dry white wine
- 1 teaspoon sugar
- salt and pepper

Alternative fish: herring
or sardines

 288

Sgombri al ribes

MACKEREL WITH REDCURRANTS

Preheat the oven to 180°C / 350°F / Gas Mark 4. Put the redcurrants in a bowl, add warm water to cover and let soak. Meanwhile, make several diagonal slashes in each side of the fish and put them into an ovenproof dish. Melt the butter in a saucepan, add the onion and garlic and cook over low heat, stirring occasionally, for about 10 minutes. Drain the redcurrants, reserving the soaking liquid. Set 120 g (¾ cup) aside and squeeze the remainder over the bowl of soaking liquid, then discard. Pour the wine and soaking liquid into the pan, stir in the sugar and season with salt and pepper. Heat to simmering point, then remove from the heat and pour the mixture over the fish. Bake for about 10 minutes, then add the reserved redcurrants, return the dish to the oven and cook for another 10 minutes. Serve with the sauce.

Serves 4
Preparation time: 25 mins
Cooking time: 6–10 mins

- ½ bread roll (bun)
- 400 g (14 oz) mackerel fillets, skinned
- 25 g (2 tablespoons) butter, softened
- 2 tablespoons chopped flat-leaf parsley
- pinch of freshly grated nutmeg
- plain (all-purpose) flour, for dusting
- olive or vegetable oil, for deep-frying
- salt and pepper

Alternative fish: herring
or salmon

 288 290

Frittelle di sgombri

MACKEREL CROQUETTES

Tear the bread into small pieces, put it into a bowl, add 3–4 tablespoons water and let soak for 5 minutes, then squeeze out. Meanwhile, put the fish fillets into a food processor and process to a purée, then scrape into a bowl. Stir in butter, soaked bread, parsley and nutmeg and season with salt and pepper. Shape the mixture into small balls and dust them with flour. Heat the oil in a deep-fryer to 180–190°C (350–375°F) or until a cube of day-old bread browns in 30 seconds. Add the fish balls to the hot oil, in batches if necessary, and cook for 3–5 minutes, until golden brown. Remove and drain on paper towels, then keep warm while you cook the remaining batch. Serve hot.

Serves 4
Preparation time: 10 mins
Cooking time: 20 mins

· 4 mackerel, cleaned and
  heads removed
· plain (all-purpose) flour,
  for dusting
· 50 g (4 tablespoons) butter
· juice of ½ lemon, strained
· 2 tablespoons chopped
  flat-leaf parsley
· salt
· lemon slices, to garnish

Alternative fish: sole or
salmon

 288

Sgombri alla mugnaia

MACKEREL MEUNIÈRE

Dust the mackerel with flour. Melt half the butter in
a large frying pan or skillet, add the mackerel and cook
for 10 minutes on each side. Season with salt. Melt the
remaining butter in a small saucepan and heat until pale
golden brown. Remove the pan from the heat. Open out
the fish and remove the backbone and any attached bones.
Put the fish on a serving platter and sprinkle with the
lemon juice, lightly browned butter and chopped parsley.
Garnish with lemon slices and serve immediately.

Serves 4
Preparation time: 10 mins
Cooking time: 20 mins

· 4 mackerel, cleaned
· plain (all-purpose) flour,
  for dusting
· 3 tablespoons olive oil
· 25 g (2 tablespoons) butter
· 4 rashers (slices) smoked bacon
· salt

Alternative fish: herring or
sardines

 288

Sgombri fritto con pancetta

FRIED MACKEREL WITH BACON

Dust the fish with flour, shaking off the excess. Heat the
oil in a large frying pan or skillet, add the mackerel and cook
over medium heat for 5 minutes on each side. Remove with
a fish slice (spatula) and drain on paper towels. Season
lightly with salt and keep warm. Melt the butter in a small
frying pan or skillet, add the bacon and cook for 2–3 minutes
on each side. Remove the bacon from the pan and wrap
a slice around each fish, put them on a serving plate and
serve immediately.

Serves 4
Preparation time: 1hr
+ 15 mins marinating
Cooking time: 20 mins

· 4 mackerel, cleaned and
  heads removed
· 1 lemon wedge
· red wine vinegar, for drizzling
· 2 tablespoons chopped mint
· juice of ½ lemon, strained
· 6 tablespoons olive oil
· 1 garlic clove, finely chopped
· 1 tablespoon chopped
  flat-leaf parsley
· salt and pepper

Alternative fish: herring
or salmon

 288

MARINATED MACKEREL WITH MINT

Put the fish into a flameproof casserole (Dutch oven), pour in water to just cover the fish, add the lemon wedge, cover and cook over low heat for 10 minutes. Remove the fish with a fish slice (spatula) and let cool. Skin and fillet the fish, then put the fillets in a shallow dish. Drizzle with vinegar, season with salt and pepper and sprinkle with half the mint. Cover with clingfilm (plastic wrap) and let marinate for 15 minutes. Meanwhile, whisk together the lemon juice, olive oil, garlic, parsley and remaining mint until combined. Drain the fish fillets, put them on a serving platter and drizzle with the dressing. Chill in the refrigerator until you are ready to serve.

Photograph opposite

Serves 4
Preparation time: 25 mins
Cooking time: 10 mins

· 4 mackerel, cleaned
· plain (all-purpose) flour,
  for dusting
· 25 g (2 tablespoons) butter
· juice of ½ lemon, strained
· salt

For the sage butter:
· 100 g (½ cup) butter
· 15 sage leaves
· salt

Alternative fish: herring
or sardines

 288

MACKEREL WITH SAGE BUTTER

Make several diagonal slashes on each side of the mackerel, then dust lightly with flour, shaking off the excess. Melt the butter in a frying pan or skillet, add the fish and cook over medium heat for about 5 minutes on each side. Meanwhile, make the sage butter. Melt the butter in a saucepan. When it starts to colour add the sage leaves, season with salt and cook for a few minutes, until the leaves are crisp, then remove from the heat. Season the fish with salt and transfer to a warm serving dish. Spoon a little of the sage butter over each fish and sprinkle with the lemon juice. Serve immediately.

Serves 6
Preparation time: 15 mins
Cooking time: 20–25 mins

- 300g (11oz) fusilli
- olive oil, for drizzling
- 250g (1⅔ cups) green beans
- 200g (7oz) canned tuna in oil, drained and flaked
- 1 small onion, thinly sliced
- 4–6 basil leaves, torn, to garnish
- salt and pepper

Alternative fish: canned salmon or fresh tuna

Insalata di fusilli e tonno

FUSILLI AND TUNA SALAD

Bring a large saucepan of salted water to a boil, add the pasta, bring back to a boil and cook for 8–10 minutes, until tender but still firm to the bite. Drain, cool under cold running water and drain again. Tip the pasta into a bowl, drizzle with oil and set aside in a cool place. Cook the green beans in salted boiling water for 10–15 minutes, until tender-crisp, then drain and cut into short lengths.

Put all the ingredients into a salad bowl and sprinkle with torn basil leaves. Drizzle with a little olive oil, season with salt and pepper and serve.

Serves 6
Preparation time: 35 mins
Cooking time: 15 mins

· 2 onions, sliced
· 400 g (14 oz) potatoes, diced
· 1 small green bell pepper,
  seeded and quartered
· 1 small yellow bell pepper,
  seeded and quartered
· 3 tablespoons olive oil
· 1 garlic clove, peeled
· 1 tablespoon chopped
  flat-leaf parsley
· 1.2 kg (2½ lb) tuna, cut
  into cubes
· 200 ml (scant 1 cup)
  dry white wine
· 200 g (7 oz) tomatoes, sliced
· pinch of dried chilli flakes
· 6 slices bread, toasted
· salt

Alternative fish: swordfish
or salmon

Tonno in tegame con verdure miste

TUNA WITH MIXED VEGETABLES

Blanch the onions, potatoes and bell peppers in a saucepan of salted boiling water for 2 minutes, then drain and set aside.

Heat the olive oil with the garlic clove in a pan. When the garlic starts to brown, remove and discard it. Add the parsley to the pan and cook over low heat, stirring gently, for 1 minute, then add the fish. Cook, stirring occasionally, for 2 minutes. Add the wine and cook until the alcohol has evaporated.

Add the blanched vegetables, tomatoes and chilli flakes, stir, heat through briefly and season with salt. Remove from the heat and serve immediately with slices of toasted bread.

Serves 4
Preparation time: 10 mins
Cooking time: 10 mins

· 2 tablespoons olive oil
· 4 tuna steaks
· 100 ml (scant ½ cup) dry
  white wine
· 100 g (1 cup) olives, pitted
  and chopped
· 25 g (¼ cup) blanched
  almonds, chopped
· 25 g (¼ cup) pine nuts, chopped
· grated zest of 1 lemon
· ½ clove garlic, chopped
· 1 tablespoon chopped marjoram
· 1 tablespoon chopped thyme
· 1 tablespoon chopped
  flat-leaf parsley
· salt and pepper

Alternative fish: swordfish
or grouper

TUNA WITH ALMONDS, PINE NUTS AND OLIVES

Heat the oil in a frying pan or skillet, add the tuna and cook over medium heat for 4 minutes on each side. Add the wine and cook until the alcohol has evaporated, then season with salt and pepper. Cook for another few minutes, then transfer the fish to a serving platter and keep warm. Mix together the olives, almonds, pine nuts, lemon zest, garlic, marjoram, thyme and parsley in a bowl, add to the pan and cook over low heat, stirring constantly, for 1 minute. Remove from the heat, sprinkle the mixture over the tuna and serve.

Photograph opposite

Serves 4
Preparation time: 20 mins
Cooking time: 55 mins

· 2 tablespoons olive oil
· 4 tuna steaks, halved
· 1 shallot, chopped
· 200 g (1½ cups) carrots, chopped
· 200 g (1½ cups) turnips, chopped
· 200 g (1¾ cups) green beans,
  halved
· 1 thyme sprig
· 1 rosemary sprig
· 100 ml (scant ½ cup) white wine
· salt and pepper

Alternative fish: salmon or
monkfish

SLOW-COOKED TUNA

Heat the olive oil in a large shallow pan, add the tuna and cook over high heat until browned on both sides. Remove the tuna from the pan, skim off any excess fat, then add the shallot and cook, stirring occasionally, for about 5 minutes. Add the carrots, turnips, beans, thyme and rosemary, season with salt and pepper and cook over medium heat, stirring occasionally, for about 10 minutes. Put the tuna on top of the vegetables, add the wine and 150 ml (⅔ cup) warm water, reduce the heat, cover and simmer for 30 minutes. Remove and discard the herbs and transfer the tuna and vegetables to a warm serving dish. Serve immediately.

Serves 6
Preparation time: 35 mins
Cooking time: 15 mins

· 200g (7oz) canned cannellini
  beans, drained and rinsed
· 2 heads chicory (Belgian
  endive), trimmed and cut
  into strips
· 1 bunch rocket (arugula),
  chopped
· 400g (14oz) cooked
  langoustines, peeled
· 200g (7oz) canned tuna,
  drained and coarsely flaked
· 1 teaspoon curry powder
· 4 tablespoons olive oil
· salt

Alternative fish: canned
salmon or prawns (shrimp)

Insalata di tonno e scampi

TUNA WITH LANGOUSTINES, BEANS AND CHICORY (BELGIAN ENDIVE)

Put the beans, chicory (Belgian endive) and rocket
(arugula) in a salad bowl and add the langoustines and
tuna. Whisk together the curry powder and oil to taste
in a bowl and season with salt. Pour the dressing over
the salad, toss gently and serve.

Photograph opposite

Serves 4
Preparation time: 10 mins
Cooking time: 30 mins

· 3 tablespoons olive oil
· 1 garlic clove, sliced
· 4 tuna steaks
· 1 flat-leaf parsley sprig, chopped
· 2 tablespoons white wine vinegar
· salt and pepper

Alternative fish: salmon or
swordfish

Tonno all'aceto

TUNA IN VINEGAR

Heat the olive oil in a large, shallow pan, add the garlic
and cook for a few minutes, then add the tuna and
2 tablespoons water. Season with salt and pepper to taste
and sprinkle with the parsley. Cover and cook over low
heat for about 20 minutes. Add the vinegar and cook until
it has evaporated, then serve.

Serves 8–10
Preparation time: 40 mins
Cooking time: 50 mins

· 2 tablespoons olive oil
· 2 red onions, chopped
· 1 celery stalk, chopped
· 3 garlic cloves, chopped
· 1 bunch flat-leaf parsley,
  chopped
· 5 tomatoes, chopped
· 2 kg (4½ lb) assorted fish,
  such as salmon, mackerel,
  scorpion fish, gurnard (sea
  robin), conger eel, grouper,
  cuttlefish and squid, cleaned
  and cut into pieces
· 3 litres (13 cups) boiling water
· 1 kg (6 cups) precooked
  (instant) couscous
· salt and pepper

Alternative fish: grouper,
red mullet, scallops or tuna

 288 302

FISH COUSCOUS

Heat the oil in a large deep-sided frying pan or skillet,
add the onions, celery, garlic, parsley, tomatoes and fish
and cook over medium-low heat, stirring occasionally,
for about 10 minutes. Pour in the boiling water and season
with salt and pepper. Reduce the heat to low, cover and
simmer for 30 minutes. Remove the fish from the pan, set
aside and keep warm. Carefully drain off about one-third
of the cooking liquid into the bottom of a steamer and
return the pan of vegetables to low heat. Add 1 litre
(4¼ cups) to the cooking liquid and bring to a boil.

Meanwhile, put the couscous in a sieve (strainer) and
run it under cold water until all the grains are thoroughly
moistened. Line the top of the steamer with muslin
(cheesecloth), add the couscous and set it over the bottom.
Cover and steam for about 10 minutes, until all the grains
are tender and fluffed up. (If using uncooked couscous,
follow the packet instructions.) Fluff up the grains with
as fork and transfer the couscous to a warm serving
platter. Add half the sauce and mix well, then place the
fish on top. Serve immediately, handing the remaining
sauce separately.

Serves 4
Preparation time: 30 mins
Cooking time: 10 mins

· 1 kg (2¼ lb) mixed small
  oily fish, such as anchovies,
  scaled and cleaned
· plain (all-purpose) flour,
  for dusting
· olive oil, for frying
· 4 sage leaves, plus extra
  to garnish
· 1 lemon, cut into wedges
· salt and freshly ground
  white pepper

Alternative fish: sardines,
smelts or sprats

 297

FRITTO MISTO

Rub off the scales from the fish with your fingers, then rinse under cold running water. Cut off and discard the heads. Slit open the fish along the length of the belly, pull out and discard the guts and rinse the cavity under cold running water. Open out the fish and put it skin side uppermost on a chopping (cutting) board. Press firmly along the backbone with your thumb or the palm of your hand.

When the fish is completely flat, turn it over, pull away the backbone and snip it off at the tail end. Remove any remaining small bones with tweezers. Prepare the remaining fish in the same way.

Dust the fish with flour, shaking off excess. Heat plenty of oil with the sage leaves in a large frying pan or skillet. Add the larger fish first and cook for about 1 minute, then add smaller ones and cook for another few minutes, until the flesh flakes easily. You may need to cook them in batches. Remove with a fish slice (spatula) and drain on paper towels. Keep warm until all the fish have been cooked. Put the fish on a serving dish, garnish with wedges of lemon and sage leaves, season with salt and white pepper and serve immediately.

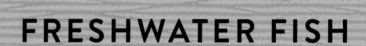

FRESHWATER FISH

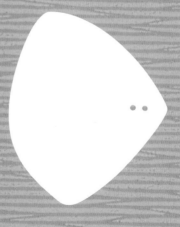

Freshwater fish are numerous and feature prominently in some cuisines, particularly in Italy. In other countries there is less interest in them in a culinary sense, but they are popular with recreational anglers who fish on a catch-and-release basis. Carp today is the most extensively farmed fish in the world because it is particularly prized in China and in Eastern European countries including Hungary and Poland.

With a round and bony body structure, freshwater fish generally have a thick layer of slime on the body that make them slippery and a challenge to handle. They also have a thick layer of scales that need to be removed prior to cooking. Freshwater fish include pike, carp, trout, perch and eel.

These fish have often have a strong flavour and earthy texture that take on robust flavours very well. They take well to roasting, grilling (broiling), pan-frying and barbecuing and fish such as pike and carp are used to make fish mousselines that are poached or baked.

CARP

Carpa
Cyprinidae

Average weight range:
400g–2.2kg (14oz–4½lb)
Average length: 10–100cm
(4–40 inches)

Recipes on pages 185

Hugely popular with communities that have little or no access to the coast, carp is the key member of a large family of freshwater fish including minnows, tench and roach, and popular species include the common carp, grass carp and mirror carp. They have beautiful golden skin and varying amounts of scales (depending on the species) over deep flanks. Today it is the most extensively farmed fish in the world.

Carp is most often sold whole and ungutted. Like most freshwater fish, it naturally has a heavy layer of slime that requires careful removal before preparing. When preparing carp, it is important to leave them under cold, running water or soak them in water acidulated with a little vinegar for several hours so their flesh loses any slight muddy taste it may have retained. It can then be cleaned and scaled. If the fish is to be cooked whole, be sure to remove the gills and blood line, which are bitter and can taint the flavour of the flesh.

With a white, textured flesh, it has a distinctive, earthy taste. Carp is delicious roasted whole but can also be filleted and pinboned for quicker and easy cooking, if preferred. *Carpa al burro maître d'hôtel* (Carp in maître d'hôtel butter, see page 185) is a simple and tasty recipe with just butter, parsley and lemon.

Other fish such as tilapia, catfish, pike and freshwater bream are good alternatives.

PERCH

Pesce persico
Percidae

Average weight range:
300g–1.3kg (11oz–3lb)
Average length: 20–50cm
(8–20 inches)

Recipes on pages 186–188

Considered to be one of the finest of all freshwater fish, perch can be found near the banks of lakes and slow-flowing rivers in central and other regions of Italy and Sicily, and are also found in many other parts of Europe and North America. It has a plump, round body with dark olive-green colouration and the fins and tail are often a vibrant orange. It has a heavy armour of scales and, if straight from the water, a thick layer of slime, making it slightly difficult to handle. It is known to have a fierce, predatory temperament.

Perch can be sold whole and cleaned and many chefs recommend scaling the fish immediately after landing because scales can adhere to the skin. Dipping the fish into boiling water for 5 seconds and then plunging it directly into ice cold water will allow the scales and skin to be peeled off in one go. The sharp fins should be carefully trimmed with scissors before any other preparation. While fillets are easier to prepare, the fine bones are a little easier to locate if the fish is cooked whole. When preparing fillets, be careful when removing pinbones.

Its delicate, flaky white flesh is subtle and sweet and lacks the intense earthiness of many other freshwater fish. Ideal for pan-frying, steaming and baking, the fillets can be coated in flour, egg and breadcrumbs before frying. A classic dish is *Pesce persico alla salvia* (Perch with sage, see page 188). Since it may be difficult to obtain in many countries (unless you know a keen fisherman), freshwater bream, redfish, hybrid striped trout or rainbow trout make suitable alternatives.

PIKE

Luccio
Escocidae

Average weight range:
1–5kg (2¼–11lb)
Average length: 50–90cm
(20–35 inches)

Recipes on pages 189–192

With a head and flat snout shaped like a duck's bill and a sleek, elongated body, this aggressive and predatorial fish can be found in slow-flowing freshwater streams, rivers and lakes in central northern Italy, northern Europe and North America. It has yellow eyes and greenish skin bespeckled with gold. Female pike roe (the eggs) is a deep golden colour and a delicacy in some parts of Europe. Buy it ready prepared and avoid eating it raw, which can be poisonous.

Pike is often sold cleaned and whole, but can be filleted and skinned. With firm, white and very bony flesh, it is classically used for mousselines because the bones can be removed when the mixture is sieved (strained).

The meaty flesh has a strong, almost gamey flavour that combines superbly with robust flavours and can be prepared in a variety of ways such as pan-frying, poaching, baking and roasting. In Italy, it may be served with a creamy mushroom sauce, such as in *Luccio in blanquette* (Pike blanquette, see page 189) or even as a delicate *Mousse di luccio* (Pike mousse, see page 192). Other highly regarded freshwater fish such as zander or pike-perch would be the closest alternatives.

SALMON TROUT

Trota salmonata
Salmo trutta

Average weight range:
500g–6kg (1lb 2oz–13lb)
Average length: 60–100cm
(2–3 feet)

Recipes on pages 193–198

The salmon trout, also known as sea trout, is the migratory variety of the freshwater brown trout, known as *fario* in Italy, and native to Europe. With a long silver body dotted with black, the salmon trout has a distinct appearance with a bent head and a jaw line that extends past the eyes. It has a shorter legal fishing season than salmon and is just as threatened in the wild. It is also widely farmed. Other members of the this freshwater family include whitefish, char and grayling, all of which bear resemblance to the trout group – whitefish in particular are well utilized in Italy.

Fine, sweet, delicately flavoured, salmon trout has oil-rich, flaky pink flesh that can easily dry out if over-cooked. It is usually sold whole and cleaned and is occasionally available cold-smoked. It may also be sold in fillets, in which case, if large enough, they can be cut into steaks.

The best cooking methods include poaching, pan-frying, grilling (broiling), roasting and baking. Classic herbs – such as dill, chervil and fennel – work incredibly well with the fish, while seasonal sea vegetables, such as samphire, make fine accompaniments. Both salmon and salmon trout are relatively new additions to Italian cuisine, but these fish are so versatile that they are often used in recipes more commonly associated with swordfish and tuna. Alaskan salmon and Arctic char are the best alternatives, although trout can also be used.

STURGEON

Storione
Acipenseridae

Average weight range:
2–8 kg (4½–17½ lb)
Average length: 60–120 cm
(2–4 feet)

Recipes on pages 200–202

The sturgeon has changed little in appearance over the last few thousand years and has a prehistoric appearance with a long, pointed snout and dark black, slimy body. More than 20 species can be found in fresh water, the seas of Europe and on both sides of the Atlantic Ocean. A number of sturgeon are famously caught in the Caspian Sea, where for years sturgeon has been aggressively harvested for caviar. It is a slow-growing, late-maturing fish that has been hunted relentlessly for its roe and is now one of the most endangered of all fish. Because stocks of wild sturgeon are so seriously endangered by over-fishing and pollution of their habitat, only farmed fish should be purchased for eating. A good alternative to use is sustainably caught common or conger eel.

Rich and oily, sturgeon's white, firm and tasty flesh is excellent for poaching, grilling (broiling) or frying. If sold whole, the fish requires trimming and cleaning before cooking. The fillets are usually quite thick and need to be cooked for at least 6–8 minutes on each side. Although the fresh fillets are excellent, it is most often smoked, a very popular Sicilian speciality.

TROUT

Trota
Salmonidae

Average weight range:
300 g–2 kg (11 oz–4½ lb)
Average length: 25–50 cm
(10–20 inches)

Recipes on pages 202–207

Like many other freshwater fish, trout is a favourite Italian treat. The two main varieties are *fario* or brown trout, which are caught in lakes, streams and rivers in Italy, and the rainbow trout, which is native to the United States and a fast-growing species that is both farmed and used to stock lakes and rivers. It has a dark green back with silver scales, black spots and a vibrant rainbow-like flash of iridescent blue and pink along the flank. The migratory form of brown trout is a salmon trout (see page 182). The migratory variety of rainbow trout in the United States is known as steelhead trout and is similar in appearance and taste to salmon trout.

The flavour of this oil-rich fish varies depending on where it is harvested. Farmed over a gravel riverbed, it has a delicate, slightly earthy flavour reminiscent of mushrooms, but if caught in muddy waters, this earthiness can be intense and unpleasant.

It can be sold whole and cleaned, as fillets and both hot- and cold-smoked. A classic method of cooking trout is *au bleu*, whereby very fresh trout is poached in an acidulated court-bouillon, causing the fish to turns a magnificent shade of blue, but it can also be grilled (broiled), roasted, baked in *cartoccio* (wrapped in a paper parcel or package). In northern Italy, trout pan-fried in butter (a dish called *trotelle*) is popular while trout garnished with truffles is a classic of central Italy's Umbrian region. Salmon trout may be used as an alternative.

Serves 4
Preparation time: 15 mins
Cooking time: 10 mins

· 50 g (4 tablespoons) butter,
  softened
· juice of 1 lemon, strained
· 1 tablespoon chopped
  flat-leaf parsley
· 4 × 350-g (12-oz carp), scaled
  and cleaned
· olive oil, for brushing
· salt

Alternative fish: pike or tilapia

 288

Carpa al burro maitre d'hotel

CARP IN MAÎTRE D'HÔTEL BUTTER

Beat the butter with 3 tablespoons of the lemon juice,
the parsley and a pinch of salt until thoroughly combined.
Shape the mixture into cubes and chill in the refrigerator
until required. Preheat the grill (broiler). Brush the
fish with oil and remaining lemon juice and grill (broil)
for 5 minutes on each side, until the flesh flakes easily.
Transfer to a warm serving dish, garnished with the
flavoured butter and serve immediately.

Serves 4
Preparation time: 15 mins
Cooking time: 1¼ hrs

· 50 g (4 tablespoons) butter
· 2 tablespoons olive oil
· 2 carrots, finely chopped
· 2 onions, finely chopped
· 1 celery stalk, finely chopped
· 1 × 1-kg (2¼-lb) carp, scaled
  and cleaned
· 500 ml (2 cups) red wine
· salt and pepper

Alternative fish: freshwater
bream or trout

 288

Carpa al vino

CARP IN WINE

Melt half the butter with the olive oil in a large frying pan
or, add the carrots, onions and celery and cook over low
heat, stirring occasionally, for 15 minutes. Add the carp,
season with salt and pepper and pour in the wine and
5 tablespoons water. Bring to a boil, then cover and simmer
gently for 45 minutes. Transfer the fish to a serving dish.
Pass the vegetables through a food mill and return them to
the pan with the cooking juices. Cook until thickened and
stir in the remaining butter. Serve the carp with the sauce.

Serves 4
Preparation time: 10 mins
Cooking time: 10 mins

· 8 perch fillets, skinned
· 50 g (4 tablespoons) butter
· 4 tablespoons chopped chervil
· 4 tablespoons chopped basil
· 4 tablespoons chopped
  flat-leaf parsley
· 200 ml (scant 1 cup) dry
  white wine
· 200 ml (scant 1 cup) double
  (heavy) cream
· 120 g (2 cups) fresh breadcrumbs
· salt and pepper

Alternative fish: freshwater
bream, pike or cod

⌂ 288   ⌐ 290   ∏ 296

Persico con panna ed erbe

PERCH BAKED WITH CREAM AND HERBS

Preheat the oven to 200°C/400°F/Gas Mark 6. Put the
fish fillets in a roasting pan, dot with the butter, sprinkle
with the chervil and basil and season with salt and pepper.
Pour the wine and cream over the fish and sprinkle with
the breadcrumbs. Bake for 10–15 minutes, until the fish
flakes easily, then serve immediately.

Photograph opposite

- -

Serves 4
Preparation time: 15 mins
Cooking time: 20 mins

· 3 tablespoons olive oil, plus
  extra for brushing
· 1 onion, finely chopped
· 1 courgette (zucchini), finely
  chopped
· 150 g (1¼ cups) shelled walnuts,
  finely chopped
· 1 tablespoon chopped flat-leaf
  parsley, plus extra to garnish
· 800 g (1¾ lb) perch fillets
· 1 lemon, thinly sliced
· salt and pepper

Alternative fish: pike, freshwater
bream or cod

⌂ 288   ⌐ 290   ∏ 296

Filetti di persico al forno alle noci

PERCH WITH WALNUTS

Preheat the oven to 200°C/400°F/Gas Mark 6. Brush an
ovenproof dish with oil. Heat 2 tablespoons of the oil, add
the onion and cook over low heat, stirring occasionally, for
5 minutes, until translucent. Add the courgette (zucchini)
and cook, stirring occasionally, for another 5–8 minutes,
until softened, then add the walnuts and parsley. Season
with salt and pepper, stir and remove from the heat. Put
the fish into the prepared dish, sprinkle with the onion and
walnut mixture and drizzle with the remaining oil, then bake
for 15 minutes. Remove the dish from the oven, sprinkle
with more chopped parsley, garnish with lemon slices
and serve immediately.

Serves 4
Preparation time: 25 mins
Cooking time: 20 mins

· 8 perch fillets, skinned
· plain (all-purpose) flour,
  for dusting
· 50g (4 tablespoons) butter
· 1 tablespoon olive oil
· 3 white onions, cut into thin
  julienne strips
· 2 tablespoons clear honey
· 4 potatoes, thinly sliced
· 2 tomatoes, sliced
· 2 tablespoons Dijon mustard
· pinch of fresh marjoram
· balsamic vinegar, for drizzling
· salt and freshly ground white
  pepper

Alternative fish: cod, trout
or freshwater bream

288   290   296

Pesce persico con sauté di patate, miele e aceto balsamico

BAKED PERCH WITH POTATOES, HONEY AND BALSAMIC VINEGAR

Preheat the oven to 200°C/400°F/Gas Mark 6. Lightly dust
the fish with flour. Melt the butter with the oil in a flameproof
casserole (Dutch oven), then add a layer of onions, pour
over 1 tablespoon of the honey, cover with the potato slices,
then add the remaining onions and top with the tomato
slices. Bake for 10 minutes, then remove from the oven and
put the fish fillets on top of the vegetables. Spread with the
mustard, season with salt and white pepper, sprinkle with
the marjoram and return to the oven. Cook for another
10 minutes, until the fish is crisp. Remove the casserole
from the oven, drizzle with balsamic vinegar and serve.

Serves 4
Preparation time: 10 mins
Cooking time: 6–8 mins

· 600g (1lb 5oz) perch
  fillets, skinned
· plain (all-purpose) flour,
  for dusting
· 50g (4 tablespoons) butter
· 8 fresh sage leaves
· salt and pepper

Alternative fish: pike, carp
or tilapia

288   290   296

Pesce persico alla salvia

PERCH WITH SAGE

Lightly dust the fish fillets with flour and shake off any
excess. Melt the butter with the sage in a large frying
pan or skillet, add the fish and cook over medium heat
for 3–4 minutes on each side, until light golden brown all
over. Season with salt and pepper and serve immediately.

Serves 4
Preparation time: 30 mins
Cooking time: 30–35 mins

· 2 tablespoons olive oil
· 1 × 1-kg (2½-lb) pike, cleaned
  filleted and skinned
· 5 tablespoons dry white wine
· 1 onion, thinly sliced
· ½ garlic clove, chopped
· 50 g (4 tablespoons) butter,
  softened and cut into pieces
· juice of ½ lemon, strained
· 100 g (3½ oz) smoked pancetta,
  cubed
· salt and pepper
· chopped flat-leaf parsley,
  to garnish

Alternative fish: carp,
freshwater bream or trout

Luccio all'antica

OLD-FASHIONED PIKE

Heat the olive oil in a large frying pan or skillet. Season
the fish fillets with salt and pepper on both sides, add
to the pan and cook over high heat until golden brown
on both sides. Transfer the fish to a plate and keep warm.
Pour the wine into the pan, add the onion and garlic and
cook, stirring occasionally, until the liquid has reduced by
half. Add the butter, a little at a time, and mix well. Finally,
stir in 3 tablespoons warm water and the lemon juice. Keep
warm over very low heat. Put the pancetta in a pan and heat
until the fat runs, then remove with a slotted spoon. Put
the fish in the butter sauce, add the pancetta and simmer
gently for 10–15 minutes. Transfer the pike fillets and sauce
to a serving dish, garnish with parsley and serve.

Serves 4
Preparation time: 25 mins
Cooking time: 30–35 mins

· 1 × 1-kg (2¼-lb) pike, cleaned,
  skinned and cut into chunks
· plain (all-purpose) flour,
  for dusting
· 50 g (4 tablespoons) butter
· 200 g (3 cups) thinly sliced
  mushrooms
· 2 egg yolks
· 200 ml (scant 1 cup) double
  (heavy) cream
· salt and pepper

Alternative fish: freshwater
bream, perch or cod

 288

Luccio in blanquette

PIKE BLANQUETTE

Lightly dust the pieces of fish with flour. Melt the butter
in a large pan and, when it has turned light golden brown,
add the fish, then cook until evenly browned on both sides.
Add the mushrooms, season with salt and pepper to taste
and cook over low heat for about 20 minutes. Meanwhile,
beat together the egg yolks and cream in a small bowl
and season lightly with salt. Remove the pan from the
heat and pour the egg mixture over the fish. Return to very
low heat and heat through gently. Transfer the fish pieces
to a warm serving dish and spoon the sauce over them.
Serve immediately.

Serves 4
Preparation time: 20 mins
Cooking time: 30 mins

· 1 × 1-kg (2¼-lb) pike, scaled
  and cleaned
· 1 small onion slice
· 1 flat-leaf parsley sprig
· 1 garlic clove
· 3 tablespoons butter, melted
· salt and pepper

For the beurre blanc:
· 3 shallots, finely chopped
· 1 tablespoon white wine vinegar
· 1 tablespoon dry white wine
· 200g (¾ cup plus 2 tablespoons)
  butter, softened and cut into
  small pieces
· juice of ½ lemon, strained
· salt and white pepper

Alternative fish: salmon or
red mullet

 288

Luccio al burro bianco

PIKE IN BEURRE BLANC

Preheat the oven to 180°C/350°F/Gas Mark 4. Season
the cavity of the pike with salt and pepper and place the
onion, parsley and garlic inside it, then season the fish
with salt and pepper. Brush the melted butter over the
fish, put it into an ovenproof dish and bake for 30 minutes,
brushing every 5 minutes with the remaining melted butter.

Meanwhile, make the beurre blanc. Put the shallots
in a saucepan with the vinegar and wine and cook over
medium-high heat until reduced. Remove the pan from
the heat and whisk in the butter, a little at a time. Return
the pan to the heat for a few seconds after each addition.
Stir in the lemon juice and season with salt and pepper
to taste. Serve the pike with the beurre blanc on the side.

Photograph opposite

Serves 4
Preparation time: 15 mins
Cooking time: 20 mins

· 15g (½ oz) dried mushrooms
· 50g (4 tablespoons) butter
· 1 × 1-kg (2¼-lb) pike, scaled,
  cleaned and cut into pieces
· 2 flat-leaf parsley sprigs
· 2 thyme sprigs
· 1 bay leaf
· 1 tablespoon plain
  (all-purpose) flour
· 150 ml (⅔ cup) Fish Stock
  (see page 78)
· 200 ml (scant 1 cup)
  dry white wine
· 2 egg yolks
· juice of ½ lemon, strained
· salt and pepper

Alternative fish: carp or
freshwater bream

 288

Luccio in fricassea

PIKE FRICASSÉE

Put the mushrooms into a bowl, pour in warm water to
cover and let soak for 20 minutes, then drain, squeeze out
and chop. Melt the butter in a pan, add the fish and cook
over medium heat, turning occasionally, for 5 minutes, until
lightly browned. Tie the parsley, thyme and bay together
and add to the pan with the mushrooms. Sprinkle with the
flour, season with salt and pepper and pour in the stock
and wine. Reduce the heat and simmer for 20 minutes.
Using a slotted spoon, transfer the pieces of fish to a
serving dish and keep warm. Remove the herbs from the
pan and discard. Beat the egg yolks with the lemon juice
in a bowl and stir into the pan. Stir over low heat until
thickened but do not let the sauce boil. Spoon the sauce
over the fish and serve immediately.

Serves 10
Preparation time: 30 mins
Cooking time: 40 mins

· 175 g (¾ cup) butter, plus
  extra for greasing
· 1 shallot, chopped
· 500 g (1lb 2oz) pike fillets
· 2 tablespoons brandy
· 5 eggs
· 1½ tablespoons caster
  (superfine) sugar
· 500 ml (2 cups) double
  (heavy) cream
· 150 g (⅔ cup) cream cheese
· salt

For the sauce:
· 1 tablespoon olive oil
· 1 shallot, chopped
· 2 carrots, diced
· 2 tablespoons mixed chopped
  flat-leaf parsley, thyme and
  chervil
· 300 ml (1¼ cups) dry white wine
· 500 ml (2 cups) vegetable stock
· 20 g (1½ tablespoons) butter
· 3 tablespoons double
  (heavy) cream
· 50 g (¼ cup) cream cheese
· salt and pepper

Alternative fish: salmon

288   290   296

PIKE MOUSSE

Preheat the oven to 180°C/350°F/Gas Mark 4. Grease
10 ramekins with butter. Melt 15 g (1 tablespoon) butter
in a pan. Add the shallot and cook over low heat, stirring
occasionally, for 3 minutes, until softened. Add the fish
fillets and cook gently for about 10 minutes. Pour in the
brandy and, standing well back, ignite it. When the flames
have died down, remove the pan from the heat and allow
to cool. Transfer the mixture to a food processor.

Melt the remaining butter in a saucepan. Add the melted
butter, eggs, sugar, cream, cheese and a pinch of salt to the
food processor and process until smooth and thoroughly
combined. Pass the mixture through a sieve (strainer) into
a bowl, then divide among the prepared ramekins. Cover
them with foil, put them into 1–2 roasting pans and pour
in hot water to come about halfway up the sides. Bake for
30 minutes.

Meanwhile, make the sauce. Heat the oil in a saucepan,
add the shallot, carrot and herbs and cook over low heat,
stirring occasionally, for 5 minutes. Pour in the wine and
cook until it has reduced to 2 tablespoons, then pour in
the stock, bring to a boil and cook for 5 minutes. Remove
the pan from the heat and strain the liquid into a clean
saucepan. Return to the heat and cook until the sauce
starts to thicken. Stir in the butter and cream, season with
salt and pepper and add the fresh cheese. Pass the sauce
through a sieve (strainer). Turn out the fish mousse onto
individual plates, spoon over the sauce and serve.

Serves 6
Preparation time: 50 mins
Cooking time: 25 mins

For the stock:
· 800 g (1¾ lb) heads from
  white fish, such as sole
  and turbot, gills removed
· 1 onion, cut into wedges
· 1 carrot, cut into chunks
· 1 leek, cut into chunks

· butter, for greasing
· 1 × 1-kg (2-¼ lb) salmon trout,
  cleaned, filleted and skinned
· 2 egg yolks
· 1 tablespoon potato flour
· 250 ml (1 cup) double
  (heavy) cream
· 1 tablespoon chopped
  flat-leaf parsley
· 1 tomato, peeled, de-seeded
  and diced
· salt and pepper

For the vegetable garnish:
· 25 g (2 tablespoons) butter
· 2 celery stalks, cut into
  thin strips
· 1 courgette (zucchini),
  cut into thin strips
· 2 carrots, cut into thin strips
· 1 leek, cut into thin strips
· salt and pepper

For the sauce:
· 1 tablespoon potato flour
· pinch of saffron threads,
  lightly crushed
· 100 ml (scant ½ cup)
  dry white wine
· 25 g (2 tablespoons) butter
· salt and pepper

Alternative fish: salmon or trout

288   290   296

Timballo di trota salmonata

SALMON TROUT TIMBALES

First make the stock. Put the fish heads, onion, carrot and leek in a large saucepan, pour in 1 litre (4¼ cups) water, bring to a boil and simmer for 15 minutes. Strain into a clean saucepan, return to high heat and cook until reduced by half. Remove from the heat and let cool.

Meanwhile, preheat the oven to 180°C/350°F/Gas Mark 4. Grease 6 ramekins with butter. Cut the salmon trout into pieces, put them into a food processor, season with salt and pepper and process to a purée. Add the egg yolks, potato flour and all but 1 tablespoon of the cream and process again. Divide the mixture among the prepared ramekins, put them into a roasting pan and pour in hot water to come about halfway up the sides. Bake for 20 minutes.

To make the vegetable garnish, melt the butter in a large frying pan or skillet, add the celery, courgettes (zucchini), carrots and leeks and cook over medium-high heat, stirring continuously, for 5 minutes, until softened but not coloured. Remove the pan from the heat, cover and keep in a warm place.

To make the sauce, stir the potato flour into the cold fish stock, then set over medium-low heat and bring to a boil, stirring constantly. Add the saffron and the reserved tablespoon of cream, bring back to a boil and season with salt and pepper. Pour in the wine, bring to a boil and simmer gently for a few minutes. Remove the pan from the heat and stir in the butter, then spoon a little of the sauce onto a warm serving dish. Spoon the vegetable garnish on top. Remove the ramekins from the oven and gently turn out the flans on top of the vegetable garnish. Sprinkle with chopped parsley and garnish with the tomato. Serve immediately, passing the remaining sauce separately in a sauceboat.

SALMON TROUT WITH PUMPKIN AND HORSERADISH

Serves 6
Preparation time: 20 mins
+ 1hr standing
Cooking time: 25–35 mins

· 350 g (2⅔ cups) chopped pumpkin
· 2 tablespoons caster (superfine) sugar
· 1 tablespoon balsamic vinegar
· 100 g (3½ oz) horseradish, peeled and coarsely chopped
· 50 g (½ cup) shelled walnuts
· 2–3 tablespoons olive oil, plus extra for brushing
· 900 g (2 lb) salmon trout fillets
· salt and pepper

Alternative fish: salmon or char

 288   290   296

Put the pumpkin into a heatproof dish, put it in the top of a steamer and cook for 20 minutes. Remove from the heat and pass it through a sieve (strainer) into a bowl. Stir in the sugar and balsamic vinegar, season with salt and let stand for at least 1 hour. Put the horseradish and walnuts into a blender or food processor and process, then stir the mixture into the pumpkin purée. Stir in olive oil to taste.

Brush a large non-stick frying pan or skillet with oil and set over medium heat. Add the fish fillets and cook for 3 minutes on each side (you may need to do this in batches). Season with salt and pepper and serve immediately, passing the pumpkin purée separately.

Serves 6
Preparation time: 40 mins
Cooking time: 40 mins

· 50 g (4 tablespoons) butter,
  plus extra for greasing
· 50 g (½ cup) plain
  (all-purpose) flour
· 500 ml (2 cups) milk
· pinch of freshly grated nutmeg
· 200 g (7oz) smoked salmon
  trout, chopped
· 2 eggs, separated
· 3 tablespoons double
  (heavy) cream
· 2 tablespoons chopped
  blanched almonds
· salt and pepper

  For the vegetables:
· 25 g (2 tablespoons) butter
· 500 g (1lb 2oz) sorrel, coarse
  stalks removed
· 500 g (1lb 2oz) spinach,
  coarse stalks removed
· 1 tablespoon double
  (heavy) cream
· salt and pepper

  Alternative fish: salmon
  or char

SMOKED SALMON TROUT WITH ALMONDS AND GREENS

Melt the butter in a saucepan, stir in the flour and cook, stirring constantly, over low heat for 2 minutes. Remove the pan from the heat and gradually stir in the milk, a little at a time. Add a pinch of nutmeg. Return the pan to the heat and bring to a boil, stirring constantly. Cook until thickened, then remove from the heat and let cool.

Meanwhile, preheat the oven to 220°C/425°F/Gas Mark 7. Grease 6 ramekins with butter. Stir the fish and egg yolks into the cooled sauce and season with salt and pepper. Whisk the egg whites in a grease-free bowl until stiff, then fold into the fish mixture. Divide the mixture among the prepared ramekins, put them in a roasting pan and pour in hot water to come about halfway up the sides. Bake for 25 minutes.

To prepare the vegetables, melt the butter in a saucepan, add the sorrel and spinach and cook over low heat, stirring occasionally, for 5–10 minutes. Season with salt and pepper, stir in the cream and remove the pan from the heat. Spread out the mixture the bottom of an ovenproof dish. Remove the roasting pan from the oven and reduce the oven temperature to 180°C/350°F/Gas Mark 4. Turn out the moulds on top of the vegetables, drizzle with the cream and sprinkle with the almonds. Bake for about 15 minutes, then serve immediately.

Serves 4
Preparation time: 15 mins
Cooking time: 20 mins

- 2½ tablespoons sultanas
  or golden raisins
- 3 tablespoons olive oil
- 1 small onion, chopped
- 1 celery stalk, chopped
- 1 garlic clove, chopped
- 1 rosemary sprig
- 1 × 1-kg (2¼-lb) salmon
  trout, scaled and cleaned
- grated zest of 1 lemon
- 4 tablespoons white wine
  vinegar
- 250 ml (1 cup) Fish Stock
  (see page 78)
- 2 tablespoons plain
  (all-purpose) flour
- salt

Alternative fish: salmon
or red mullet

 288

Trota salmonata alla piemontese

PIEDMONTESE-STYLE SALMON TROUT

Put the sultanas or golden raisins into a small bowl, pour in lukewarm water to cover and let soak until required. Heat the olive oil in a frying pan or skillet, add the onion, celery, garlic and rosemary and cook over low heat, stirring occasionally, for 5 minutes. Drain the sultanas and squeeze out. Add the fish to the pan, sprinkle with the grated lemon zest and sultanas and add the vinegar and stock. Season with salt and pepper and simmer for about 10 minutes. Lift out the salmon trout with a fish slice (spatula), remove the fillets and put them on a warm serving platter. Remove and discard the rosemary from the pan, pour in 100 ml (scant ½ cup) lukewarm water, sprinkle in the flour, and simmer gently, stirring constantly, until thickened. Spoon the sauce over the fish fillets and serve immediately.

Serves 4
Preparation time: 10 mins
Cooking time: 10 mins

- 4 × 250-g (9-oz) whitefish,
  cleaned
- plain (all-purpose) flour,
  for dusting
- 80 g (6 tablespoons) butter,
  melted
- 12 fresh sage leaves
- salt

Alternative fish: char or
salmon

 288

Lavarello alla salvia

WHITEFISH WITH SAGE

Preheat the oven to 200°C/400°F/Gas Mark 6. Season the cavities of the fish with salt and dust lightly with flour. Put them into an ovenproof dish in a single layer. Pour the melted butter over the fish, add the sage leaves and bake, basting once with the cooking juices, for 10 minutes. Remove from the over and serve immediately straight from the dish.

Photograph opposite

Serves 4
Preparation time: 15 mins
Cooking time: 25 mins

· 1 bunch flat-leaf parsley,
  chopped
· 2 tablespoons chopped sage
· 1 tablespoon chopped rosemary
· 1 garlic clove, chopped
· 650 g (1lb 7oz) sturgeon fillet
· 120 g (4oz) prosciutto, sliced
· 2 tablespoons olive oil
· 1 shallot, chopped
· 200 ml (scant 1 cup) dry
  white wine
· salt and pepper

Alternative fish: pike or carp

288   290   296

Storione aromatico al forno

AROMATIC BAKED STURGEON

Mix together the parsley, sage, rosemary and garlic on a
large plate. Season the sturgeon with salt and pepper and
roll it in the herb mixture until completely coated. Wrap it in
the slices of prosciutto and tie securely with kitchen string.
Preheat the oven to 180°C / 350°F / Gas Mark 4. Heat the oil
in a flameproof casserole (Dutch oven), add the shallot
and cook over low heat, stirring occasionally, for 3 minutes.
Add the fish and cook, turning occasionally, until evenly
browned. Pour in the white wine and cook until the alcohol
has evaporated. Cover the casserole with foil and prick a
few holes in it with a fork. Bake for about 20 minutes. Turn
off the heat, remove the foil and let the casserole stand
in the cooling oven for a few minutes, then remove from the
oven, transfer the fish to a serving platter and serve.

Photograph opposite

Serves 4
Preparation time: 20 mins
Cooking time: 35 mins

· olive oil, for brushing and
  drizzling
· 1 × 1-kg (2½-lb) sturgeon,
  scaled and cleaned
· 4 flat-leaf parsley sprigs
· 200 g (7oz) onions, very
  thinly sliced
· 1 tablespoon paprika
· 100 ml (scant ½ cup) dry
  white wine
· 100 ml (scant ½ cup) crème
  fraîche
· salt and pepper

Alternative fish: char or cod

288

Storione alla paprica

STURGEON WITH PAPRIKA

Preheat the oven to 240°C / 475°F / Gas Mark 9. Brush an
ovenproof dish with oil. Season the fish inside and out
with salt and pepper and put the parsley sprigs in the
cavity. Spread out the onions in the dish, put the fish
on top, sprinkle with the paprika and drizzle with olive oil.
Bake for 15 minutes, then remove the dish from the oven
and pour the wine over the fish. Return the dish to the
oven and bake for another 15 minutes. Remove the dish
from the oven, transfer the fish to a serving platter and keep
warm. Pour the cooking juices into a saucepan, stir in the
crème fraîche and cook over low heat, stirring constantly,
until the sauce thickens. Pour the sauce over the fish and
serve immediately.

Serves 4
Preparation time: 15 mins
Cooking time: 30 mins

- 1 × 1-kg (2¼-lb) sturgeon
  steak cut from the middle
- 25 g (1 oz) fat bacon, cut
  into larding strips
- 20 g (1½ tablespoons) butter
- 2 tablespoons olive oil
- 250 ml (1 cup) vegetable stock
- juice of 1 lemon, strained
- salt and pepper

Alternative fish: pike or salmon

 288   290

Storione in umido

BRAISED STURGEON

Skin the sturgeon, wrap the bacon around it, then tie in place with kitchen string and season with salt and pepper. Melt the butter with the olive oil in a flameproof casserole (Dutch oven), add the sturgeon and cook over low heat, turning once, until browned on both sides. Add half the stock and simmer gently, occasionally adding the remaining stock, for about 30 minutes. Sprinkle with the lemon juice just before removing the casserole from the heat, season with salt and pepper and serve immediately.

- -

Serves 4
Preparation time: 15 mins
Cooking time: 45 mins

- 1 tablespoon olive oil
- 250 g (9 oz) trout, skinned
  and filleted
- 35 g (2½ tablespoons) butter
- 1 shallot
- 200 g (7 oz) red Treviso
  radicchio
- 300 g (1½ cups) risotto rice
- 500 ml (2 cups) Fish Stock
  (see page 78), hot
- salt and pepper

Alternative fish: salmon
or mackerel

288   290   296

Risotto alla trota

TROUT RISOTTO

Preheat the oven to 180°C/350°F/Gas Mark 4. Pour the oil into a roasting pan, add the fish and season with salt and pepper. Cook in the oven for 15 minutes. Meanwhile, melt the butter in a saucepan over medium-low heat, add the shallot and cook for 5 minutes, stirring until softened. Add the radicchio and cook for another 5 minutes. Add the rice and stir for a few minutes, then add the stock, one ladle at a time, stirring frequently, until the rice is half cooked (about 8 minutes). Add the trout fillets and continue to cook for 10 minutes, or until the rice is tender but retains some bite. Serve immediately.

Serves 4
Preparation time: 10 mins
Cooking time: 25 mins

- 3 mandarin oranges
- 1½ tablespoons olive oil
- 4 trout, cleaned
- 5–6 green olives, pitted
- 2 flat-leaf parsley sprigs
- 1 teaspoon capers, rinsed
- 1 gherkin (dill pickle)
- 20g (1½ tablespoons) butter
- 120 ml (½ cup) brandy
- 2 egg yolks
- salt and pepper

Alternative fish: salmon
or char

 288

TROUT WITH MANDARIN ORANGE JUICE

Squeeze the juice from 1 mandarin. Pour some water into a fish kettle (poacher) or pan large enough to hold all the fish, stir in the mandarin juice, a pinch of salt and 1 tablespoon of the olive oil and add the fish. Bring just to a boil, then reduce the heat to very low and poach the trout for 10 minutes.

Meanwhile, squeeze the juice from the other mandarins. Using a fish slice (spatula), transfer the fish to a chopping (cutting) board, remove and discard the skins and lift the fillets off the bones onto a warm serving dish. Keep hot.

Chop the olives, parsley, capers and gherkin together. Melt the butter with the remaining oil in a small saucepan, add the chopped herb mixture and cook over low heat, stirring occasionally, for 2–3 minutes. Pour in the brandy and the remaining mandarin juice. Bring to a boil and cook for 5–10 minutes, until reduced. Reduce the heat to very low and quickly whisk in the egg yolks but do not let the mixture boil. Remove the pan from the heat, season with salt and pepper, pour the sauce over the trout and serve immediately.

Serves 4
Preparation time: 10 mins
Cooking time: 15 mins

· large pinch saffron threads,
  lightly crushed
· 100 ml (scant ½ cup) double
  (heavy) cream
· 25 g (2 tablespoons) butter
· 1 shallot, finely chopped
· 4 trout fillets
· 2 tablespoons dry Marsala
· 3 tablespoons pistachios,
  toasted and chopped
· salt and pepper

Alternative fish: char or
salmon trout

 288   290   296

Trota in giallo

TROUT WITH SAFFRON AND PISTACHIOS

Put the saffron in a small bowl, stir in 2 tablespoons of the cream and set aside. Melt the butter in a frying pan or skillet, add the shallot and cook over low heat, stirring occasionally, for 5 minutes. Add the fish, skin side down, increase the heat to medium and cook for 10 minutes. Sprinkle with the Marsala and cook until it has evaporated, then add the pistachios, remaining cream and the saffron mixture. Season with salt and pepper and cook, gently stirring occasionally, for another few minutes, until the sauce thickens. Transfer the fish fillets to a serving platter, spoon the cream sauce over them and serve immediately.

Photograph opposite

Serves 4
Preparation time: 15 mins
Cooking time: 20 mins

· 4 trout, scaled and cleaned
· plain (all-purpose) flour,
  for dusting
· 40 g (3 tablespoons) butter
· 40 g (⅓ cup) flaked (slivered)
  almonds
· juice of 1 lemon, strained
· 1 tablespoon chopped
  flat-leaf parsley
· salt and pepper

Alternative fish: mackerel
or salmon

 288

Trota alle mandorle

TROUT WITH ALMONDS

Dust the trout with flour, shaking off the excess. Melt the butter in a large frying pan or skillet, add the fish and cook over medium heat for 6–7 minutes on each side, until evenly browned and cooked through. Transfer them to a serving platter and keep warm. Add the almonds to the pan and cook, stirring constantly, for 2 minutes, then add the lemon juice, and parsley and season with salt and pepper. Cook for another few minutes, then sprinkle the mixture all over the fish and serve immediately.

Serves 4
Preparation time: 15 mins
Cooking time: 15–20 mins

- 1 tablespoon olive oil, plus extra for brushing
- 2 garlic cloves, chopped
- 2 rosemary sprigs, chopped
- 2 sage sprigs, chopped
- 2 thyme sprigs, chopped
- 2 marjoram sprigs, chopped
- 2 mint sprigs, chopped
- 4 × 225-g (8-oz) trout, scaled and cleaned
- salt and pepper

Alternative fish: grey (striped) mullet or mackerel

 288

Trota alle erbe

TROUT WITH HERBS

Light a barbecue. Brush a hinged wire rack with oil. Combine the garlic and herbs in a bowl, season with salt and pepper and stir in the olive oil. Divide the herb mixture among the cavities of the trout. Season the trout with salt and pepper and brush generously with oil. Put the trout in the prepared rack with plenty of oil mixed with salt and pepper. Grill over a medium-hot barbecue for 10–12 minutes, then turn over, brush with a little more oil and grill for another 5 minutes, until the flesh flakes easily. Transfer the fish to individual plates and serve immediately.

Note: If a little mint and rosemary is added to the barbecue, their aroma will intensify as they burn and add more flavour to the trout.

Photograph opposite

Serves 4
Preparation time: 15 mins
Cooking time: 20 mins

- 1 carrot, sliced into rounds
- 1 bay leaf
- 1 thyme sprig
- 2 flat-leaf parsley sprigs
- 8 trout fillets
- 200 ml (scant 1 cup) dry white wine
- 200 ml (scant 1 cup) white wine vinegar
- 4 juniper berries
- salt

Alternative fish: grey (striped) mullet or mackerel

 288   290   296

Trota al ginepro

TROUT WITH JUNIPER

Put the carrot, bay leaf, thyme and parsley in a saucepan, pour in 500 ml (2 cups) water and bring to a boil. Put the fish fillets in a steamer, set it over the pan, cover and cook for 10 minutes. Remove the steamer and increase the heat under the pan to reduce the liquid. Meanwhile, remove the fish, drain on paper towels and put into a dish. When the liquid in the pan has reduced, add the wine, vinegar, juniper berries and a pinch of salt. Bring to a boil, then remove from the heat and pour the mixture over trout. Let cool to room temperature before serving.

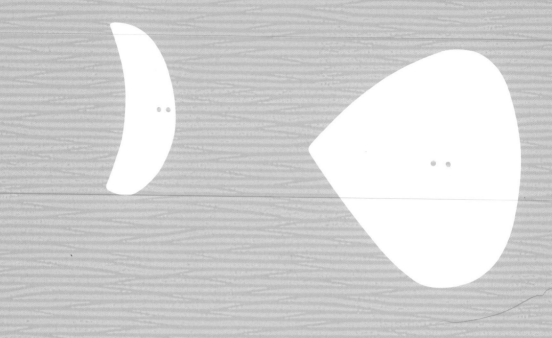

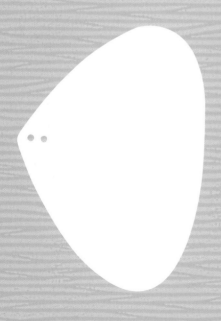

SEAFOOD

Seafood include two main groups: crustaceans and molluscs. Most are rich in calcium, magnesium, sodium chloride, iodine, omega 3 and, above all, iron.

Crustaceans are those with an intricate jointed shell – such as lobster, crabs and prawns (shrimp) – and they are sold live or raw, cooked or frozen. They have a sweet, delicate flavour that is prized around the world. Lobsters and langoustines require careful cooking and can be either boiled, baked or grilled (broiled), whereas larger species of crab are simply boiled. Prawns (shrimp) can be fried, poached, barbecued or grilled. The firm meaty texture and intensely sweet flavour works well just about anything from flavoured butters to spices and chilli.

Molluscs are made up of three groups: the first are sea snails or gastropods (univalves) such as periwinkles, whelks and abalone. The second are bivalves or filter feeders – such as clams, mussels, scallops and oysters – and inhabit two shells that are held together by a strong abductor muscle. They feed by filtering water through their system and picking up nutrients, and must always be cooked from live as they deteriorate very quickly after they die. Although they do not have shells, cephalopods make up the third group of molluscs and include squid, octopus and cuttlefish. Cephalopods offer the most versatility because they can be cooked very slowly or rapidly.

All seafood must be absolutely fresh. Always buy from a reliable supplier and never gather them from the seashore yourself. If purchased alive they must only be kept for a short period of time before cooking and must be cooked from live. Eating shellfish that is not fresh or alive when cooked can cause poisoning as toxins build rapidly. If they are frozen, defrost and cook as soon as you can.

LOBSTER

Astice (European lobster)/
Aragosta (spiny lobster)
Nephropidae

Average weight range:
300g–2kg (11oz–4½lb)

Average length: 50–90cm
(20–35 inches)

Recipes on pages 223–227

Amongst the finest and most highly prized shellfish, lobsters vary in colour when they are alive, but the shell contains a heat-sensitive pigment that turns a vivid coral red on cooking. European and American lobsters (above) have large claws and are, respectively, dark blue and dark green in colour, while the spiny or rock lobster has a craggy, prickly carapace and insignificant claws. Some countries have sustainability issues with lobsters, but generally, the supply is good. Large prawns are a cheaper alternative.

Lobsters are available live, freshly cooked or frozen. The tail meat is also sold frozen, raw or cooked and in or out of the shell. To cook a fresh lobster, split it in half and grill (broil) or boil it. A lobster weighing between 700–900g (1¾–2lb) is ideal for a single serving but for a sharing platter, choose one that is about 1–1.2kg (2¼–2¾lb). A larger lobster will require a longer cooking time because the claws are heavier – calculate 10 minutes per 500g (1½lb). Be careful not to over boil, which causes the meat to become tough. Heavy lobsters (weighing upwards of 1.5kg [3lb]) are old, tough and best avoided. Also avoid buying females that are carrying eggs under their tail shell.

Live lobsters should be placed in the freezer before being immersed in boiling water. Place the lobster in a large quantity of boiling water and cover immediately with a lid. Bring the water to a boil and simmer for the calculated cooking time. They can also be cooked for a shorter length of time, then split in half and put on the grill. Once cooked, plunge the lobster into ice water. Split the lobster in half and remove the dark intestinal tract with the point of a knife and discard. Remove the stomach sac that is just behind the eye in the carapace (head shell).

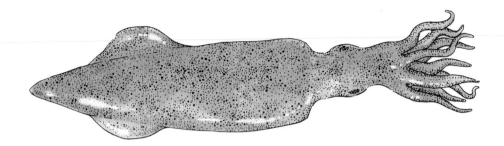

SQUID

Calamaro
Loligo forbesi

Average weight range:
50–750 g (2 oz –1 lb 10 oz)

Average length: 10–90 cm
(4–35 inches)

Recipes on pages 228–233

There are a number of species of squid, all with a body or mantle (often referred to as a tube), with a pair of fins that resemble wings. Inside the body is a translucent feather-like piece of cartilage known as the quill or pen. Squid also contain a small ink sac that is extracted and used to colour pasta and rice. Covering the body is a thin, light brown, patterned membrane. The body itself is pure white when fresh, turning a light shade of pink as it deteriorates. Some methods of fishing for squid are considered unsustainable. Although it has the potential to be one of the most widely consumed types of seafood in the world because it is found in all seas, squid is still under utilized in some countries.

Squid is available fresh and unprepared or as prepared frozen tubes and tentacles. When preparing fresh squid (see page 302), the body can be opened out into a sheet to cook whole or cut into slices or rings. Whether pan-fried, grilled (broiled) or deep-fried, squid requires only a couple of minutes to cook to perfection. Avoid overcooking squid, which will cause it to be tough and rubbery. Squid can also dried, smoked and cooked and preserved in brine.

A favourite Italian dish has whole tubes stuffed and slowly braised whereas baby squid, known as *calamaretti*, is often fried in *fritto misto*, such as in *Fritto misto con verdure* (Seafood and vegetable fritto misto, see page 280). Alternatives are cuttlefish and, in some cases, octopus.

SCALLOPS

Capesante
Pectinidae

Average size: 7 cm (2¾ inches)
across

Recipes on pages 234–237

With pretty, fan-shaped corrugated shells, scallops
are an appreciated shellfish from most seas. Scallops are
bivalve molluscs but, unlike other molluscs, are harvested
from deeper waters and move freely by expelling water
from their shells. They are both harvested in the wild and
farmed in some countries. Harvesting by hand-divers is
more environmentally sound than dredging. In the absence
of the great or king scallop, the smaller and sweeter queen
(bay) scallop or monkfish cheeks are good alternatives.

A freshly opened scallop reveals a frill or skirt around
the edge, gills and intestinal sac, all of which are discarded.
The edible jewels are the white disc of meat (abductor
muscle) and the coral coloured roe. The white meat is
sweet, succulent and tender, while the coral has a stronger
flavour and in some countries is either dried for use in
sauces or discarded all together. Scallop dishes are often
served in the shells so even if you're buying prepared
scallops, it's worth asking the fish store for the upper,
curved half-shell.

The simplest way of enjoying scallops is to pan-fry them,
which sears the outside and makes the scallops particularly
sweet. They may be served with mayonnaise or with oil
and lemon juice, or even skewered with vegetables as in
Spiedini di capesante (Skewered scallops, see page 236).
In Italy, scallops are often added to a pasta sauce or simply
fried in sage-infused butter.

MUSSELS

Cozze
Mytilus edulis

Average size up to 6 cm
(2½ inches)

Recipes on pages 238–242

These popular bivalve molluscs have an oval blue-black shell, and the mussel meat varies in colour from a deep ochre to pale taupe, depending on where they have been harvested. They are harvested in the wild, but are also extensively farmed on ropes or stakes and in sheltered beds and are commonly regarded as one of the most sustainable types of seafood.

Available year round, mussels are sold live in the shell, precooked or canned in brine or vinegar. Smoked mussels are also available. Although most commercially available mussels are farmed, which guarantees a high level of cleanliness, they should still be thoroughly scrubbed under cold, running water, but not left to soak in the water (see page 300). Live mussels should be prepared and eaten as soon after purchase as possible but may be briefly stored, lightly covered, in the refrigerator, but not in direct contact with water because this kills them quickly. Discard any mussels with broken or damaged shells or open ones that do not shut immediately when sharply tapped.

With a sweet flavour and creamy texture, mussels can be steamed with lemon and parsley or stuffed and baked to make a classic antipasti. Mussels can be substituted with clams.

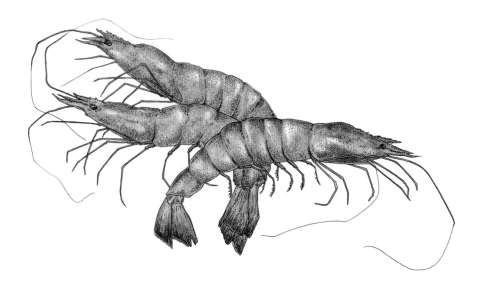

PRAWNS / SHRIMP

Gamberi / Gamberetti
Pandalus penaeus

Average weight and length depends on species

Recipes on pages 243–249

Prawns (shrimp) are hugely sought after and are both caught in the wild and extensively farmed. The word 'shrimp' is inclusive of all varieties in the United States, but in other English-speaking countries, it is used only for a couple of tiny species. They vary in colour when alive, but most turn pink-orange when cooked. There are many environmental and sustainability issues surrounding the harvesting of wild prawns and the methods of farming them, but there are some excellent sources. For those unable to eat this and other crustaceans, monkfish or scallops make good alternatives.

They can be sold cooked or raw, whole or shelled or, very occasionally, live. Prawns should be deveined (see page 307) as the gritty intestinal tract can be unpleasant to eat.

Prawns are very meaty, dense and sweet compared to the more intense flavour and delicate textures of the cold water crustaceans. Prawns can be grilled (broiled) or pan-fried and served with lemon and olive oil. They are better left unpeeled when grilled because they are less likely to dry out. Be careful to avoid over-cooking, which makes them tough. The shells make excellent stock that can be used for risotto and soup.

CRAB

Granchio / Granceola
Cancridae

Average weight range:
100g–2kg (3½oz – 4½lb)

Recipes on pages 250–253

Found on every continent, the array of varieties of both small and large crabs makes this a favourite shellfish around the world. Little mud crabs are perfect for soups and stocks, Dungeness crabs (above) provide wonderfully sweet white meat, shore crabs in their molted state are a delicacy (and known as soft-shell crabs) and the magnificent King crab is favoured for its leg meat. Many crabs are harvested sustainably as they are landed live. Lobster and prawns (shrimp) are good substitutes.

Crab contains two types of meat; white meat is extracted from the legs, claws and central body, while brown meat is located in the carapace or shell that contains its main organs. White meat is generally the more popular because it is sweet and delicate. Brown meat, or meat from the body of the crab, has a stronger and more pronounced flavour and varies in consistency.

Crab is sold live, cooked and unprepared, and cooked and dressed (which means that the inedible parts have been removed). Fresh, pasteurized and canned crab meat is also available, usually separated into white and brown. Cooked crab should always be purchased from a reliable source; it should have a lovely sweet seafood aroma. To remove the meat from a cooked crab, place it on its back and break off the claws and legs, then break off the tail flap. Insert a heavy-bladed knife between the body shell and the back shell, twist and then prise (pry) apart with your thumbs. Remove and discard the 'dead man's fingers' (gills). Using a spoon, scoop the brown meat out into a bowl. Halve the body with a sharp knife and carefully pick out the meat. Finally, press on the back shell just behind the eyes, then remove and discard the mouth and stomach sac. Scoop out the remaining brown meat.

OYSTERS

Ostrice
Ostreidae

Average weight range: graded
by size at production and range
from 50–70g (2–2¾oz) to 110g
(3¾oz). European oysters are
graded by size, 1 being the
largest.

Recipes on pages 254–257

Pacific oysters are oval, European are flat and round and American oysters (above), from the Eastern Seaboard, are similar but with a more uniform shape. With a powerful muscle that holds the shell shut, oysters filter nutrients from the vast quantities of seawater they take in daily and can be difficult to open. A number of oyster varieties, notably Pacific oysters, are farmed extensively. Oysters must be harvested from purified or unpolluted water once landed to ensure they are safe to eat.

Oysters are available live in the shell, canned in brine and smoked. Live oysters should be kept chilled and lightly covered, with the flat shell uppermost to prevent loss of the salty liquor. There are various methods of opening oysters (see page 306). If prising (prying) them open with a knife, a proper oyster knife is the safest option because a more flexible blade can snap and cause injury. If they are to be cooked, you can put them into a very hot oven for a few moments until they open.

The whorls on the shells and, more importantly, the flavour of oysters greatly depends on the diet – flavours can be sweet, metallic, grassy or nutty. The texture of a raw oyster will vary by type and season, ranging from soft and creamy to firm and meaty. During the summer they become milky and soft. They are most often served simply with a squeeze of lemon juice, but in some regions of Italy, they are baked with olive oil, breadcrumbs and parsley.

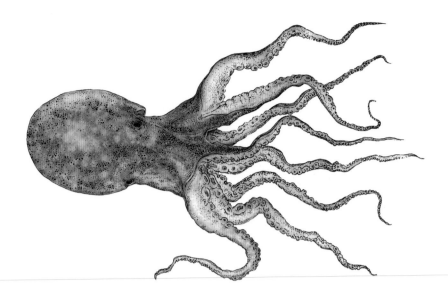

OCTOPUS

Polpo
Octopus vulgaris

Average weight range:
750g–1.3kg (1lb 10oz – 3lb)

Average length: 50–100cm
(20–40 inches)

Recipes on pages 258–260

The many species of octopus are found in temperate seas and popular particularly in the Mediterranean and Japan. Unlike other cephalopods, the octopus does not have an internal shell and the body, of course, has eight long tentacles. The common octopus, the species found in the Mediterranean, has tentacles with double rows of suction pads that often contain grit. In some parts of the world, where it is considered a delicacy, it is over-exploited and alternatives, such as cuttlefish and squid, can be used.

It is sold fresh and unprepared and also cleaned and frozen, but not skinned. To clean and tenderize a whole octopus, beat it against a hard surface or dip it alternately into boiling and iced water because this breaks down the protein slowly. Carefully wash the tentacles in several changes of water to remove sand and grit.

Larger octopuses are best prepared using slow-cooking methods, such as braising or stewed in casseroles, whereas smaller specimens can be grilled (broiled), fried or poached. Octopus can also be boiled or poached, then thinly sliced and dressed with olive oil, lemon juice, garlic and parsley, such as in the simple *Seppioline alla napoletana* (Neapolitan-style baby octopus, see page 259).

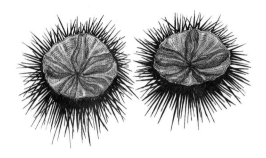

SEA URCHIN

Riccio di mare
Echinidae

Average weight range:
50–250g (2–9oz)

Average size: up to 15cm
(6 inches) depending on species

Recipes on pages 261–262

Though not common in homecooking, sea urchins are included in the classic cuisines of Italy, Spain, France and Japan. These spiny creatures are gathered for the gonads, usually called roe or coral, and only available during the late spring and the autumn (fall) when the coral is fully developed. Over-exploited only in areas where they are considered a delicacy, they do not have any real substitute, although other fish roes, including soft herring roe (for texture) and keta or salmon roe (for colour), could be used.

Sea urchins are sold live and require careful handling because of the spines. Turn the urchin onto its back, snip a disc around the mouth with scissors and remove it. Pour away any liquid and pull out and discard all black parts from inside the shell. Extract the coral from the shell with a teaspoon.

With a deep orange colour, a strong, salty seafood flavour and a creamy texture, sea urchin coral is an acquired taste boasting an intense smell and flavour of the sea. Traditionally, it is eaten raw, scooped straight from the shell, and sprinkled with lemon juice. Unsuitable for long cooking, it can add a salty intensity to creamy sauces, omelettes and pasta dishes such as *Linguine ai ricci di mare* (Linguine with sea urchins, see page 262).

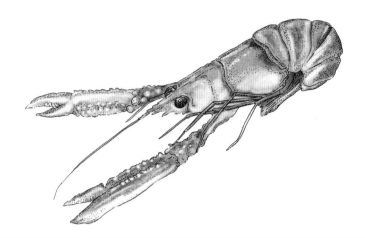

LANGOUSTINE

Scampo
Nephrops norvegicus

Average weight range:
50–225 g (2–8 oz)

Average length: 8.5–35 cm
(3½–14 inches)

Recipes on pages 262–267

Known by a variety of names – including Dublin Bay prawns, Norwegian lobster, scampi and lobsterettes – langoustines are coral in colour and become paler upon cooking. Most of their weight is made up of shell, with slender claws, tiny legs and long carapace (head shell). Langoustine are not commonly available in the United States and can be replaced with large fresh prawns (shrimp) or crawfish.

Langoustines are just one of several crustaceans consumed in Italy – other species include the Mantis shrimp and slipper lobster. They are available live or chilled, raw or cooked and both fresh and frozen. They should be eaten extremely fresh because their flesh deteriorates very quickly. The only edible part is the tail, which is sweet, succulent and tender, not unlike lobster. They are easier to peel after cooking as the meat is very delicate, although some recipes suggest removing them from the shell first.

Langoustines may be poached in a court bouillon, roasted or split in half, brushed with butter or oil and grilled (broiled) to be enjoyed straight from the shell. The cooking time will vary according to size. When added to boiling water, allow 5 minutes from when the water returns to a boil. If added to cold water, allow 3 minutes after it comes to a boil. The cooked meat may turn powdery in texture if overcooked or when the langoustine has lost its condition. The tail shell is sharp but gently pinching it together shatters the underside, making it easier to peel. The shells can be crushed and used to make a superb shellfish stock or to infuse oil or butter.

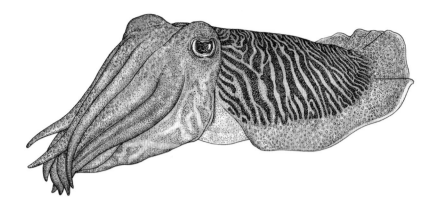

CUTTLEFISH

Seppia
Sepia officinalis

Average weight range:
300 g – 1 kg (11 oz – 2¼ lb)

Average length: 20–40 cm
(8–16 inches)

Recipes on pages 268–272

Cuttlefish are cephalopods with long tentacles and a characteristic oval bone, called a quill or cuttlebone. The body is covered with a thick, dark maroon, mottled and patterned membrane. A frilled fin surrounds the edge of the body, which has eight short, thick tentacles and two longer tentacles. They thrive in most oceans with the exception of northern American waters. Cuttlefish is seasonal and can sometimes be difficult to obtain; however, both squid and octopus are good alternatives. Cuttlefish ink is also sold pasteurized and in small packs as *nero de seppia*, traditionally used to colour pasta and risotto an intense black.

Cuttlefish is usually sold uncleaned. To prepare, cut off the tentacles just in front of the eyes and discard the beak in their centre. Separate and skin the tentacles and pull off the skin from the body. Cut along the back and remove the cuttlebone, then remove the ink sac. Remove and discard the innards and the head. Take care when removing the ink sac because the ink is thick and any stains are impossible to remove. If you need to reserve the ink sac, put it in a small bowl of water until required. For additional detail, see page 302.

The body, with a sweet seafood flavour and a tender texture, can be thinly sliced and flash-fried for a few seconds in hot butter or oil. It may also be left whole and opened out as a sheet and lightly scored to let the heat penetrate quickly, marinated and grilled (broiled) or cooked on the barbecue. The tentacles are tough and best suited to long slow-cooking methods.

CLAMS

Vongole
Veneridae

Average length: 6–8cm
(2½–3¼ inches)

Recipes on pages 273–275

Clams have a round, meaty body with a small amount of roe and come in myriad sizes and colours. Clams are usually sold live because they deteriorate rapidly after death. However, some are cooked, extracted from the shell and canned in brine or juice or packed in vinegar. They should be cooked immediately after purchase but may be stored briefly in the refrigerator. Do not add water to them because it will kill them.

To prepare, rinse them thoroughly under cold, running water to remove as much grit as possible. Make sure that the shells are closed, or close immediately when sharply tapped. Discard any that remain open and any with cracked or damaged shells. Clams can be eaten raw if they are harvested from areas where they have been properly treated or come from very clean water. After shucking, they are usually served sprinkled with lemon juice or a sauce.

Clams are often steamed in a small quantity of liquid, such as stock, wine or water, for 2–3 minutes, or until the shell has opened completely. If cooked for too long, they become tough. They may be eaten straight from the shell or removed to add to sauces or salads. The cooking liquid is a flavoursome addition to clam dishes, but should be filtered through a sieve (strainer) lined with muslin (cheesecloth) to remove any traces of grit.

Serves 4
Preparation time: 20 mins
Cooking time: 40 mins

- 40 g (3 tablespoons) butter, plus extra for greasing
- 1 × 1-kg (2¼-lb) cooked lobster (see page 211)
- 3 tablespoons olive oil
- 1 teaspoon hot mustard
- juice of 1 lemon, strained
- pinch of dried oregano
- 1 basil sprig, chopped
- 120 ml (½ cup) brandy
- 120 ml (½ cup) Marsala
- 100 g (2 cups) fresh breadcrumbs
- salt and pepper

Alternative fish: langoustines or prawns (shrimp)

LOBSTER WITH MUSTARD AND LEMON SAUCE

Preheat the oven to 200°C/400°F/Gas Mark 6. Grease an ovenproof dish with butter. To remove the meat, put the lobster belly side down and with its legs splayed out on a chopping (cutting) board. Using a heavy sharp knife, cut it in half through the middle of the head, then turn the board around and complete the cut through the tail. Open and lift out the tail meat. Remove the black intestinal tract with the point of the knife and discard.

Break off the claws, then break the claws at the joints. Hit with the handle of the knife to break the shells in the claws and pick out the meat in as large pieces as you can. Cut the meat into thin slices and put them into the prepared dish.

Whisk together the oil, mustard, lemon juice, oregano, basil, brandy, Marsala and breadcrumbs in a bowl until thoroughly combined and season with salt and pepper. Pour the sauce over the lobster, dot with the butter and bake for 20 minutes. Serve immediately.

Serves 4
Preparation time: 40 mins
+ 2 hrs freezing
Cooking time: 1 hr 20 mins

· 2 × 800–900-g (1¾–2-lb) lobsters
· olive oil, for brushing and
  drizzling
· 2 red bell peppers, halved
  and seeded
· 2 tablespoons double
  (heavy) cream
· 1 tablespoon finely chopped
  flat-leaf parsley
· 200 g (1 cup) long-grain rice
· juice of ½ lemon, strained
· 200 ml (scant 1 cup)
  dry white wine
· 200 g (7 oz) asparagus tips
· salt and pepper

Alternative fish: white crabmeat,
langoustines or monkfish

LOBSTER AND RICE SALAD

Put the lobsters in plastic bags in the freezer for 2 hours.
Meanwhile, preheat the oven to 180°C/350°F/Gas Mark 4.
Brush an ovenproof dish with olive oil, put the bell peppers
in the dish in a single layer and drizzle generously with
olive oil. Roast for 35–40 minutes, then remove from the
oven and let cool. Peel off the skins from the cooled bell
peppers, put the flesh in a blender or food processor
and process to a purée. Scrape it into a bowl, stir in the
cream and parsley and set aside.

Plunge the lobsters into a large saucepan of salted boiling
water, cover and cook for 20 minutes. Remove the lobsters
from the pan and let cool. To remove the meat, put a lobster
belly side down and with its legs splayed out on a chopping
(cutting) board. Using a heavy sharp knife, cut it in half
through the middle of the head, then turn the board around
and complete the cut through the tail. Open and lift out the
tail meat. Remove the black intestinal tract with the point
of the knife and discard. Break off the claws, then break the
claws at the joints. Hit with the handle of the knife to break
the shells on the claws and pick out the meat in as large
pieces as you can. Cut the tail meat into chunks.

Cook the rice in a large saucepan of salted boiling water
for about 20 minutes, then drain, rinse under cold running
water and spread it out on a clean cloth to cool completely.
Pour 150 ml (⅔ cup) water into a small saucepan, add the
lemon juice and wine and bring to a boil. Add the asparagus
tips and simmer for 10 minutes, then drain. Arrange the
rice, lobster meat and asparagus tips in a large salad
bowl and dress with the bell pepper and cream mixture.
Serve immediately.

Serves 4
Preparation time: 20 mins
+ 2 hrs freezing
Cooking time: 10 mins

· 4 × 500-g (1 lb 2-oz) live lobsters

For the court-bouillon:
· 1 carrot
· 1 onion
· juice of 1 lemon, strained
· 200 ml (scant 1 cup) white wine
· 1 teaspoon white wine vinegar

· 5 vine tomatoes, peeled,
  de-seeded and diced
· 2 celery stalks, chopped
· 1 basil sprig, chopped
· 6 tablespoons olive oil
· juice of ½ grapefruit, strained
· juice of ½ lemon, strained
· 50 g (½ cup) black olives, pitted
  and chopped
· salt and pepper

Alternative fish: langoustines
or monkfish

LOBSTER AND GRAPEFRUIT SALAD

Put the lobsters in plastic bags in the freezer for 2 hours. Meanwhile, make the court-bouillon. Put the carrot, onion, lemon juice, wine and vinegar into a large saucepan, add 3 litres (13 cups) water and bring to a boil, then reduce the heat and simmer for 20 minutes. Bring to a boil again, add the lobsters, cover and cook for 10 minutes.

Remove the lobsters from the pan and let cool. To remove the meat, put a lobster belly side down and with its legs splayed out on a chopping (cutting) board. Using a heavy sharp knife, cut it in half through the middle of the head, then turn the board around and complete the cut through the tail. Open and lift out the tail meat. Remove the black intestinal tract with the point of the knife and discard. Break off the claws, then break the claws at the joints. Hit with the handle of the knife to break the shells on the claws and pick out the meat in as large pieces as you can. Cut the tail meat into chunks.

Put the tomatoes, celery and basil in a fairly large bowl and add the lobster. Whisk together the olive oil and grapefruit and lemon juice in a bowl until thoroughly combined and season with salt and pepper. Drizzle the dressing over the salad, mix gently and season with salt and pepper, divide among individual plates and garnish with the olives.

Serves 4
Preparation time: 25 mins
Cooking time: 30–35 mins

· 2 × 800-g (1¾-lb) freshly
  cooked spiny lobsters
  (see page 211)
· 100g (7 tablespoons) butter
· 1 onion, finely chopped
· 1 celery stalk, finely chopped
· 1 carrot, finely chopped
· 4 tablespoons brandy
· 1 teaspoon herb mustard
· 1 fresh tarragon sprig,
  finely chopped
· 175 ml (¾ cup) dry white wine
· juice of ½ lemon, strained
· salt and pepper

Alternative fish: prawns (shrimp)
or crab claws

Aragosta in salsa di dragoncello

LOBSTER IN TARRAGON SAUCE

Cut open the lobsters and remove the meat (see page 211), reserving the tomalley and coral. Melt 50g (4 tablespoons) of the butter in a saucepan, add the onion, celery and carrot and cook over low heat, stirring occasionally, for 5 minutes. Add the lobster meat and cook until lightly browned, then season. Add half the brandy and cook until it has evaporated, then add the mustard and tarragon. Pour in the wine, cover and simmer for 10 minutes.

Remove the pan from the heat, transfer the lobster meat to a serving plate and keep warm. Strain the cooking liquid into a clean saucepan. Chop the tomalley and coral and add to the pan with the remaining butter, remaining brandy and the lemon juice. Cook over medium heat until slightly reduced, then season and spoon the sauce over the lobster meat. Serve immediately.

Serves 4
Preparation time: 45 mins
Cooking time: 25 mins

· 200 g (7 oz) baby squid, cleaned
· juice of ½ lemon, strained
· 4 baby globe artichokes
· 2 tablespoons olive oil
· 1 garlic clove, peeled
· 100 ml (scant ½ cup)
  dry white wine
· 5 cherry tomatoes, quartered
· 250 g (9 oz) fusilli
· 6 basil leaves, torn
· salt and pepper

Alternative fish: cuttlefish,
octopus or prawns (shrimp)

 302

PASTA SALAD WITH BABY SQUID

Rinse the squid well under cold running water and peel off the skin. Fill a bowl halfway with water and stir in the lemon juice. To prepare the artichokes, break off the stems, remove any coarse outer leaves and cut into small slices. (Baby artichokes will not yet have developed an inedible choke.) Heat the oil in a frying pan or skillet, add the garlic clove and cook over low heat, stirring occasionally, for a few minutes, until beginning to colour, then remove and discard. Add the artichoke slices to the pan and cook, stirring occasionally, for 3 minutes. Pour in the white wine and cook until the alcohol has evaporated, then add the squid sacs and tentacles and cherry tomatoes and cook for 6 minutes, adding 1 tablespoon hot water, if necessary.

Season with pepper, remove from the heat, transfer the mixture to a salad bowl and let cool to room temperature. Bring a large saucepan of salted water to a boil. Add the pasta, bring back to a boil and cook for 8–10 minutes, until al dente. Drain and refresh under cold running water, then drain again and add to the salad bowl. Toss the ingredients together, sprinkle with the basil and let stand for 5 minutes before serving.

Serves 4
Preparation time: 15 mins
Cooking time: 40 mins

· 800 g (1¾ lb) baby squid, cleaned
· 1 tablespoon capers preserved
  in salt, rinsed and chopped
· 1 garlic clove, chopped
· 1 fresh basil sprig, chopped
· ½ chilli, chopped
· 2 tablespoons olive oil
· 100 ml (scant ½ cup)
  dry white wine
· ½–1 teaspoon grated
  fresh ginger
· 4 ripe tomatoes, peeled,
  seeded and coarsely chopped
· salt

Alternative fish: monkfish
cheeks, baby octopus or
langoustines

 302

Calamaretti piccanti

SPICY BABY SQUID

Rinse the squid well under cold running water and peel off the skin. Mix together the capers, garlic clove, basil and chilli in a bowl. Heat the olive oil in a saucepan, add the caper mixture and cook over low heat stirring occasionally, for 3–4 minutes. Add the squid, pour the wine and cook until it has evaporated. Stir in the ginger, season with salt, cover and cook for 10–15 minutes. Add the tomatoes, cover and simmer for another 20 minutes, then remove the lid, season with more salt if necessary and simmer until the sauce has reduced. Transfer to a serving platter and serve.

Photograph opposite

Serves 4
Preparation time: 30 mins
Cooking time: 12 mins

· 12 sea urchins
· 25 g (2 tablespoons) butter
· 3 tablespoons olive oil
· 1 shallot, finely chopped
· 8 squid, cleaned
· sea salt and pepper

Alternative fish: cuttlefish
or monkfish cheeks

 302

Misto di calamari e ricci di mare

SQUID WITH SEA URCHINS

Open the sea urchins, reserving any liquid, then clean and scoop out the coral with a spoon (see page 219). Strain the reserved liquid into a bowl and store in the refrigerator until required. Melt the butter with the oil in a large frying pan or skillet, add the shallot and cook over low heat, stirring occasionally, for 5 minutes, until softened. Season with salt and pepper, add the squid body sacs and tentacles, the coral and reserved liquid of the sea urchin and 1 tablespoon water. Cover and cook for 6–7 minutes. Remove from the heat and season with salt and pepper. Transfer to a warm serving platter and serve immediately.

Serves 4
Preparation time: 40 mins
Cooking time: 1 hr

· 12 large squid, cleaned
· 150 g (5 oz) cooked small
  prawns (shrimp), peeled
  and finely chopped
· 4 tablespoons fresh
  breadcrumbs
· 10 basil leaves, chopped
· 1 tablespoon chopped
  flat-leaf parsley
· ½ garlic clove, finely chopped
· 3 tablespoons olive oil, plus
  extra for drizzling
· salt and pepper

Alternative fish: scallops
or monkfish

 302   307

SQUID STUFFED WITH PRAWNS (SHRIMP)

Finely chop the squid tentacles and put them in a bowl.
Add the prawns (shrimp), breadcrumbs, basil, parsley and
garlic, season with salt and pepper and drizzle with olive
oil. Mix well and divide among the body sacs of the squid,
without over-filling them. Secure each with 1–2 wooden
cocktail sticks or toothpicks.

Heat the olive oil in a flameproof casserole (Dutch oven),
add the stuffed squid and cook over medium heat, gently
shaking the casserole, for 2 minutes, then cover, reduce the
heat to low and cook for about 1 hour, occasionally adding
a little lukewarm water to prevent the squid from scorching.
Lift out the stuffed squid, remove and discard the cocktail
sticks or toothpicks, arrange on a serving platter and
serve immediately.

Serves 6
Preparation time: 35 mins
+ 5 mins standing
Cooking time: 30 mins

- 24 scallops, shucked and
  cleaned, with shells reserved
- 3 tablespoons olive oil
- 1 garlic clove, peeled
- pinch of fresh thyme leaves
- 2 tablespoons brandy
- 250 ml (1 cup) Fish Stock
  (see page 78)
- 1 onion, finely chopped
- 300 g (1½ cups) long-grain rice
- salt and pepper

For the sauce:
- 6 egg yolks
- 175 g (¾ cup) butter, softened
- juice of ½ lemon, strained
- salt

Alternative fish: monkfish
cheeks, skate knobs or
prawns (shrimp)

 304

SCALLOP GRATIN WITH THYME

Wash the bottom scallop shells under cold running water,
dry and set aside. Heat the olive oil with the garlic in a
frying pan or skillet over medium-high heat. When it starts
to colour, remove and discard the garlic. Add the thyme
and scallops and cook for 2 minutes, then add the brandy
and cook until it has evaporated. Season lightly with salt
and pepper and remove the pan from the heat.

Preheat the oven to 180°C/350°F/Gas Mark 4. Pour the
fish stock into a flameproof casserole (Dutch oven) and
bring to a boil. Meanwhile, make the sauce. Beat the egg
yolks, with the butter, lemon juice and a pinch of salt in
a bowl until thoroughly combined. Set aside. Add the onion
to the stock, bring it back to a boil and add the rice. Cover,
transfer to the oven and cook for about 18 minutes, until
the rice has absorbed all the liquid. Remove the casserole
from the oven but do not switch it off.

Spoon the rice evenly onto an ovenproof serving platter
and put place the reserved scallop shells on top. Put
a scallop in each and add a tablespoon of the egg sauce.
Transfer to the oven and bake for a very few minutes, until
lightly browned. Remove from the oven and let stand for
5 minutes before serving.

Serves 4
Preparation time: 30 mins
Cooking time: 20 mins

· 250 ml (1 cup) dry white wine
· 16 live scallops in their
  shells, rinsed
· 25 g (2 tablespoons) butter
· 500 g (1 lb 2 oz) spinach,
  coarse stalks removed
· 1 thyme sprig
· 40 g (½ cup) grated
  Parmesan cheese
· salt and pepper

For the béchamel sauce:
· 25 g (2 tablespoons) butter
· 25 g (¼ cup) plain
  (all-purpose) flour
· 300 ml (1¼ cups) milk
· pinch of freshly grated nutmeg
· salt and pepper

Alternative fish: scallops or
langoustines

SCALLOP AND SPINACH GRATIN

First make the béchamel sauce. Melt the butter in a saucepan over low heat, add the flour and cook, stirring constantly, for 1–2 minutes. Gradually stir in the milk, a little at a time, then bring to a boil, stirring constantly. When the sauce has thickened, remove the pan from the heat, season with salt and pepper and stir in the nutmeg. Set aside until required and stir occasionally.

Heat the wine in a saucepan, gently lower the scallops into it with a slotted spoon and cook for 5 minutes. Lift out and drain the scallops. Holding a scallop with the flat shell uppermost, slide the blade of a sharp flexible knife between the shells and cut through the upper ligament. Lift off the top shell, then pull out and discard the skirt and black stomach sac. Slide the knife blade underneath the scallop and cut through the second ligament. Pull off any remaining ligament attached to the white muscle meat, but keep the orange corals if you like. Shuck the remaining scallops in the same way and keep warm.

Preheat the oven to 180°C/350°F/Gas Mark 4. Put the butter into an ovenproof dish and put the dish in the oven to melt it. Put the spinach with just the water clinging to the leaves after washing in a saucepan and cook for about 5 minutes, until wilted, then drain well, squeeze out the excess moisture and chop. Remove the dish from the oven, add the spinach and thyme leaves, put the scallops on top and season with salt and pepper. Spoon the béchamel sauce over them to cover completely and sprinkle with the cheese. Return the dish to the oven and bake for 5 minutes, until the top is lightly browned. Serve immediately. You can also bake the scallops in 4 individual gratin dishes.

Serves 4
Preparation time: 20 mins
Cooking time: 6–10 mins

· 40 g (3 tablespoons) butter
· 8 fresh sage leaves
· 16 scallops, shucked and
  cleaned with corals reserved
· salt and freshly ground
  white pepper

Alternative fish: monkfish
cheeks or prawns (shrimp)

 304

Capesante al burro e alla salvia

SCALLOPS WITH BUTTER AND SAGE

Melt the butter with the sage leaves in a frying pan or skillet, add the scallops with their coral and cook over low heat for 3–5 minutes on each side, until lightly browned. Season with salt and pepper and serve.

Serves 6
Preparation time: 20 mins
+ 10 mins marinating
Cooking time: 3 mins

· juice of 2 limes, strained
· 1 garlic clove, crushed
· 24 scallops, shucked
  and cleaned
· 1 green bell pepper
· 1 red bell pepper
· olive oil
· salt and pepper

Alternative fish: baby squid
or monkfish cheeks

 304

Spiedini di capesante

SKEWERED SCALLOPS

Pour the lime juice into a shallow dish, season with salt and pepper, add the garlic and scallops and let marinate in a cool place for 10 minutes. Meanwhile, peel the bell peppers with a vegetable peeler, remove the seeds and chop into 24 pieces. Preheat the grill (broiler). Drain the scallops and thread 4 onto each of 6 skewers, alternating with the chunks of red and green bell peppers. Brush with oil and grill (broil) for 1½ minutes on each side. Remove from the heat, season with salt and pepper, transfer to a serving dish and serve.

Photograph opposite

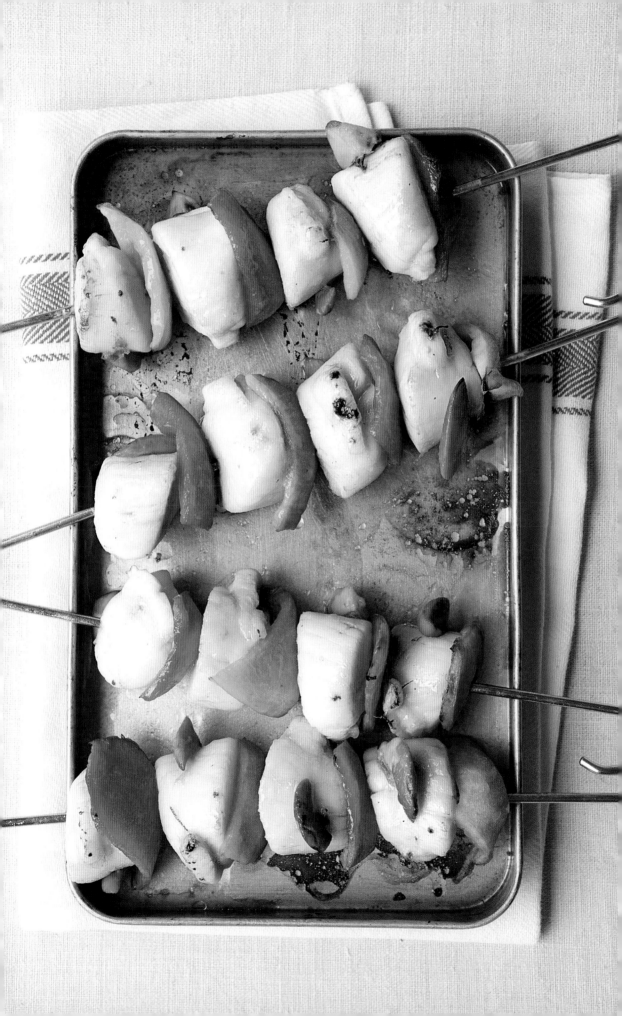

Serves 4
Preparation time: 35 mins
+ 5 mins standing
Cooking time: 20 mins

· 500 g (1 lb 2 oz) mussels,
  cleaned
· 2 garlic cloves, chopped
· 1 bunch flat-leaf parsley,
  chopped
· 4 tablespoons olive oil,
  plus extra for drizzling
· 2 onions, thinly sliced
· 400 g (14 oz) cherry tomatoes,
  chopped
· 20 g (¼ cup) grated
  Pecorino cheese
· 300 g (11 oz) potatoes, cut
  into rounds
· 300 g (1½ cups) long-grain rice
· salt and pepper

Alternative fish: clams,
oysters or langoustines

 300

OVEN-BAKED RICE WITH MUSSELS

Preheat the oven to 180°C/350°F/Gas Mark 4. Discard any mussels with damaged shells or that do not shut immediately when sharply tapped. To open the mussels, push the tip of a small knife between the shells and run the tip all around the edge. Ease open the top shell and run the knife all around the inside edge, then snap it off. Run the knife around the inside edge of the bottom shell and remove the meat.

Mix together the garlic and parsley in a bowl. Pour the oil into an ovenproof dish and add the onions. Cover with half the tomatoes, then add half the garlic and parsley mixture and sprinkle with the cheese. Add half the potato rounds, all the rice and top with the mussels. Sprinkle with the remaining garlic and parsley mixture and cover with the remaining tomatoes and remaining potato rounds. Season with salt, drizzle with olive oil and add enough water to cover. Bake for about 20 minutes, until the rice is tender. Remove the dish from the oven, let stand for 5 minutes and then serve.

Serves 4
Preparation time: 40 mins
Cooking time: 35 mins

· 1 kg (2¼ lb) mussels, cleaned
· 4 tablespoons olive oil
· 50 g (4 tablespoons) butter
· 1 tablespoon anchovy paste
· 100 g (1 cup) black olives,
  pitted and sliced
· 250 g (9 oz) tomatoes, peeled,
  seeded and diced flesh
· 320 g (11½ oz) bucatini
· 1 garlic clove, finely chopped
· 1 tablespoon finely chopped
  flat-leaf parsley
· salt and pepper

Alternative fish: clams
or oysters

 300

BUCATINI WITH MUSSELS

Discard any mussels with damaged shells or that do
not shut immediately when sharply tapped. Put them into
a large saucepan with half the oil, cover and cook over
high heat, shaking the pan occasionally for 5–6 minutes,
until the shells have opened. Remove the pan from the
heat and discard any mussels that remain shut. Reserve
a few mussels in their shells for garnish and remove
the remainder. Strain the cooking liquid through a sieve
(strainer) lined with muslin (cheesecloth) into a bowl.

Melt the butter with the remaining oil in frying pan or
skillet, stir in the anchovy paste, then add the olives,
tomatoes and 3–4 tablespoons of the reserved mussel
cooking liquid and heat gently.

Meanwhile, bring a large saucepan of salted water to
a boil, add the pasta, bring back to a boil and cook for
8–10 minutes, until al dente. Stir the garlic and parsley
into the sauce and cook for another few minutes. Drain
the bucatini, tip it into a serving dish, add the sauce and
shelled mussels and season with pepper. Toss to mix,
garnish with the reserved mussels in their shells and
serve immediately.

Serves 4
Preparation time: 10 mins
Cooking time: 15 mins

· 2 tablespoons olive oil
· 1 garlic clove, peeled
· 250 g (9 oz) shelled mussels
· 350 g (12 oz) tomatoes, peeled,
  seeded and chopped
· pinch of saffron threads,
  lightly crushed
· 2 tablespoons chopped
  flat-leaf parsley
· salt and pepper

For the gnocchi:
· 1 kg (2¼ lb) potatoes
· 200 g (1¾ cups) plain
  (all-purpose) flour, plus
  extra for dusting
· 1 egg, lightly beaten
· salt

Alternative fish: baby squid
or clams

 300

GNOCCHI WITH MUSSELS AND SAFFRON

To make the gnocchi, steam the potatoes for 25–30 minutes, until tender, then mash in a bowl or pass through a potato ricer into a bowl while they are still hot. Stir in the flour, egg and a pinch of salt and knead to a soft elastic dough. Shape the dough into long rolls about 1.5 cm (⅔ inch) in diameter, then cut into 2-cm (¾-inch) lengths. Press them gently against the side of a grater and spread out on a lightly floured dish towel.

To make the sauce, heat the olive oil with the garlic clove in a saucepan. When the it begins to colour, remove and discard the garlic. Add the mussels and tomatoes to the pan and cook for about 10 minutes. Meanwhile, put the saffron into a small bowl, add a little lukewarm water and let soak. Stir the saffron and its soaking water into the sauce, season with salt and pepper, stir in the parsley and remove from the heat. Bring a large saucepan of salted water to a boil, add the gnocchi in batches and cook until they rise to the surface. Remove with a slotted spoon and add to the sauce. When all the gnocchi have been added, transfer to a serving dish and serve immediately.

Serves 4
Preparation time: 30 mins
Cooking time: 10 mins

· 2 kg (4½ lb) mussels, cleaned
· 2 tablespoons olive oil, plus
  extra for deep-frying
· 1 flat-leaf parsley sprig, chopped
· 1 marjoram sprig, chopped
· 1 oregano sprig, chopped
· 1 bay leaf
· 1 garlic clove, peeled
· 200 ml (scant 1 cup) dry
  white wine
· juice of 1 lemon, strained

For the batter:
· 40 g (⅓ cup) plain
  (all-purpose) flour
· 1 egg
· 2 tablespoons milk
· salt and pepper

Alternative fish: oysters or
prawns (shrimp)

 300

GOLDEN MUSSELS

Discard any mussels with damaged shells or that do not shut immediately when sharply tapped. Put the olive oil, parsley, marjoram, oregano, bay leaf and garlic clove in a frying pan or skillet. Add the mussels and set over high heat. Pour in the wine and cook until it has evaporated. Cover and cook, shaking the pan occasionally, for about 4 minutes, until the shells have opened. Remove the pan from the heat and let cool. Meanwhile, make the batter. Sift the flour into a bowl and beat in the egg until smooth. Stir in the milk and season. Discard any mussels that remain shut and remove the meat from the shells. Heat the oil in a deep-fryer to 180–190°C / 350–375°F or until a cube of day-old bread browns in 30 seconds. Using a slotted spoon, dip the mussels in the batter and then lower them into the hot oil one at a time. Cook for 1–2 minutes, until crisp. Remove, drain and sprinkle with lemon juice. Serve immediately.

Serves 4
Preparation time: 25 mins
Cooking time: 5 mins

· 1.5 kg (3¼ lb) mussels, cleaned
· 3 tablespoons finely chopped
  flat-leaf parsley
· pepper

Alternative fish: clams

 300

MUSSELS MARINARA

Discard any mussels with damaged shells or that do not shut when sharply tapped. Put them in a large frying pan or skillet over high heat with plenty of pepper but no water and cook for about 5 minutes, until they have opened. Discard any that remain closed. Drain, reserving the cooking juices, and tip into a deep serving dish. Strain the cooking juices thorough a sieve (strainer) lined with muslin (cheesecloth) into a bowl. Stir in the parsley, pour the mixture over the mussels and serve immediately.

Serves 4
Preparation time: 20 mins
Cooking time: 20 mins

· 200 g (scant 1½ cups) polenta
· 200 g (7oz) asparagus tips
· 2 tablespoons olive oil
· 1 garlic clove, finely chopped
· 1 tablespoon chopped
  flat-leaf parsley
· 200 ml (scant 1 cup)
  dry white wine
· 200 g (7oz) Mediterranean or
  tiger prawn (jumbo shrimp) tails
· ½ teaspoon potato flour or
  cornflour (cornstarch)
· salt and pepper

Alternative fish: scallops or
monkfish

 307

POLENTA WITH PRAWNS (SHRIMP) AND ASPARAGUS

Cook the polenta (see page 125). Meanwhile, cut the asparagus tips in half lengthwise and then in half crosswise. Blanch them in boiling water for 2 minutes and drain. Heat the olive oil in a frying pan or skillet, add the garlic and parsley and cook over low heat, stirring occasionally, for 2–3 minutes. Pour in the wine and cook until it has reduced by two-thirds, then add the prawns (shrimp). Mix the potato flour or cornflour (cornstarch) to a paste with 2 teaspoons water in a small bowl, add to the pan and cook, stirring constantly, for a few minutes, until the mixture thickens slightly. Add the asparagus, stir gently, remove from the heat and season with salt and pepper to taste. Serve the polenta and the prawn mixture in separate dishes.

Serves 4
Preparation time: 20 mins
Cooking time: 30 mins

· 1 litre (4¼ cups) vegetable stock
· 250 g (2 cups) mixed diced
  carrots, diced courgettes
  (zucchini) and shelled peas
· 1 large potato, grated
· 60 g (2¼ oz) small prawns
  (shrimp)
· 2 tablespoons chopped
  flat-leaf parsley
· 3 tablespoons olive oil
· salt

Alternative fish: scallops or
baby squid

 307

PRAWNS (SHRIMP) WITH VEGETABLES

Bring the stock to a boil in a large saucepan, add the vegetables and simmer for 15 minutes. Add the prawns (shrimp) and parsley, season with salt and simmer for another 10 minutes, until the soup thickens slightly. Serve immediately, drizzled with the olive oil.

Serves 6
Preparation time: 35 mins
Cooking time: 14 mins

· 300 g (3 cups) young
  green beans
· 2 kg (4½ lb) uncooked
  Mediterranean or tiger prawns
  (jumbo shrimp)
· 1 garlic clove, crushed
· 1 large celery stalk,
  coarsely chopped
· 50 g (scant ½ cup) capers, rinsed
· 3–4 canned anchovy fillets,
  drained
· 5 hard-boiled egg yolks
· grated zest of ½ lemon
· 1½ tablespoons red wine vinegar
· 100 ml (scant ½ cup) chilli oil

Alternative fish: monkfish
cheeks or langoustines

 307

PRAWNS (SHRIMP) WITH PEVARADA SAUCE

Cook the beans in salted boiling water for 5–10 minutes, until tender, then drain. Peel the prawns (shrimp) and reserve the roe. Put the prawns in the top of a steamer and steam for 4 minutes, then remove from the heat. Put the garlic, celery, capers, anchovies, hard-boiled egg yolks, beans, lemon zest, vinegar and chilli oil in a food processor and process to a smooth purée. Pour this sauce evenly over a serving platter, top with the prawns, garnish with the reserved roe and serve immediately.

Serves 4
Preparation time: 15 mins
Cooking time: 10 mins

· 500 g (1 lb 2 oz) raw large
  prawns (shrimp)
· 500 g (1 lb 2 oz) Treviso
  radicchio
· 4 tablespoons olive oil
· 1 apple, peeled, cored and
  cut into thin julienne strips
· salt and freshly ground
  white pepper

For the dressing:
· 150 ml (⅔ cup) plain full-fat
  (whole milk) yogurt
· 2 tablespoons mayonnaise
· 120 g (5 cups) very finely chopped
  rocket (arugula)
· 2 shallots, very finely chopped
· salt and freshly ground
  white pepper

Alternative fish: scallops

 307

PRAWN (SHRIMP) AND RED CHICORY SALAD

To make the dressing, mix together the yogurt and mayonnaise in a bowl, season with salt and pepper and stir in the rocket (arugula) and shallots. Set aside in a cool place. Steam the prawns (shrimp) for 10 minutes. Divide the radicchio among 4 individual plates, season with salt and pepper and drizzle with the olive oil. Sprinkle the apple strips over each serving and top with the prawns. Add the yogurt dressing to each portion and serve immediately.

Serves 6
Preparation time: 40 mins
Cooking time: 35 mins

· 2 tablespoons olive oil, plus
  extra for brushing
· 500g (1lb 2oz) long aubergines
  (eggplants), thinly sliced
  lengthwise
· 450g (1lb) courgettes (zucchini),
  thinly sliced lengthwise
· 500g (1lb 2oz) langoustines,
  peeled but with heads intact
· 700g (1½lb) uncooked tiger
  prawns (jumbo shrimp),
  peeled but with heads intact
· 2 oregano sprigs, chopped
· 2 marjoram sprigs, chopped
· 2 shallots, chopped
· 1kg (2¼lb) tomatoes, peeled,
  seeded and diced
· 2 mint sprigs, leaves shredded,
  plus extra to garnish
· salt and freshly ground white
  pepper

Alternative fish: scallops or
huss (dogfish)

 307

VEGETABLE-WRAPPED SHELLFISH

Preheat the oven to 180°C/350°F/Gas Mark 4. Brush
a sheet of foil with oil. Spread out the aubergines
(eggplant) and courgettes (zucchini) slices on the sheet
of foil and cook in the oven for 20 minutes, then remove
from the oven but do not turn off the heat.

Meanwhile, season the langoustines and prawns (shrimp)
with salt and pepper. Brush another sheet of foil with oil.
When the aubergines and courgettes are cool enough
to handle, sprinkle the prawns with the oregano and wrap
them in the courgette slices. Sprinkle the langoustines
with the marjoram and roll them up in the aubergine slices.
Put the shellfish rolls on the prepared sheet of foil and
cook in the oven for 4 minutes.

Heat the olive oil in a saucepan, add the shallot and
cook over low heat, stirring occasionally, for 5 minutes,
until translucent. Add the tomatoes and mint leaves,
season with salt and pepper and simmer for 10 minutes.
Pour the sauce into a serving dish, put the vegetable
and shellfish rolls on top, garnish with mint leaves and
serve immediately.

Serves 6
Preparation time: 1¾ hrs
Cooking time: 10 mins

· 24 raw tiger prawns
  (jumbo shrimp)
· 6 tablespoons olive oil
· 2 carrots, finely chopped
· 2 celery stalks, finely chopped
· ½ onion, finely chopped
· 1 leek, chopped
· 200 ml (scant 1 cup) dry
  white wine
· 1 thyme sprig
· 1 bay leaf
· 2 tomatoes, chopped
· 2 large lemons
· 1 tablespoon caster
  (superfine) sugar
· plain (all-purpose) flour,
  for dusting
· 120 ml (½ cup) brandy
· 50 g (⅓ cup) sultanas or
  golden raisins
· 1 tablespoon pine nuts
· salt and pepper

Alternative fish: scallops
or huss (dogfish)

 307

SWEET AND SOUR PRAWNS (SHRIMP)

Peel the prawns (shrimp), reserving the heads and shells. Heat 2 tablespoons of the oil in a saucepan, add the prawn heads and shells and cook over medium heat, stirring and mashing with a wooden spoon, for 5 minutes. Pour in 1 litre (4¼ cups) water, and bring to a boil. Reduce the heat, cover and simmer for 1 hour. Remove from the heat, pour the mixture into a blender and process.

Heat 2 tablespoons of the remaining oil in a large saucepan, add the carrots, celery, onion and leek and cook over low heat, stirring occasionally, for 8–10 minutes, until they start to brown, then pour in the wine and bring to a boil. Add the prawn stock, thyme, bay leaf and tomatoes and simmer, uncovered, for 20–30 minutes, until much of the liquid has evaporated.

Remove the pan from the heat and strain into a small saucepan, pressing down on the flavourings in the sieve (strainer) with the back of a ladle. Return to the heat and cook until reduced to 100 ml (scant ½ cup). Remove from the heat and set aside. Squeeze the juice from the lemons and pare the zest thinly, then cut into very thin strips. Blanch the strips in boiling water for a few minutes, then drain. Repeat the process twice more, then put them in a small saucepan, sprinkle with the sugar and 2 tablespoons water and cook until candied.

Heat the remaining oil in a frying pan or skillet. Lightly dust the prawns with flour, add to the pan and cook over high heat, stirring and tossing, for 4–5 minutes, until they start to brown. Pour in the brandy and cook until it has evaporated, then stir in the prawn reduction, lemon juice, candied lemon zest, sultanas and pine nuts. Season with salt and pepper, heat through briefly and serve.

Serves 4
Preparation time: 15 mins
Cooking time: 23 mins

- 1.5 litres (6¼ cups) Fish Stock
  (see page 78)
- 25 g (2 tablespoons) butter
- 2 tablespoons olive oil
- 1 shallot, chopped
- 320 g (1⅓ cups) risotto rice
- 200 ml (scant 1 cup)
  dry white wine
- ¼ red bell pepper, seeded
  and cut into thin strips
- 150 g (1¼ cups) shelled peas
- pinch of saffron threads,
  lightly crushed
- ½ teaspoon paprika
- ½ teaspoon mild curry powder
- 150 g (5 oz) peeled cooked
  prawns (shrimp)
- salt

Alternative fish: scallops or squid

 307

Risotto speziato ai gamberetti

SPICY PRAWN (SHRIMP) RISOTTO

Pour the stock into a saucepan and bring to a boil. Melt half the butter with the oil in a flameproof casserole (Dutch oven), add the shallot and cook over low heat, stirring occasionally, for 4–5 minutes, until softened. Add the rice and cook, stirring constantly, for a few minutes, until all the grains are coated with fat. Add the wine and cook until the alcohol has evaporated. Add a ladleful of the hot stock and cook, stirring, until it has been completely absorbed. Continue adding the stock, a ladleful at a time, and stirring until each addition has been absorbed, about 18–20 minutes. Halfway through the cooking time, add the bell pepper and peas. Mix the saffron with a little hot stock in a bowl and stir into the rice. Stir in the paprika and curry powder. Add the prawns about 5 minutes before the end of the cooking time. When the rice is tender and creamy, remove the pan from the heat, stir in the remaining butter, season and serve.

Photograph opposite

Serves 4
Preparation time: 15 mins
Cooking time: 25 mins

- 2 tablespoons olive oil
- 1 shallot, finely chopped
- 2 courgettes (zucchini), sliced
- 2 tablespoons dry white
  vermouth
- 350 g (12 oz) spaghetti
- 12 cooked small prawns
  (shrimp), peeled
- 6 courgette (zucchini) flowers,
  pistils removed, cut into strips
- salt and pepper

Alternative fish: scallops or
baby squid

 307

Spaghetti ai gamberetti

SPAGHETTI WITH PRAWNS (SHRIMP)

Heat the oil in a frying pan or skillet, add the shallot and cook over low heat, stirring occasionally, for 5 minutes, until softened. Add the courgettes (zucchini) and cook, stirring occasionally, for another 5 minutes. Stir in the vermouth. Meanwhile, bring a large saucepan of salted water to a boil, add the pasta, bring back to a boil and cook for 8–10 minutes, until al dente. Drain and tip into the pan with the courgettes. Add the prawns and courgette flowers and season with salt and pepper. Cook for another few minutes to let the flavours mingle, then remove from the heat and serve.

Serves 4
Preparation time: 20 mins
Cooking time: 5–7 mins

· 3 tablespoons olive oil, plus
  extra for deep-frying
· 3 garlic cloves, chopped
· 1 onion, chopped
· 500 g (1 lb 2 oz) fresh white
  crab meat, flaked (see page 216)
· pinch of chilli flakes
· 1 tablespoon chopped
  flat-leaf parsley
· 600 g (1 lb 5 oz) boiled potatoes
· plain (all-purpose) flour,
  for dusting
· 2 eggs, beaten
· 150 g (3 cups) fresh white
  breadcrumbs
· salt

Alternative fish: salt cod
or salmon

Polpettine di granchio

CRAB CAKES

Heat the oil in a frying pan or skillet, add the garlic and onion and cook over low heat, stirring occasionally, for 5 minutes. Add the crab meat, chilli flakes and parsley, season with salt and cook for a few minutes. Remove from the heat and let cool. Pass the potatoes through a potato ricer into a bowl, add the crab mixture and mix gently. Taste and adjust the seasoning if necessary.

Lightly dust your hands with flour and shape the mixture into 4 patties. Lightly beat the eggs in a shallow dish and spread out the breadcrumbs in another shallow dish.

Heat the oil for frying in a deep-fryer to 180–190°C (350–375°F) or until a cube of day-old bread browns in 30 seconds. Dip the crab cakes first into the beaten egg and then roll them in the breadcrumbs. Add to the hot oil and cook for 5–7 minutes, until golden brown. Remove with a fish slice (spatula), drain on paper towels and serve immediately.

Serves 4
Preparation time: 30 mins

· 4 freshly cooked spider crabs
 (see page 216)
· 4–8 lettuce leaves
· 2 tablespoons lemon juice
· 5 tablespoons olive oil
· salt and pepper

Alternative fish: langoustines

Granceola all'olio e limone

SPIDER CRAB WITH OIL AND LEMON

Remove the meat from the crab (see page 216). When the meat has been removed from all the crabs, wash the shells thoroughly and dry with paper towels, then line each with 1–2 lettuce leaves. Divide the brown and white crab meat among them, keeping it separate. Drizzle with the olive oil and lemon juice and season with salt and pepper.

If the crabs contained coral, mix it with a little olive oil and use to garnish the crab. If you prefer a stronger-flavoured dressing, add a little chopped fresh parsley and a clove of garlic to the oil and lemon juice.

Serves 4
Preparation time: 30 mins
Cooking time: 35 mins

· 25 g (2 tablespoons) butter
· 2 tablespoons olive oil
· 2 shallots, thinly sliced
· 100 ml (scant ½ cup)
  lukewarm water
· 8 globe artichoke hearts,
  cut into quarters
· 200 g (7oz) crab meat, drained
  if canned, thawed if frozen
· 100 ml (scant ½ cup) double
  (heavy) cream
· 350 g (3 cups) farfalle (bow
  tie pasta)
· salt and pepper

Alternative fish: scallops
or salmon

FARFALLE WITH CRAB

Melt the butter with the oil in a shallow pan, add the shallots and cook over low heat, stirring occasionally, for 5 minutes. Pour in the lukewarm water, add the artichoke hearts and crab meat, stir and cook for 15 minutes. Pour in the cream, season with salt and pepper, cover and simmer for another few minutes.

Bring a large saucepan of salted water to a boil, add the pasta, bring back to a boil and cook for 8–10 minutes, until tender but still firm to the bite. Drain and tip into the pan with the sauce. Increase the heat and toss well. Transfer to a warmed serving dish and serve immediately.

Serves 8
Preparation time: 40 mins
Cooking time: 50 mins

· 24 large oysters, shucked
  (juices reserved), with shells
· 3 shallots, finely chopped
· 2 apples, peeled, cored
  and grated
· 4 tablespoons Calvados
· 4 tablespoons dry (hard) cider
· 100 ml (scant ½ cup) double
  (heavy) cream
· 1 loaf brioche bread, sliced
· freshly ground white pepper

Alternative fish: scallops

 306

OYSTERS WITH CALVADOS

Put the shucked oysters in their lower shells and place them on a baking sheet. To make the sauce, put the shallots, apples, Calvados and cider into a saucepan, bring to a boil and cook over high heat until the liquid has reduced by three-quarters. Reduce the heat to low, stir in the cream and simmer for about 10 minutes.

Meanwhile, preheat the grill (broiler). Strain the reserved oyster juices, including any juices that have collected in the lower shells, into the sauce. Stir, and as soon as the sauce starts to thicken enough to coat the back of the spoon, remove from the heat and strain. Spoon a little of the sauce over each oyster in the half-shell, season lightly with pepper and carefully place in the grill (broiler) pan.

Grill (broil) the oysters for about 3 minutes, until they are just very lightly browned. Serve immediately with slices of brioche.

Serves 4
Preparation time: 15 mins
Cooking time: 15 mins

· 2 eggs
· juice of 1 lemon, strained
· 120 g (generous ¾ cup)
  fine polenta
· olive oil, for frying
· 20 oysters, shucked

  For the dressing:
· 200 ml (scant 1 cup) tomato
  ketchup
· 1 teaspoon cider vinegar
· 1 tablespoon lemon juice
· pinch of dried chilli flakes
· salt

  Alternative fish: mussels
  or monkfish

 306

FRIED OYSTERS

First make the dressing. Whisk together all the ingredients in a bowl until thoroughly combined and set aside in a cool place. Beat the eggs with the lemon juice in a shallow dish and spread out the polenta in another shallow dish. Heat the oil in a deep-fryer to 180–190°C/350–375°F or until a cube of day-old bread browns in 30 seconds. Dip the oysters first in the beaten egg and then in the polenta to coat. Add them to the hot oil and cook for 1–1½ minutes, until lightly browned. Remove with a slotted spoon and drain on paper towels. Serve immediately with the dressing.

Serves 4
Preparation time: 50 mins
Cooking time: 4–5 mins

· 16 oysters, shucked, with
  shells reserved
· 200 g (7 oz) courgettes
  (zucchini), cut into rounds
· 50 g (4 tablespoons) butter
· coarse salt, for the baking sheet
· 4 egg yolks
· 1 shallot, finely chopped
· 100 ml (scant ½ cup) sparkling
  dry wine
· salt and pepper

Alternative fish: scallops
or monkfish

 306

BAKED OYSTERS WITH SABAYON

Wash the bottom shells of the oysters under cold running water. Bring a saucepan of salted water to a boil, add the courgettes (zucchini) and cook for 5 minutes, then drain and process to a purée in a blender or food processor. Scrape the purée into a small saucepan, add half the butter and a pinch of salt and cook over low heat, stirring occasionally, for 5 minutes, then remove from the heat. Dice the remaining butter and let stand at room temperature.

Preheat the oven to 220°C / 425°F / Gas Mark 7. Make a thick layer of salt on a baking sheet. Put the yolks into a heatproof bowl, add the shallot and beat in the wine. Set the bowl over a saucepan of barely simmering water and cook, whisking constantly, for about 10 minutes, until thickened. Do not let mixture boil. Remove the bowl from the heat and stir in the remaining butter and a pinch each of salt and pepper. Nestle the reserved oyster shells on the prepared baking sheet and add a tablespoonful of courgette purée to each. Put an oyster on top and cover with a tablespoonful of sabayon sauce. Bake for 4–5 minutes, then remove from the oven and serve immediately.

Serves 4
Preparation time: 30 mins
+ 1hr standing
Cooking time: 10–15 mins

- 1 kg (2¼ lb) baby octopus,
  cleaned
- 150 ml (⅔ cup) olive oil
- 3 tablespoons flat-leaf parsley
- 2 garlic cloves, finely chopped
- juice of 1 lemon, strained
- salt and pepper

Alternative fish: cuttlefish
or scallops

 301

Seppioline alla napoletana

NEAPOLITAN-STYLE BABY OCTOPUS

Cook the octopus in a little salted boiling water for
10–15 minutes, until tender. Drain and cut into pieces.
Whisk together the olive oil, parsley, garlic and lemon
juice in a bowl and season with salt and pepper. Pour
the dressing over the octopus, stir, let stand in a cool
place for 1 hour to let the flavours mingle, then serve.

Photograph opposite

. . . .

Serves 4
Preparation time: 30 mins
+ 2 hrs marinating

- 1 lemon
- 1 flat-leaf parsley sprig,
  finely chopped
- 300 g (11 oz) baby octopus,
  cleaned and cut into pieces
- olive oil, for drizzling
- salt and freshly ground white
  pepper

Alternative fish: baby squid
or monkfish

 301

Insalata di seppioline

BABY OCTOPUS SALAD

Zest the lemon and chop the zest finely. Squeeze the juice
and strain it into a bowl. Add the parsley and lemon zest
to the lemon juice, season with salt and white pepper and
mix well. Put the octopus into a dish, add the lemon juice
mixture and toss to coat. Cover with clingfilm (plastic wrap)
and let marinate in the refrigerator for 2 hours. Remove
the dish from the refrigerator, drizzle the octopus with
olive oil and serve.

Serves 6
Preparation time: 1hr
Cooking time: 1¼hrs
+ 45mins for the polenta

· 100ml (scant ½ cup) olive oil
· 1 clove garlic, peeled
· 1 bay leaf
· 3 shallots, chopped
· 4 tablespoons chopped
  flat-leaf parsley
· 1.5kg (3¼lb) baby octopus,
  cleaned
· 400ml (1⅔ cups) dry white wine
· 800g (1¾lb) tomatoes, peeled,
  deseeded and puréed
· 2 pinches of ground ginger
· ½ green chilli, finely chopped
· salt and pepper

For the polenta:
· 1½ litres (6¼ cups) water
· 400g (generous 2¾ cups)
  coarse polenta
· salt

Alternative fish: cuttlefish
or squid

 301

Polipetti in umido con polenta morbida

BABY OCTOPUS STEW
WITH SOFT POLENTA

Heat 2 tablespoons of the olive oil with the garlic and bay
leaf in a flameproof casserole (Dutch oven). When they
are beginning to brown, remove and discard the garlic and
bay leaf. Add the shallots and parsley and cook over low
heat, stirring occasionally, for 5 minutes. Add the octopus,
pour in the wine and cook until the alcohol has evaporated.
Add 200ml (scant 1 cup) water and the puréed tomatoes,
season with salt and pepper and cook over medium heat
for 1 hour. Remove the casserole from the heat and stir
in the ground ginger and chill.

To cook the polenta, pour the water into a large saucepan
and bring to a boil, then add a generous pinch of salt.
Sprinkle in the polenta, stirring constantly, and cook,
stirring constantly, for 35–45 minutes, until the polenta
has thickened and starts to come away from the sides
of the pan. Just before the polenta is ready, gently reheat
the octopus mixture. Transfer the polenta to a serving
platter, top with the octopus and sauce on top, drizzle
with the remaining olive oil and serve.

Serves 4
Preparation time: 30 mins
Cooking time: 50 mins

· 500 g (1 lb 2 oz) potatoes,
  cut into cubes
· 4 leeks, white parts only,
  sliced
· 12 sea urchins
· 40 g (3 tablespoons) butter
· 200 ml (scant 1 cup) double
  (heavy) cream
· 200 ml (scant 1 cup) warm milk
· sea salt and pepper

Alternative fish: caviar,
salmon roe or bottarga

SEA URCHINS WITH POTATO CREAM

Put the potatoes and leeks in a large saucepan, pour
in 1 litre (4¼ cups) water and bring to a boil over medium
heat. Reduce the heat, cover and simmer for 40 minutes.
Meanwhile, open the sea urchins, reserving any liquid,
clean and scoop out the coral with a spoon (see page 219).
Strain the reserved liquid into a bowl and store in the
refrigerator until required.

Using a slotted spoon, transfer the potatoes and leeks
to a food processor or blender and process until smooth.
Reserve the cooking water. Pour the potato mixture
into a saucepan, add the butter, cream, warm milk and
reserved liquid from the sea urchins. Heat gently, stirring
occasionally, adding a few tablespoons of the reserved
cooking water, if necessary, to obtain the desired
consistency. Season with salt and pepper and remove
from the heat. Spoon the hot potato cream into 4 individual
bowls, top with the sea urchin corals and serve immediately.

Serves 6
Preparation time: 30 mins
Cooking time: 25 mins

· 3 tablespoons olive oil
· 1 garlic clove
· 500g (1lb 2oz) ripe but firm
  tomatoes, peeled, seeded
  and coarsely chopped
· 30 sea urchins, opened and
  cleaned (see page 219)
· 500g (1lb 2oz) linguine
· salt and pepper

Alternative fish: caviar
or bottarga

Linguine ai ricci di mare

LINGUINE WITH SEA URCHINS

Heat the oil with the garlic in a frying pan or skillet. When
the garlic starts to colour, remove and discard it. Add the
tomatoes and 150 ml (⅔ cup) water to the pan, season with
salt and pepper and simmer for 15 minutes. Extract the
coral from the sea urchins with a spoon, put it into a bowl
and set aside. Bring a large saucepan of salted water
to a boil, add the pasta, bring back to a boil and cook for
8–10 minutes, until tender but still firm to the bite. Drain,
reserving 1–2 tablespoons of the cooking water, tip it into
the pan and toss with the sauce. Add the sea urchin coral
and heat for a few seconds, adding the reserved pasta
cooking water if necessary. Transfer to a warmed serving
platter and serve immediately.

Photograph opposite

Serves 4
Preparation time: 30 mins
+ 1hr marinating
Cooking time: 10–12 mins

· 20 langoustines, peeled
· juice of 2 lemons, strained
· 20 sage leaves
· 20 rashers (slices)
  smoked bacon
· olive oil, for brushing
· salt and pepper

Alternative fish: prawns
(shrimp) or scallops

Scampi alla salvia e pancetta

LANGOUSTINES WITH
SAGE AND BACON

Put the langoustines in a bowl, season with salt and pepper,
pour the lemon juice over them and let marinate for 1 hour.
Preheat the grill (broiler). Drain the langoustines, reserving
the marinade. Wrap each one, together with a sage leaf, in
a rasher (slice) of smoked bacon and secure with a wooden
cocktail stick or toothpick. Lightly brush with oil and grill
(broil), turning twice and brushing occasionally with the
reserved marinade, for 10–12 minutes. Serve immediately.

Serves 4
Preparation time: 30 mins
Cooking time: 5–15 mins

- 1 grapefruit
- 4 tablespoons oil
- 2 tablespoons white wine vinegar
- 8 cooked langoustines (see page 220)
- 1 head curly endive, separated into leaves
- 1 tablespoons finely chopped chervil
- 1 tablespoon finely chopped chives
- salt and pepper

Alternative fish: crab claws, scallops or salmon

Insalata di scampi, pompelmo e indivia

LANGOUSTINE, ENDIVE AND GRAPEFRUIT SALAD

Peel the grapefruit, removing all traces of bitter pith. Using a small, sharp knife, cut out the segments and discard the membranes. Thinly slice the segments. Whisk together the oil and vinegar in a small bowl and season with salt and pepper.

Arrange the grapefruit slices on a serving platter, lay the langoustines on top and surround with the curly endive leaves. Drizzle with the dressing and sprinkle with the chervil and chives.

Serves 6
Preparation time: 35 mins
Cooking time: 20 mins

· 300 g (2⅓ cups) plain
  (all-purpose) flour
· 1 tablespoon cornflour
  (cornstarch)
· 750 ml (3 cups) sparkling
  mineral water, chilled
· 10 baby globe artichokes,
  trimmed
· 4 tablespoons olive oil,
  plus extra for deep-frying
· 6 courgettes (zucchini),
  cut into rounds
· 2.5 kg (5½ lb) langoustines,
  peeled
· salt

Alternative fish: prawns
(shrimp) or scallops

LANGOUSTINE AND VEGETABLE FRITTERS

Whisk the flour, cornflour (cornstarch), a pinch of salt
and the mineral water in a bowl until smooth. Remove and
discard the tough outer leaves from the artichokes and slice
them. Heat the oil in a deep-fryer to 180–190°C/350–375°F
or until a cube of day-old bread browns in 30 seconds.
Dip the baby artichokes and courgette (zucchini) rounds
in the batter, drain off the excess, add to the hot oil, in
batches, and cook until crisp and golden. Remove with
a slotted spoon and drain on paper towels.

Dip the langoustines in the batter, allow the excess
to drip off, and add to the hot oil in batches. Cook until
crisp and golden. Remove with a slotted spoon and
serve immediately with the vegetable fritters.

Serves 6
Preparation time: 30 mins
+ 2 hrs freezing
Cooking time: 45 mins

· 150 g (5 oz) bacon
· 1.2 kg (2½ lb) cuttlefish,
  cleaned
· 2 tablespoons olive oil
· 1 kg (2¼ lb) young spinach,
  cut into large strips
· salt and pepper

For the sauce:
· 2 tablespoons olive oil
· 2 shallots, finely chopped
· 100 ml (scant ½ cup)
  dry white wine
· 4 tablespoons Fish Stock
  (see page 78)
· juice of ½ lemon, strained
· 50 g (4 tablespoons) butter,
  chilled
· 1 tablespoon cuttlefish ink
· salt and pepper

Alternative fish: squid or
scallops

 302

CUTTLEFISH AND SPINACH WITH BACON

Line a freezer-proof tray with foil. Cut the bacon rashers (slices) crosswise in half or into four pieces. Pinch these pieces to gather them together in their centres so that they resemble butterflies, lay them on the prepared tray and put the tray in the freezer for 2 hours. Remove the bacon butterflies from the freezer, put them into a non-stick saucepan, season with salt and pepper and set aside until you are ready to fry them. Cut the cuttlefish into strips.

To make the sauce, heat the olive oil in a frying pan or skillet, add the shallots and cook over low heat, stirring occasionally, for 7–8 minutes, until lightly coloured. Sprinkle with 1 tablespoon water, season with salt and pepper and remove from the heat. Transfer the mixture to a food processor or blender and process at high speed, then scrape the purée back into the pan and set over medium heat. Pour in the wine and cook until it has evaporated, then pour in the fish stock and simmer for 10 minutes. Stir in the lemon juice and butter, remove the pan from the heat and stir in the cuttlefish ink.

To cook the cuttlefish, heat the olive oil in a frying pan or skillet, add the cuttlefish and spinach and cook, stirring occasionally, for 10 minutes, then season with salt and pepper. Meanwhile, cook the bacon in a separate frying pan or skillet without any added oil, carefully turning once, for 5–8 minutes, until fairly crisp. Put the bacon butterflies on one half a serving plate and spoon the sauce over them. Spoon the spinach and cuttlefish mixture onto the other half of the serving plate and serve immediately.

Serves 4
Preparation time: 25 mins
Cooking time: 1¾ hrs

· 4 tablespoons olive oil
· 1 garlic clove
· 800 g (1¾ lb) cuttlefish,
  cleaned and cut into strips
· 175 ml (¾ cup) dry white wine
· 700 g (5 cups) shelled
  fresh of frozen peas
· salt and pepper

Alternative fish: squid
or monkfish

 302

CUTTLEFISH WITH PEAS

Heat the olive oil with garlic clove in a saucepan over medium heat. When the garlic begins to colour, remove and discard it. Add the cuttlefish to the pan, season with salt and pepper, stir well and cook for a few minutes. Pour in the wine and cook until it has evaporated. Pour in just enough water almost to cover the cuttlefish and bring to a boil. Reduce the heat, cover and simmer for about 1½ hours. Shortly before serving, add the peas and cook for about 5–10 minutes until tender. Transfer to a warm serving dish and serve immediately.

Photograph opposite

Serves 4
Preparation time: 15 mins
Cooking time: 1¾ hrs

· 4 anchovies preserved in
  salt, rinsed
· 1 garlic clove, peeled
· 2 tablespoons olive oil
· 1 kg (2¼ lb) cuttlefish, cleaned
  and chopped
· 200 ml (scant 1 cup)
  dry white wine
· 4 ripe tomatoes, peeled,
  seeded and chopped
· 350 g (scant 2½ cups) polenta
· butter, for greasing
· salt and pepper

Alternative fish: octopus
or monkfish

 302

Polenta e seppioline

POLENTA WITH CUTTLEFISH

Pat the anchovies dry with paper towels, then pull off the heads, pinch along the top edges of the fish and pull out the backbones. Put them in a frying pan or skillet with the garlic clove and olive oil. Heat gently, crushing the anchovies with a wooden spoon. Increase the heat to high, add the cuttlefish pieces and cook, stirring frequently, for a few minutes, until lightly browned. Add the wine and cook until the alcohol has evaporated. Reduce the heat, add the tomatoes, season with salt and pepper and simmer for 1 hour. Meanwhile, make the polenta (see page 125). Generously grease a ring mould (tube pan) with butter and pour the cooked polenta into it. Let stand for a few minutes until the mixture cools slightly and sets, then unmould onto a serving platter. Spoon the cuttlefish and sauce into the centre of the polenta ring and serve immediately.

Serves 4
Preparation time: 1hr
Cooking time: 50 mins

· 350g (12oz) baby cuttlefish,
  cleaned
· 3 tablespoons olive oil
· 1 onion, chopped
· 200ml (scant 1 cup)
  dry white wine
· 3 tablespoons diced
  tomato flesh
· 2 tablespoons chopped
  flat-leaf parsley
· 320g (11½oz) linguine
· salt and pepper

Alternative fish: squid or
huss (dogfish)

 302

LINGUINE WITH CUTTLEFISH

Cut the cuttlefish into strips. Heat the olive oil in a
saucepan, add the cuttlefish and onion and cook over
medium-high heat, stirring frequently, for 5 minutes. Pour
in the wine and cook until it has evaporated, then stir in
the tomato and season with salt and pepper. Reduce the
heat to low, cover and simmer for 20 minutes, then stir
in the cuttlefish ink and cook for about 5 minutes, until
the sauce thickens a little. Stir in the parsley and remove
from the heat.

Bring a large saucepan of salted water to a boil, add the
linguine, bring back to a boil and cook for 8–10 minutes,
until al dente. Drain the pasta, add to the cuttlefish sauce,
toss lightly and serve.

Serves 4
Preparation time: 15 mins
Cooking time: 25 mins

· 1 litre (4¼ cups) Fish Stock
  (see page 78) or chicken stock
· 225 g (1½ cups) shelled peas
· 2 tablespoons olive oil
· 2 garlic cloves, lightly crushed
· 300 g (11oz) clams, shucked
· 200 ml (scant 1 cup) dry
  white wine
· 200 ml (scant 1 cup) passata
  (puréed canned tomatoes)
· 300 g (1½ cups) risotto rice
· 1 tablespoon finely chopped
  flat-leaf parsley
· salt and pepper

Alternative fish: mussels
or scallops

 300

Risotto con vongole e piselli

RISOTTO WITH CLAMS AND PEAS

Pour the stock into a saucepan and bring to a boil, then reduce the heat and simmer. Blanch the peas in salted boiling water for 5 minutes, then drain and set aside. Heat the olive oil in a large saucepan, add the garlic cloves and cook over low heat for a few minutes, until they begin to colour, then remove and discard them. Add the clams and cook, stirring frequently, for 2 minutes, then add the wine and cook until it has evaporated. Add the passata (puréed canned tomatoes) and peas, season and cook for 3–4 minutes. Stir in the rice and cook, stirring constantly, until it has absorbed all the liquid. Add a ladleful of the hot stock and cook, stirring constantly, until it has been absorbed. Continue adding the stock, a ladleful at a time, and stirring until each addition has been absorbed. This will take 18–20 minutes. Sprinkle the risotto with the parsley, season with pepper and serve immediately.

Serves 4
Preparation time: 20 mins
Cooking time: 25 mins

· 1.5 kg (3¼ lb) small clams,
  cleaned
· 3 tablespoons olive oil
· 1 garlic clove, peeled
· 1 bunch flat-leaf parsley,
  chopped
· 2 egg yolks
· juice of 1 lemon, strained
· salt and pepper

Alternative fish: mussels
or cod cheeks

 300

Vongole in salsa d'uovo al limone

CLAMS IN EGG AND LEMON SAUCE

Discard any clams with broken shells or that do not shut when sharply tapped. Put them into a frying pan or skillet, add the oil, garlic clove and parsley and cook over high heat for 3–4 minutes, until the shells have opened, then remove from the heat. Discard any that remain shut. Beat together the egg yolks and lemon juice in a bowl. Transfer the clams to a clean saucepan set over very low heat, pour the egg and lemon mixture over them and stir until thickened. As soon as the clams are coated in the sauce, remove the pan from the heat. Be careful not to cook over too high heat or for too long or the eggs will scramble. Serve immediately.

Serves 4
Preparation time: 25 mins
Cooking time: 30 mins

· 1 kg (2¼ lb) small clams,
  cleaned
· 200 ml (scant 1 cup) olive oil
· 2 garlic cloves, peeled
· 2 tablespoons chopped
  flat-leaf parsley
· 320 g (11½ oz) spaghettini
· salt and pepper

Alternative fish: mussels
or scallops

 300

SPAGHETTINI WITH CLAMS

Discard any clams with damaged shells or that do not
shut immediately when sharply tapped. Heat the oil with
the garlic cloves in a large saucepan. When they are
beginning to colour, remove and discard the garlic cloves.
Add the clams to the pan and cook, occasionally shaking
the pan, for 3–4 minutes, until the shells have opened.
Remove the pan from the heat and lift out the clams with
a slotted spoon and put them in a shallow dish. Discard
any that remain shut. Remove the clams from their shells.
Strain any juices left behind in the dish into the pan, then
add the clams and parsley and season with salt and pepper.
Cook over low heat for 10 minutes.

Meanwhile, add the spaghettini to a large saucepan
of salted boiling water, bring back to a boil and cook for
8–10 minutes, until al dente. Drain, tip into the pan with
the clams, toss over high heat and serve.

Note: Another way to cook spaghetti with clams is to
drain the pasta when it is half-cooked and to finish cooking
it in the juices left behind in the pan after opening the
shellfish. This makes the dish especially flavoursome.
For a variation on this plain clam sauce, you can add
a few chopped tomatoes.

Serves 6
Preparation time: 45 mins
Cooking time: 20 mins

· 500g (1lb 2oz) mussels, cleaned
· 300g (11oz) clams, cleaned
· 1 red bell pepper, seeded
  and sliced
· 1 green bell pepper, seeded
  and sliced
· 2 dried chillies, crumbled
· 4 garlic cloves, chopped
· 1 bunch fresh mixed herbs,
  such as marjoram, thyme, basil,
  sage and chives, chopped
· 100ml (scant ½ cup) olive oil
· 200ml (scant 1 cup) red wine
· 300g (11oz) octopus, cleaned
· 300g (11oz) cuttlefish, cleaned
  and halved if large
· 300g (11oz) baby octopus,
  cleaned
· 100ml (scant ½ cup) white rum
· pinch of freshly grated nutmeg
  (optional)
· pepper

Alternative fish: squid, monkfish
cheeks or huss (dogfish)

300 301 302

Zuppa di pesce del pirata

PIRATE'S FISH SOUP

Place a cup of water in a large saucepan and bring to
the boil. Place the clams and the mussels in a steamer
basket or colander over the boiling water. Steam the clams
and the mussels until the shells open wide. Remove the
shellfish as they open and set aside. Cover with foil to keep
warm and reserve the cooking liquid.

Put the bell peppers and olive oil in a flameproof casserole
(Dutch oven) and cook, covered, over medium-low heat
for 8 minutes. Add the dried chilies and garlic and cook for
another 2 minutes. Add the wine and bring to the simmer.
Stir in the octopus, then the squid. Cook for 2–3 minutes
or until the pieces turn from transparent to opaque. Do not
overcook or the fish will become tough.

Add the rum, reserved steaming liquid (minus any grit)
from the bottom of the cup, clams and the mussels to
the casserole. Sprinkle with the nutmeg, if using, freshly
ground black pepper and the chopped herbs. Ladle into
bowls and serve immediately.

Serves 8–10
Preparation time: 50 mins
Cooking time: 1hr

· 300 g (11oz) mussels, cleaned
· 300 g (11oz) clams, cleaned
· 4–5 tablespoons olive oil
· 1 onion, finely chopped
· 300 g (11oz) large cuttlefish,
  cleaned
· 1 green bell pepper, seeded
  and sliced
· 5 just-ripe tomatoes, peeled,
  seeded and chopped
· 1 fresh chilli, seeded and finely
  chopped
· 100 ml (scant ½ cup) white
  wine vinegar
· 2.5 kg (5½ lb) mixed fish, such
  as scorpion fish, monkfish fillet,
  mackerel and red mullet, cleaned
  and cut into chunks if necessary
· 300 g (11oz) mantis shrimp,
  slipper lobsters or langoustines
· 300 g (11oz) small cuttlefish,
  cleaned
· salt and pepper

Alternative fish: prawns
(shrimp), scallops or huss
(dogfish)

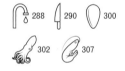
288   290   300
302   307

MARCHE-STYLE FISH SOUP

Discard any mussels and clams with broken shells or that
do not shut immediately when sharply tapped. Put them in
2 separate frying pans or skillets over high heat for about
2 minutes, until they have opened. Discard any that remain
closed. Remove some of the mussels and clams from their
shells and leave the rest as they are.

Heat the olive oil in a large flameproof casserole (Dutch
oven), add the onion and cook over a low heat, stirring
occasionally, for 5 minutes. Add the large cuttlefish and
cook for 10 minutes, then add the bell pepper, season
with salt and pepper and mix well. Cook over low heat for
another 10 minutes. Add the tomatoes, chilli and vinegar
and cook until the vinegar has evaporated. Gradually add
the fish and shellfish in layers, beginning with the least
delicate (such as oily fish) and finishing with the mussels
and mantis shrimp, slipper lobsters or langoustines.
Cover and simmer gently for about 20 minutes.

Note: There are as many recipes for fish soup (*brodetto*)
as there are regions along the Adriatic coast. This version
is traditionally made at San Benedetto di Tronto in Marche.

Serves 4
Preparation time: 30 mins
Cooking time: 45 mins

· 2 tablespoons olive oil
· 1 onion, thinly sliced
· pinch of ground cumin
· 2 garlic cloves, crushed
· 500 g (1 lb 2 oz) tomatoes, diced
· 1 kg (2¼ lb) assorted seafood,
  cleaned
· salt and pepper

 300 301 302

 304 307

MIXED SEAFOOD SOUP

Heat the olive oil in a large saucepan, add the onion and cook over low heat, stirring occasionally, for 5 minutes, until softened. Add the cumin, garlic and 1 tablespoon water and season with salt. Stir in the tomatoes and simmer, stirring occasionally, for 20 minutes, until they are very soft. Pour 2 litres (8¾ cups) water and bring to a boil.

Gradually add the fish and shellfish in layers, beginning with the heartier seafood (such as octopus and cuttlefish) and finishing with most delicate the mussels and prawns (shrimp). Cover and simmer gently for about 20 minutes. Serve immediately.

Serves 4
Preparation time: 20 mins
Cooking time: 15 mins

· 100 g (1½ cups) broccoli
· olive oil, for deep-frying
· 150 g (5 oz) baby squid, cleaned
· 150 g (5 oz) raw prawns
  (shrimp), peeled
· 1 baby globe artichoke,
  trimmed and thinly sliced
· 1 courgette (zucchini), cut
  into rounds
· 1 aubergine (eggplant), cut
  into rounds
· salt

For the batter:
· 100 g (scant 1 cup) plain
  (all-purpose) flour
· 1 egg white
· 175–250 ml (¾–1 cup) sparkling
  mineral water

Alternative fish: scallops,
mussels or huss (dogfish)

 302   307

SEAFOOD AND VEGETABLE FRITTO MISTO

Break the broccoli into florets. Bring a saucepan of salted water to a boil, add the broccoli and cook for 3 minutes, then drain and let cool. Meanwhile, make the batter. Sift the flour into a bowl and stir in the egg white and enough sparkling mineral water to obtain a smooth batter.

Heat the oil in a deep-fryer to 180–190°C/350–375°F or until a cube of day-old bread browns in 30 seconds. Add the prawns (shrimp), baby squid and vegetables to the batter. Lift out 1–2 tablespoons at a time, add to the hot oil and cook until crisp and golden brown. Remove with a slotted spoon, drain on paper towels, transfer to a serving dish and keep warm until all the seafood and vegetables have been cooked. Season with salt and serve.

SEAFOOD CRÊPE PARCELS

Serves 4
Preparation time: 50 mins
+ 1hr standing
Cooking time: 1hr

For the crêpes:
· 100 g (1 cup) plain
  (all-purpose) flour
· 2 eggs
· 250 ml (1 cup) milk
· 30 g (2 tablespoons) butter
· vegetable oil for brushing
· salt

For the filling:
· 1 tablespoon olive oil
· 20 uncooked Mediterranean
  or tiger prawns (jumbo shrimp),
  peeled and halved, shells
  reserved
· 1 celery stalk, coarsely chopped
· 1 carrot, coarsely chopped
· 1 leek, coarsely chopped
· 1 bay leaf
· 200 ml (scant 1 cup) white wine
· 500 ml (2 cups) vegetable stock
· 150 g (5 oz) baby octopus,
  cleaned
· 15 g (1 tablespoon) butter
· 2 red mullet or red snapper
  fillets, cut into strips
· 2 tablespoons double
  (heavy) cream
· salt and pepper

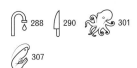 288   290   301   307

First make the crêpes. Sift the flour into a bowl, add the eggs and 3–4 tablespoons of the milk, and mix well. Gradually stir in the remaining milk to make a fairly runny batter. Melt the butter, allow to cool almost completely, then add to the batter. Season with salt, beat again for a few minutes with a small whisk, then let stand for at least 1 hour. Brush the bottom of a crêpe pan with oil and heat, then pour in 2 tablespoons of the batter. Turn and tilt the pan so that the batter covers the bottom evenly. Cook for 3–4 minutes, until the underside is set and golden brown, then flip over with a spatula and cook the other side for about 2 minutes, until golden. Slide the crêpe out of the pan onto a plate. Make 12.

To make the filling, heat the olive oil in a saucepan, add the reserved prawn (shrimp) shells and cook over low heat, stirring occasionally, for 5 minutes. Add the celery, carrot, leek and bay leaf, pour in the wine and cook until the alcohol has evaporated, then season with salt and pepper. Pour in the stock, bring to a boil, cover and simmer for 10 minutes. Remove from the heat and strain into a clean pan. Add the octopus to the pan and cook over low heat for 10 minutes, then drain them, reserving the stock.

Melt the butter in a frying pan or skillet, add the fish fillets and cook over low heat for 1–2 minutes. Sprinkle with 2 tablespoons of the stock and cook for 2 minutes, then turn the fish and cook for another 5 minutes. Add the prawns and cream and cook until the liquid has thickened.

Meanwhile, preheat the oven to 180°C / 350°F / Gas Mark 4. Grease an ovenproof dish with butter. If necessary, cut the octopus into smaller pieces, then add to the pan. Remove the pan from the heat and divide the seafood among the crêpes, spooning it into the centre of each. Fold in the sides, tops and bottoms to make parcels and carefully lift them into the prepared dish. Spoon the remaining cooking liquid over them and bake for 5–6 minutes. Serve immediately.

Serves 4
Preparation time: 25 mins
Cooking time: 1hr

· 1kg (2¼lb) mixed mussels
  and small clams, cleaned
· 200ml (scant 1cup) dry
  white wine
· 400g (14oz) broad (fava)
  beans, shelled
· pinch of saffron threads,
  lightly crushed
· 1.2 litres (5 cups) Fish Stock
  (see page 78) or chicken stock
· 2 tablespoons olive oil
· 2 shallots, chopped
· 1 garlic clove, chopped
· 300g (1½ cups) risotto rice
· 1 tablespoon chopped
  flat-leaf parsley
· salt and pepper

Alternative fish: oysters,
scallops, monkfish or huss
(dogfish)

 300

SEAFOOD RISOTTO WITH BROAD (FAVA) BEANS

Discard any mussels or clams with damaged shells or that do not shut immediately when sharply tapped. Put them in a large frying pan or skillet, pour in the wine, cover and cook over high heat, occasionally shaking the pan, for about 5 minute, until the shells open. Drain, reserving the cooking liquid, remove the mussels and clams from the shells and set aside. Discard any shells that remain closed. Strain the cooking liquid through a sieve (strainer) lined with muslin (cheesecloth) into a jug (pitcher).

Pop the beans out of their skins by pressing them gently between finger and thumb. Cook them in salted boiling water for 10–20 minutes, depending on how old they are, then drain and set aside.

Meanwhile, put the saffron into a small bowl, add 2 tablespoons of the stock and let soak. Bring the remaining stock to a boil, then reduce the heat and simmer gently. Heat the oil in a large saucepan, add the shallots and garlic and cook over low heat, stirring occasionally, for 5 minutes, until softened. Add the rice and cook, stirring constantly, for 1–2 minutes, until all the grains are coated in oil. Add the beans, the reserved cooking liquid and a ladleful of the hot stock. Cook, stirring constantly, until all the liquid has been absorbed. Continue adding the stock, a ladleful at a time, and stirring until each addition has been absorbed. When about half the stock has been added, season the risotto with salt, stir in the saffron and its soaking liquid and add the shellfish. Continue adding the remaining stock as before. Remove the risotto from the heat, sprinkle with the parsley and serve immediately.

Serves 6
Preparation time: 40 mins
Cooking time: 10 mins

· 2 canned tomatoes,
  drained and chopped
· 6 tablespoons pesto
· 2 tablespoons olive oil
· 200 g (7oz) shelled scallops
· 600 ml (2½ cups) dry
  white wine
· ½ bunch chives, snipped
· 250 ml (1 cup) double
  (heavy) cream
· 40 g (½ cup) grated mild
  pecorino cheese
· 200 g (7oz) crab meat, drained
  if canned, thawed if frozen
· 200 g (7oz) no-precook
  (oven-ready) or fresh lasagne
  sheets (noodles)
· salt and pepper

Alternative fish: prawns
(shrimp) or langoustines

 304

THREE-COLOUR SEAFOOD LASAGNE

Mix together the tomatoes and pesto in a bowl. Heat the oil in a shallow saucepan over low heat, add the scallops and cook for 2 minutes on each side. Remove from the pan and keep warm. Pour the wine into the pan, increase the heat to medium-high and cook until reduced by half. Stir in the chives and cream and cook until reduced by half again.

Meanwhile, preheat the oven to 180°C / 350°F / Gas Mark 4. Remove the pan from the heat, stir in the pecorino and crab meat and season. Make a layer of lasagne sheets (noodles) in the bottom of an ovenproof dish, spoon some of the crab filling on top and cover with a layer of seared scallops. Continue making layers in this way until all the ingredients have been used, ending with a layer of pasta. Cover with the pesto and tomato mixture. Turn off the oven and leave the lasagne in it to heat through for 10 minutes, then serve.

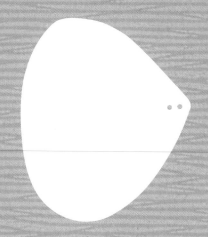

BASIC TECHNIQUES

TRIMMING, SCALING AND CLEANING

Nearly all fish need to be trimmed, scaled and cleaned before eating. A fish supplier can prepare the fish for you, but the techniques are simple enough for you to try it at home, too.

This scaling technique can be used for all fish that have a thick layer of scales including sea bass, trout, salmon and grey (striped) mullet. Some fish, such as hake, do not need scaling.

1. Place the fish on an easy-to-clean surface or chopping (cutting) board.

2. To trim the fish, use scissors to remove all the fins around the body. The easiest way to do this is to cut in the direction from tail to head.

3. To scale the fish, use a scaler or the back of a knife and brush vigorously from tail to head. Be careful to remove scales on the back and belly, which is the point of entry for the knife for gutting and filleting. This procedure can be done in a plastic bag to catch the scales.

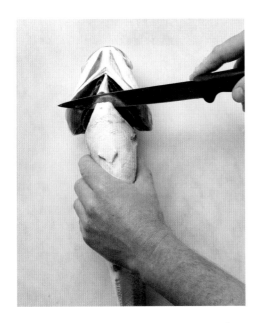

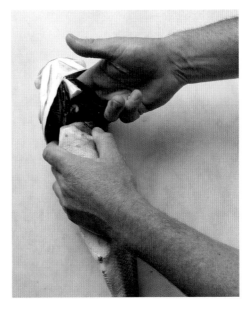

4. Turn the fish over, place it on its back and cut the throat of the fish. This will give a point of exit for the knife when gutting.

5. To release the gills, slip your fingers under the gills and pull them away. Be careful because they can be sharp.

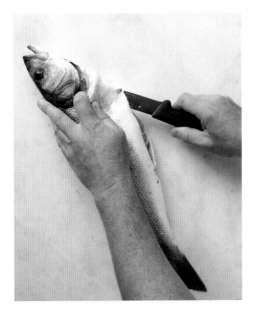

6. To gut the fish, insert the point of a filleting knife at the anal vent (the small hole two-thirds of the way down the fish) and run the knife along the belly to the gills in one action.

7. Lift out and discard the entrails and remove any traces of the blood line, which is a dark line of blood running along the spine.

FILLETING AND SKINNING ROUND FISH

When filleting or skinning fish, keep the knife clean and sharp for a much cleaner and safer cut. Use long sweeping strokes wherever possible and aim to cut away from your body.

The simple technique works for all round fish such as mackerel, sea bass, sea bream and salmon.

1. Make diagonal cuts into the back on both sides of the fish head to form a 'V'-shaped cut.

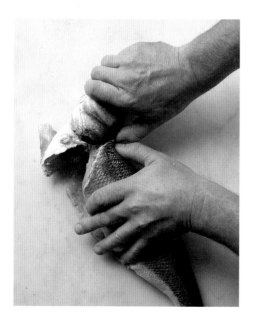

2. Snap the head off by bending it back away from the body.

3. Keeping the knife flat, cut into the skin of the top fillet above the dorsal fin and along the back. Use long sweeping cuts from head to tail to reveal the back bone. Insert the tip of the knife at the tail end and cut down to the tail to release the underside of the fillet.

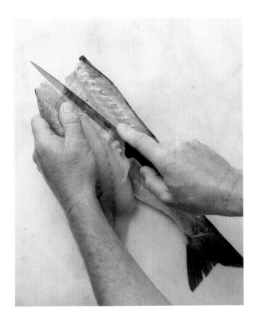

4. Release the remaining fillet by cutting over the rib bones in short smooth strokes towards the belly to release the fillet completely from the bone.

5. To remove the second fillet, turn the fish so that tail is pointing away from you. Support the belly of the fish with your free hand. Keeping the knife flat, cut into the skin along the back of the fish just above the dorsal fin and repeat the action as for the first side.

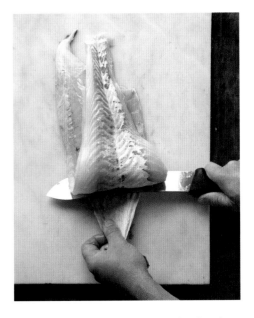

6. To remove the skin, use a flexible knife and start at the tail end or thinnest part of the fish fillet. Using the middle of the blade, cut into the fillet as far as the skin.

7. Pulling the skin taut with your other hand, shave the fillet from the skin using a gentle sawing action, keeping the knife angled slightly downwards towards the skin.

FILLETING AND SKINNING FLAT FISH

When filleting or skinning fish, keep the knife clean and sharp for a much cleaner and safer cut. Use long sweeping strokes and aim to cut away from your body. Flat fish are slightly easier to fillet than round fish and are a good fish to practice your filleting technique.

This method can be used for all flat fish including turbot, brill and sole.

1. Trim the fish by removing the fins with sharp scissors. Cut around the head with a knife and discard it (unless you wish to keep it to make stock, in which case remove the gills and rinse).

2. Place the fish on a chopping board with the dark side facing up. Slip the tip of the knife into the fillet just above the main bone and close to the central backbone, sliding the knife out to the side to release the fillet at the fin.

3. Run the tip of the knife along the backbone to release the second part of the fillet and to avoid waste.

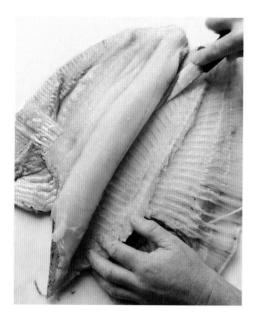

4. Turn the fish so that the bones are facing towards you. Cutting away from you, run the tip of the knife over the backbone and along the bones on the other side to release the fillet in one sweeping action.

5. Release the fillet completely to show one large flat fillet.

6. Turn the fish over and release the fillet on the other side in the exact same way. You should have two large fillets, the fish bone and trimmings at the end. The fillets can be cooked skin on or off. For skinning, see steps 6 and 7 on page 291.

SKINNING AND FILLETING MONKFISH

The technique for preparing monkfish is different from other fish because monkfish have a different bone structure and a loose skin, which peels away easily. Under the skin are a few layers of pale-coloured membrane, which should be removed as they do darken on cooking and shrink around the fillet.

Generally, monkfish is sold with the head already removed and the body is sold as 'the tail'.

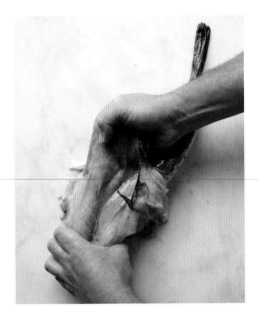

1. If skinning a headless monkfish tail, hold the body with one hand and with the other hand, peel back the dark skin towards the tail. It should come away easily.

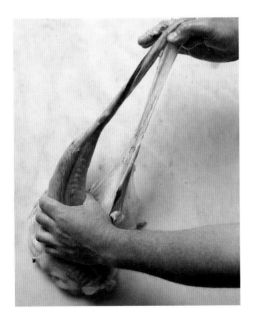

2. Continue to peel the skin away right to the tail end and remove it completely.

3. Using a knife, slip the tip of the blade between the layers of membrane and the flesh and carefully trim it away.

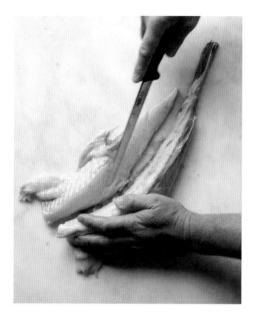

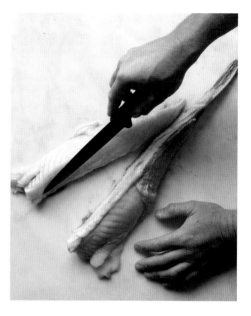

4. Using the same knife, cut through the flesh on one side of the main bone right through to the other side, keeping as close to the bone as possible.

5. Continue cutting to release the fillet right to the tail end.

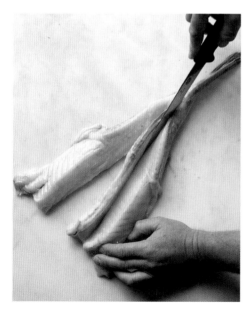

6. Repeat on the other side to create two monkfish fillets. These are now completely boneless.

7. The monkfish fillets are now completely boneless and prepared for cooking.

REMOVING PINBONES FROM A FILLET

Pinbones are 'floating' bones that are found in the centre of the thickest part of round fish fillets and are not attached to the main skeleton of the fish. The amount of pinbones in each fish will differ and they are generally found in the top third of the fillet and never in the tail end.

1. Locate the pinbones by lightly brushing the surface of the fish with your fingers.

2. Using pinbone removers or wide blade tweezers, grasp the top of each pinbone firmly. Pull the bone away from the fillet in the direction that it is lying.

SCALING AND CLEANING SMALL OILY FISH

Small fish including sardines, trout and herring have soft, loose scales. These only require the use of the back of knife or the blunt edge of a pair of scissors (as shown) to scrape them away.

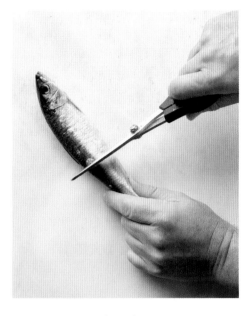

1. Using the back of a knife or scissors, scrape away the scales from tail to head.

2. To gut the sardine, support the back of the fish with your free hand. Insert the tip of the knife at the vent end and run it up the belly in one action.

3. Remove the guts and discard. Pull away the gills and briefly rinse the fish to remove the blood line (a dark line of blood that runs along the spine).

BUTTERFLY-BONING SMALL OILY FISH

Butterfly-boning removes most of the bones from small oily fish and can also create a larger cavity for stuffing. This technique is ideal for soft-boned fish such as sardines, sprats and anchovies.

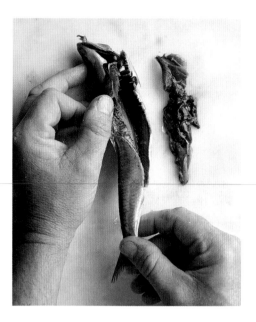

1. Use a knife to remove the head of the fish. Gut the fish as described on page 297.

2. Turn the fish onto its back. With the tip of your finger, gently loosen the bones close to the backbone.

3. Support the fillet and gently release the fine bones away from the fish.

4. Grasp the loosened bone and pull back away from the flesh.

5. Using scissors, snip the bone away from the fish at the tail end.

6. The fish is now prepared for use. Any visible fine pinbones can be pulled away with a pinbone remover or tweezers.

PREPARING MUSSELS AND CLAMS

These simple cleaning procedures remove any grit and, in the case of mussels, barnacles attached to the shell. It also allows you to locate any mussels or clams that are cracked, damaged or no longer alive making them unsafe to eat.

1. Scrub the mussels or clams with a scourer or knife to remove any barnacles. The shells should be closed. If the shell is open, sharply tap it and it will close if it is still alive. If it does not close, discard it.

2. Pull away the byssus, or beard, from the mussel. Clams do not have beards.

3. Keep the mussels or clams in a bowl covered with a cloth and not in contact with water. Discard any that are cracked or broken.

PREPARING OCTOPUS

Fish suppliers often sell octopus with the eyes, ink sac and innards removed, or will happily do so upon request. Cutting the head and removing the beak can easily be done at home.

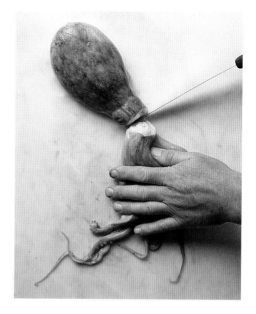

1. Cut the tentacles away from the head of the octopus with a sharp knife. Remove any other contents remaining in the body and rinse.

2. Locate the small, hard beak in the centre of the tentacles, then remove and discard it. Wash the octopus tentacles thoroughly to remove any grit.

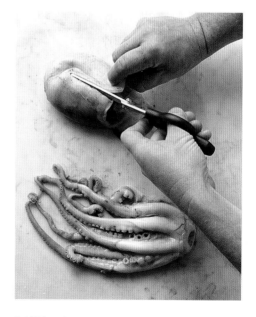

3. With scissors, snip open the head of the octopus and discard the contents. Peel away the skin from the head and rinse it.

PREPARING SQUID AND CUTTLEFISH

Whether fresh or frozen, squid is often sold cleaned and prepared. If not, they are one of the easiest fish to clean and tackle at home. This preparation also works for cuttlefish.

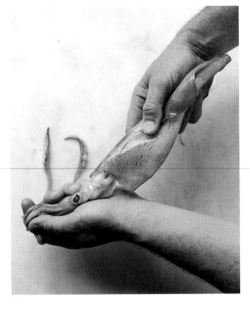

1. Hold the squid firmly in both hands and grasp the tentacles.

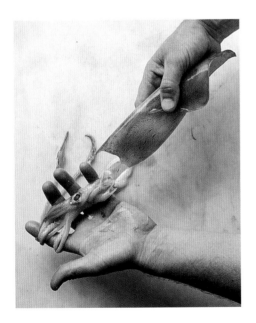

2. Pull the tentacles away from the main body of the squid.

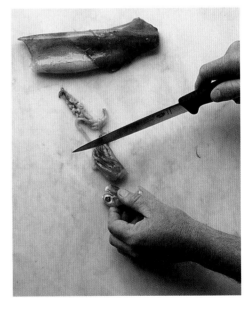

3. Cut the tentacles free from the entrails just below the eye of the squid and discard the entrails. Remove and discard any traces of the beak, which is found in the centre of the tentacles.

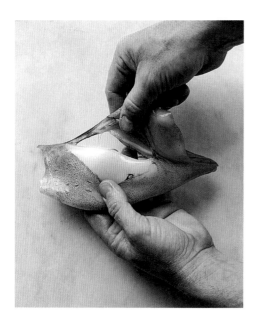

4. To prepare the body, or 'tube', pinch the fins together and gently pull away from the body. The dark membrane covering the skin should come away too. If not, you can peel it off.

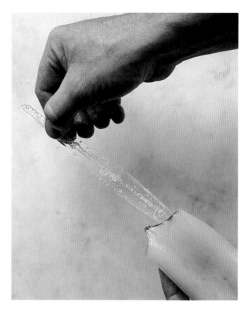

5. In the centre of the body, or tube, is a small quill-like transparent 'bone'. Pull the quill away from the body. Remove any other contents in the body and rinse.

6. The body can be left whole for stuffing or sliced into rings. To make a whole sheet, insert the knife up the centre of the body and cut the body open along the line where the quill was found.

7. To score it, use a knife to score first one way, then the other to create diamond-shaped cuts. Try to cut through half the thickness.

PREPARING SCALLOPS

Scallops are available cleaned on the half shell or completely prepared; however, live scallops in the shell are easy to prepare.

1. Fresh scallops have two sides: a flat side and a round side. Before preparation, check that the shell is tightly shut. If not, the scallop may not be safe to eat.

2. Insert a knife at the hinge of the scallop and release the muscle from the upper, rounded shell with the tip of the knife. The scallop will open easily.

3. Cut at the bottom of the scallop to be able to pull the two shells apart. It should now be possible to see the interior of the scallop and the frill located in both shells.

4. Using the tip of the knife, cut away and discard the dark intestinal sac close to the bottom of the shell and attached to the scallop. Also pull away the frill.

5. Using the tip of the knife, trim away any remaining matter and the small white muscle attached to the main muscle meat. Although edible, it is tough to eat.

6. To release the scallop, simply run a flexible knife under the meat close to the shell.

7. The scallop is now prepared for use. If you like, you can also remove the orange coral attached to the white meat, but it has a delicious flavour.

SHUCKING OYSTERS

Fresh oysters must be alive just before consumption or cooking, so it is always best to buy them whole and shuck them yourself just before eating. It is essential that the oyster is very firmly shut when they are shucked or close quickly when handled. Opening them requires a bit of skill and the best tool to use is an oyster knife.

Live oysters should be stored rounded side down in the refrigerator to prevent them from losing their natural juice if they open and close during storage.

1. Take a firm hold of the oyster and protect your hand with a thick dish cloth to help keep the oyster stable. Insert the tip of the knife, angled slightly downwards, into the hinge or pointed end of the oyster, and twist to get a good 'hold'.

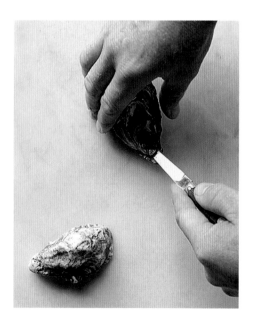

2. Once the knife is securely embedded into the hinge of the oyster, release pressure from the knife and press the handle down to break the muscle holding the oyster together.

3. Release the top, flatter shell by running the knife underneath it. Release the oyster from the bottom shell by using the tip to cut the oyster free from the shell. Be careful not to spill the juices.

PREPARING RAW PRAWNS (SHRIMP)

Prawns (shrimp) are available both peeled and unpeeled, but peeling them at home is easy. Deveining prawns (removing the dark vein that runs along the back) is not essential but the vein can be gritty and unpleasant to eat.

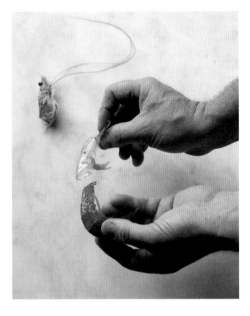

1. Pull the head of the prawn (shrimp) away from the body and peel the body shell away.

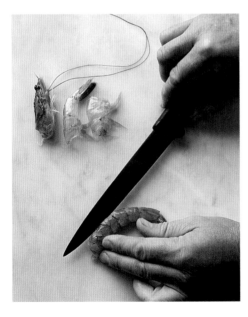

2. Make a shallow incision along the back of the prawn with the knife to partially split and reveal the digestive tract.

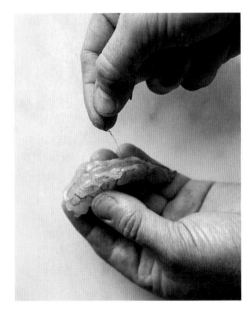

3. Pull the vein away from the body and discard it.

GLOSSARY

AL DENTE
The point during cooking at which pasta, rice and vegetables become tender but are still firm to the bite and should, therefore, be removed from the heat and drained. Vegetables cooked al dente are tastier and retain more nutrients.

BOTTARGA
Pressed, salted and dried grey (striped) mullet or tuna roe is prepared like a salami. Slices drizzled with olive oil and lemon juice or spread on toast make a tasty antipasto. Crumbled and lightly heated in oil, it makes a pleasant sauce for spaghetti. It is a Sardinian speciality.

BIVALVE
Any marine or freshwater mollusc with a shell consisting of two hinged valves. The group includes clams, oysters, scallops and mussels.

CARTILAGINOUS FISH
Fish with an internal skeleton made entirely of firm, flexible cartilage rather than hard bone. This includes sharks, rays and skates.

CEPHALOPOD
Marine molluscs with a large head and eyes, tentacles with suckers and usually an ink sac, but without an external shell. Cephalopods include octopuses, squid and cuttlefish.

COURT-BOUILLON
An aromatic liquid or stock used to poach fish and shellfish. Wine, vinegar, herbs or spices may be added and it is usually allowed to cool before using.

CRUSTACEANS
Mainly aquatic creatures with a segmented body, a hard shell and paired, jointed limbs. They include lobsters, prawns (shrimp), langoustines and crabs.

DEEP-FRY
To cook in plenty of hot oil or melted fat over high heat. Vegetable oil is best for deep-frying. If you don't have a deep-fryer with a thermostat, check that the oil is hot enough by dipping the handle of a wooden spoon into it. If the oil starts to bubble steadily, then it is hot enough for deep-frying.

FISH KETTLE
An elongated metal pan with a perforated two-handled rack and a lid, used to poach fish. Diamond-shaped kettles for poaching large flat fish, such as turbot, are also available.

FRIULI TOCAI
A white wine variety, made from grapes mostly planted in and around northeast Italy's Friuli region.

JULIENNE
Ingredients, especially vegetables, cut into very thin strips about 2.5cm (1 inch), which absorb oil, lemon juice or mayonnaise well.

LOBSTER OR CRAB PICK
A long, narrow tool, sometimes with a two-pronged fork on one end, used to extract meat from inside lobster or crab claws.

MARSALA
A sweet fortified wine produced in the region surrounding the Italian city of the same name in Sicily.

MARINATE
To steep savoury ingredients in an aromatic mixture, often based on olive oil, lemon juice, vinegar, wine, spices and herbs, in order to flavour and tenderize them.

MOLLUSC (MOLLUSK)
A soft-bodied creature, usually concealed within a hard shell. Bivalves, such as mussels and clams, have a hinged shell, gastropods, such as periwinkles and snails, have a single spiral shell, but cephalopods, such as squid and octopuses, do not have shells.

OYSTER KNIFE
A special knife with a short, thick, arrow-shaped blade with a pointed tip used to prise (pry) open an oyster shell. The best ones are fitted with a guard at the hilt to protect the hand.

PANCETTA
Like bacon, pancetta is a cut from the belly of the pig, but cured differently. It may be smoked or unsmoked, natural or rolled and flavoured with spices. It is used to add flavour to many dishes. If pancetta is not available, use bacon.

POACH
To cook food by simmering gently in liquid, such as water, stock or court-bouillon.

REDUCE
To make concentrate and/or thicken a liquid such as a stock or sauce by boiling, thus reducing the quantity of water.

ROE
The eggs or the egg-filled ovaries of female fish and shellfish are known as roe or hard roe, while the soft roe from male fish is also known as milt. Hard roes may be preserved by various techniques, such as salting and smoking. The most highly valued are caviar from sturgeon and bottarga from grey (striped) mullet.

SALMORIGLIO
Made from olive oil, lemon juice, parsley, garlic, oregano and salt, this sauce is prepared in Calabria and Sicily to season slices of grilled swordfish.

SCALE
To remove the scales covering a fish before cooking. The scales of small fish, such as sardines, can be rubbed off with the thumb. For larger fish, use a fish scaler or blunt knife. For best results work under cold running water.

SHOALED / SHOALING
When fish swim together in large numbers.

SLASH
When whole fish is to be grilled or baked, two or three diagonal slashes may be made on both sides to make it easier for the heat – and flavourings – to penetrate.

STROZZAPRETI
A type of pasta from the Emilia-Romagna region of Italy. It is short, tubular and twisted in shape.

TOMALLEY
The soft, green liver of cooked lobsters. It is added to sauces for flavour but is also considered a delicacy and may be eaten alone. It can also be used as a thickening agent.

VERMOUTH
A fortified wine that contains aromatic herbs and spices. There are different varieties but the most common are dry, white and red.

WHORL
A type of spiral or coil pattern or shape.

INDEX

RECIPE NOTES

- Butter should always be unsalted.

- Pepper is always freshly ground black pepper, unless otherwise specified.

- Unless otherwise stated, all herbs are fresh and parsley is flat-leaf parsley.

- Eggs, vegetables and fruits are assumed to be medium size, unless otherwise specified. For US, use large eggs unless otherwise specified.

- Milk is always whole, unless otherwise specified.

- Garlic cloves are assumed to be large; use two if yours are small.

- Ham means cooked ham, unless otherwise specified.

- Prosciutto refers exclusively to raw, dry-cured ham, usually from Parma or San Daniele in northern Italy.

- Cooking and preparation times are for guidance only, as individual ovens vary. If using a fan oven, follow the manufacturer's instructions concerning oven temperatures.

- To test whether your deep-frying oil is hot enough, add a cube of stale bread. If it browns in 30 seconds, the temperature is 180–190°C/350–375°F about right for most frying. Exercise caution when deep-frying: add the food carefully to avoid splashing, wear long sleeves, and never leave the pan unattended.

- Some recipes include raw or very lightly cooked fish or eggs. These should be avoided particularly by the elderly, infants, pregnant women, convalescents and anyone with an impaired immune system.

- All spoon measurements are level. 1 teaspoon = 5 ml; 1 tablespoon = 15 ml. Australian standard tablespoons are 20 ml, so Australian readers are advised to use 3 teaspoons in place of 1 tablespoon when measuring small quantities.

- Cup, metric and imperial measurements are given throughout, and US equivalents are given in brackets. Follow one set of measurements and not a mixture, as they are not interchangeable.